Perceval and Gawain in Dark Mirrors

Perceval and Gawain in Dark Mirrors
Reflection and Reflexivity in Chrétien de Troyes's Conte del Graal

Rupert T. Pickens

McFarland & Company, Inc., Publishers
Jefferson, North Carolina

All drawings are by Martha Danek.

ISBN 978-0-7864-9438-5 (softcover : acid free paper) ∞
ISBN 978-1-4766-1859-3 (ebook)

LIBRARY OF CONGRESS CATALOGUING DATA ARE AVAILABLE

BRITISH LIBRARY CATALOGUING DATA ARE AVAILABLE

© 2014 Rupert T. Pickens. All rights reserved

No part of this book may be reproduced or transmitted in any form or by any means, electronic or mechanical, including photocopying or recording, or by any information storage and retrieval system, without permission in writing from the publisher.

On the cover: Perceval gazing at drops of blood melting into the snow (drawing by Martha Danek)

Printed in the United States of America

*McFarland & Company, Inc., Publishers
Box 611, Jefferson, North Carolina 28640
www.mcfarlandpub.com*

For Nancy, my life's light,
in the fiftieth year of our marriage

Table of Contents

Preface: Chrétien de Troyes's Conte del Graal … 1
Introduction. The Prologue: "Through a glass, darkly" … 11

1. Specularity and Reflective Sequences … 17
2. The Hermitage: "He that abideth in charity" … 55
3. Gawain in the Galloway Borderland … 85
4. Apotheosis and Relapse … 104

Conclusion: "Hide your good deeds from your left hand" … 133
Appendices
    A. The *Peccatum matris* as Original Sin:
       Psalm 108/109:14 … 153
    B. The *Peccatum matris* as an Incentive to Charity:
       Foregrounding the Mother in the Vulgate Sirach … 155
    C. The Custom of Logres in the *Charrete* … 158
Chapter Notes … 161
Bibliography … 185
Index … 195

Preface
Chrétien de Troyes's *Conte del Graal*

Perceval or the Conte del Graal (*Story of the Grail*)[1] was written, probably late in the decade 1181–1190, in the court of Phillip of Alsace, count of Flanders, by Chrétien de Troyes, a native of Champagne. Earlier in his career, Chrétien had served as a clerk in the court of Henry the Liberal, Duke of Champagne, and his duchess, Marie, daughter of Louis VII of France and Eleanor of Aquitaine. The *Conte del Graal* is the capstone of a celebrated sequence of texts that began with the first Arthurian romance ever written, *Erec et Enide*. This groundbreaking work had been preceded by a narrative drawn from the Tristan matter and non–Arthurian texts such as translations from Ovid, perhaps including a *Philomena*, and an adventure romance, *Guillaume d'Angleterre*, both of which are signed by a writer named Chrétien.[2] *Erec et Enide* was followed by more romances largely centered in King Arthur's court: *Cligés*, *Lancelot* or *Li Chevaliers de la Charrete* (*Knight of the Cart*), dedicated to Marie of Champagne, and *Yvain* or *Li Chevaliers au lion* (*Knight of the Lion*).[3] The *Conte del Graal*, Chrétien's last work, represents a first for him: it is the earliest known literary work to mention a wondrous grail, a kind of serving dish, that subsequently came to be known as the Holy Grail. It is also distinguished by a cast of powerful characters who act in an intriguing and complex plot. The *Conte del Graal* is unfinished, and the crucial fact of its incompletion sparked the imagination of many followers in France and elsewhere who, within a very few years of its release, attempted to bring it to conclusion, often rewriting it in light of their personal readings of its mysteries. In fact, all works about the Grail produced

Preface

from the Middle Ages to this very day descend from Chrétien's masterpiece.

There is always something new to say about a poem as rich and intricate as the *Conte del Graal*. I have written about it before, beginning with a book published some thirty-five years ago and most recently in a companion to Chrétien de Troyes.[4] In the present book I do not often consciously refer to my previous studies and try not to repeat what I have said before; if I do, it is usually to examine old matter in a new light. Even so, little of what I have to say here clashes with the body from which the book has grown. How could it be otherwise? On the other hand, the extent to which I gratefully rely on the work of colleagues who have subsequently published works pertinent to the *Conte del Graal* and related topics will immediately become clear.

The main themes I explore are summarized in the main title, *Perceval and Gawain in a Dark Mirror*: plays of darkness, light, colors, reflective surfaces, and specularity in the *Conte del Graal*. The title also alludes to contributions by other scholars from which I have drawn inspiration: Joan Grimbert's book on ambiguity and reflexivity in Chrétien's *Yvain*,[5] Donald Maddox's paradigm of the specular encounter,[6] Norris J. Lacy's discussion of analogical relationships,[7] Antoinette Saly's studies of parallel and symmetrical structures in the *Conte del Graal*,[8] Lucien Dällenbach's seminal work on *mise en abyme*,[9] and many more.[10] It also points to St. Paul's well-known and eminently relevant anatomy of charity in 1 Corinthians 13, most notably to verse 12, which informs the *Conte del Graal* from the very beginning. He writes, to paraphrase the Vulgate, that now we perceive God—and reality—as though looking through a mirror—*per speculum*—clouded by darkness, as in an enigma, but we shall see God face to face at a time in the future.[11] In the Douay-Rheims translation, this becomes "We now see through a glass in a dark manner, but then face to face," or, more poetically, according to the Authorized King James Version (AV), "For now we see through a glass, darkly …" In the following pages, I attempt to demonstrate how specularity in its different forms interplays with other themes throughout the *Conte del Graal* to create the romance's narrative fabric.

I am interested in examining the texture of the *Conte del Graal* by identifying important thematic strands, to which I refer as reflective and sometimes specular sequences, that weave their ways through its com-

Preface

position. I also seek to account for the manner in which they come into contact with one another in certain clusters. Analysis of the text in such a perspective cannot productively be based in a linear commentary on plot development. Of necessity, discussion jumps from episode to episode and back again. Even readers already familiar with the *Conte del Graal* may appreciate a brief reminder of its episodic structure:

Prologue

(1–68). Chrétien refers to a number of biblical texts and well-known topoi to define a poetics of the seminal word and introduce the theme of charity.

Perceval Section

1. The Waste Forest (69–616, B69–634). The adolescent Perceval (as yet unnamed) meets knights for the first time in the forest where his mother owns a manor. She informs him about his genealogy and offers advice before he leaves to find King Arthur's to "be made" a knight, whereupon she falls in a dead faint.
2. The Tent Maiden I (617–812, B635–833). Perceval sees a splendid tent topped by a gleaming golden eagle and thinks it is a church. He goes in to pray and finds a beautiful maiden whose lover and attendants are absent. He attempts to seduce her and leaves. When her lover returns, he believes that she has betrayed him and begins to punish her.
3. Carlisle (Carduel) (813–1280, B834–1304). Perceval finds Arthur beset by a haughty invader, whose armor and identity as the Red Knight Perceval appropriates for himself after killing him. He leaves in search of more adventure.
4. Gornemant de Gohort (1281–1678, B 1305–1698). The untutored adolescent, bearing the Red Knight's arms, comes upon the castle of a knight who undertakes to teach him chivalric skills and courtly manners. Too soon, Perceval leaves him to search for his stricken mother.
5. Biaurepaire (1679–2937, B1699–2975). Perceval defends Gornemant's granddaughter, Blanchefleur against Clamadeus and his

seneschal, Anguigneron, who is besieging her castle. Perceval falls in love with her and defeats the invaders; following Gornemant's counsel, he refrains from killing them and sends them to be comfortably imprisoned in Arthur's court.

> Coda 1: at Disnadaron, the defeated knights are graciously received at court; they tell the story of Perceval's exploits.
>
> Coda 2: Perceval leaves Biaurepaire to continue his quest for his mother.

6. The Grail Castle (2938–3385, B2976–3421). Perceval happens upon the wounded Fisher King and his elderly father. In their castle he witnesses a spectacular procession featuring a grail and a bleeding lance. He fails to ask questions about them and is expelled from the castle the next morning.
7. The Weeping Maiden (3386–3656, B3422–3690). Later in the day, Perceval encounters his cousin, who mourns a beheaded knight, her lover and protector. She berates Perceval for his failure at the Grail Castle: had he succeeded, the Fisher King would have been healed of his wounds, a war would have ended, and the king could have ruled his lands in peace. She tells him that his mother is dead and asks his name, which he has not known, and he guesses correctly that it is "Percevax li Galois" (3541, B3757) (Perceval the Welshman). He leaves her to pursue a purposeless quest for adventure.
8. The Tent Maiden II (3657–3969, B3691–4001). Perceval meets the Tent Maiden wandering in a forest. She has suffered cruel punishment at the hands of her lover, the Orgueilleus de la Lande (Proud Knight of the Heath), who has also killed the lover of Perceval's cousin. Perceval admits his guilt to the Orgueilleus and avenges the maiden by defeating him in battle. He orders them both to go to Arthur's court after the maiden has recovered her health and beauty.
9. Carlion I (3970–4125, B 4002–4159). The Orgueilleus and his lady tell the court about Perceval's prowess and compassion. Arthur moves the court out to search for him.
10. Blood Drops in the Snow (4126–4568, B4160–4602). As he seeks adventure, Perceval becomes transfixed by a vision of

Preface

Blanchefleur when he sees blood drops melting into new-fallen snow. Arthur's court is camped nearby. Thanks to Gawain, Perceval is reunited with the king and returns to Carlion with the court.

11. Carlion II (4569–4762, B4603–4796). Amid celebration, a hideous maiden comes to berate Perceval for his failure at the Grail Castle and to propose adventures to Arthur's knights. Perceval swears to return to the Grail Castle. Gawain is diverted from undertaking his adventure to rescue a besieged maiden at Montesclere, however, when a knight comes to accuse him of murdering the former king of Escavalon, where he must prove his innocence in a trial by combat.

Gawain Adventures I

12. Tintagel (4763–5618, B4797–5654). On his way to Escavalon, Gawain is sidetracked by a tournament in Tintagel. There he champions a little girl whose sister has denigrated him. He jousts against the sister's lover and defeats him.
13. Escavalon (5619–6182, B5656–6216). The young king of Escavalon unwittingly offers hospitality to Gawain and cannot prosecute him. The trial is postponed for a year, during which Gawain must search for the Bleeding Lance, which, it is said, threatens Arthur's kingdom of Logres with destruction.

Perceval Adventures Continued

14. Hermitage Episode (6183–6478, B6217–6518). On Good Friday, after five years of adventures and insanity, Perceval comes to a hermitage where his uncle, brother to the Fisher King and Perceval's mother, hears his confession of failure at the Grail Castle and absolves him of the sin that impeded his success. This is the last we hear of Perceval.

Gawain Adventures II

15. Galloway Section (6479–9139, B6519–9188).
    (a) (6479–7189, B6519–7231). After leaving Escavalon, Gawain

enters Galloway, where he meets an old enemy, Greoreas, and his lady. Greoreas, gravely wounded, sends him to a nearby castle to face the fierce knight who has nearly beheaded him. Instead of the expected adventure, Gawain encounters the Orgueilleuse de Logres (Proud Maiden of Logres *or* the Malevolent Maiden), who puts herself under his protection. Together they ride back to the hill where Gawain left Greoreas. Gawain cures him with a medicinal herb. Healed, Greoreas recognizes Gawain as his enemy and humiliates him by taking his horse—(Le) Gringalet—and leaving him with a nag. Gawain rides away with his protégée, who mocks him ceaselessly.

(b) (7190–7328, B7232–7370). They arrive at a boat landing and see a huge castle, the Roche de Champguin (Rock of Champguin) across a wide river. A murderous knight (identified as Greoras's nephew), riding Gringalet, attacks Gawain and is defeated by him. Meanwhile, the Malevolent Maiden escapes in a boat, which she has apparently left at the dock.

(c) (7329–8329, B7371–8371). A Ferryman takes Gawain to the castle across the river and serves as his host. The following day, he leads Gawain to the castle's great hall, where Gawain successfully undergoes an arduous test of his courage and strength (the Bed of Marvels). The elder of two queens in the castle—Ygraine, Arthur's deceased mother and his own grandmother—tells him that he is the long-expected liberator of the castle and that he is now its lord. As lord, he may not leave the castle.

(d) (8330–9138, B8372–9188). Ygraine allows Gawain freedom from the castle for a day, however, when they see the Malevolent Maiden at the landing across the river with a knight who customarily fights there intruders who cross the border into Galloway. Gawain defeats the knight, and he again places the maiden under his protection. She entices him to undergo the test of the Perilous Ford, in which he eventually finds success by crossing to the other side of a deep river gorge. There he meets the lord of that territory, (Le) Guiromelant of Orqueneles, who gives him further informa-

tion about the Roche de Champguin and the Malevolent Maiden. As they converse, Guiromelant learns Gawain's identity and accuses King Lot, Gawain's father, of murdering his father and Gawain himself of murdering his cousin. The two knights agree on a trial by combat before Arthur, who is celebrating Pentecost at Orkney. Gawain returns to the Malevolent Maiden, who repents of her wicked speech and explains why she has been so hateful. He takes her to the castle, where she will gladly serve the two queens. In secret, Gawain dispatches a squire to Orkney with a message entreating Arthur to bring his court to Gawain's new domain and preside over the judicial combat against Guiromelant. Gawain then knights 500 squires who have awaited a liberator.
16. Orkney (9139–9184, B9189–9234). The messenger rides through the streets of Orkney, which teem with a sick, poverty-stricken populace who mourn the absence of their benefactor, Gawain. He arrives at the castle's great hall, where he sees a grieving Arthur. As the squire approaches the king, Chrétien lays down his pen forever.

The Narrative Fabric of the Conte del Graal: *Example of the Tent Maiden Nexus*

In nearly all narrative loci in Chrétien's last romance—episodes, discrete segments of episodes—are junctures of a variety of specular, speculative, and spectacular strands that discernibly run throughout the poem's texture. The first Tent Maiden episode serves as a useful example that is not atypically complex:

- The episode generates a secondary plot line that intersects with several others, re-emerging with the Weeping Maiden (no. 7), whose protector has been murdered by the Tent Maiden's lover, and surfacing yet again when Perceval meets her a second time, avenges her lover's mistreatment of her (no. 8), and eventually unites them with the court of King Arthur (no. 9).
- Perceval's initial belief that a dazzling tent he sees in a meadow near

Preface

a forest is a church and his bungling attempts to seduce the maiden he finds inside result from misapplications of two aspects of the advice his mother gives him when he leaves his home in the Waste Forest (no. 1).

- After Perceval leaves the Tent Maiden, her lover returns and uses his misreading of hoof prints and other signs of an intruder's presence to discredit her true account of what happened with Perceval, and he initiates a sadistic punishment directed against her and her horse for the "other knight's" abuse of her.
- Later Perceval's conversation with his cousin, the Weeping Maiden (no. 7), initiates a sequence of recapitulations of events at the Grail Castle the evening before (no. 6): at Carlion II (no. 11) and the Hermitage (no. 14), with an echo at Escavalon (no. 13) in the Gawain Adventures.
- Perceval's second meeting with the Tent Maiden and his ultimate encounter with the Orgueilleus de la Lande (no. 8) are both incidents fraught with retrospective references, of varying degrees of verifiability, going back to Perceval's intrusion into the tent (no. 2). As a condition for mercy, the Orgueilleus must restore his lady to her former beauty and elegance.
- When, at Perceval's instigation, the Orgueilleus and his lady arrive at Arthur's court in Carlisle (Carduel) (no. 9), they join a line of secondary narrators: Yonet (no. 3), Anguigneron and Clamadeus (no. 5, coda 1), and, later, the Hideous Damsel (no. 11) and even the Hermit (no. 14). All of them tell stories of Perceval's deeds and exploits: "contes de Perceval." In reaction to the Orgueilleus's confession, moreover, the king is motivated to launch a quest for Perceval, who is subsequently reunited with the court in a series of two scenes, Blood Drops in the Snow (no. 10) followed by the second Carlisle episode (no. 11), which rounds out Chrétien's discrete grouping of Perceval's adventures apart from the Hermitage episode.
- The Tent Maiden episode reflects a specular sequence defined by the consumption of food and drink (uninvited, Perceval takes a pasty and a tankard of wine that remain on a table) that begins when he demands food from his mother (no. 1) and continues in a sequence of meals, meager and lavish, in castle halls (nos. 3–5) that includes a banquet in the Grail Castle (no. 6) and culminates with

Preface

the simple meal of herbs and bread that Perceval takes with the Hermit on Good Friday (no. 14), when he learns about the Grail King's daily Eucharistic meal.
- With the gleaming eagle, the Tent Maiden episode participates as well in a sequence of mirrors of polished metal linked with shining knights' armor in the Waste Forest (no. 1) and the Grail itself (no. 6).
- Finally, it introduces the question of the Custom of Logres, which resurfaces later in the Perceval section (no. 7) and returns as a defining topic in the Gawain Adventures (no. 15a, c-d), where light is shed retrospectively on Perceval's "innocent" infraction and the Orgueilleus de la Lande's abuse of the Custom.

The list is not exhaustive, but every one of the episodes or narrative segments linked to the Tent Maiden by common reflective sequences—for example, the first Carlion episode (no. 9), in which the Orgueilleus de la Lande addresses the court—is itself a juncture of strands connected with still other episodes and narrative segments, the most evident examples of which are the various court scenes, Arthurian and non-Arthurian.

Each of the individual specular sequences has its own implications, but no sequence exists in isolation from others: significance or signification may vary with context. The strands are woven together in a fabric in which every element is involved at every moment in a poetics of prospection, retrospection, introspection, and extrospection. The fabric is multi-textured, for the strands may be variously described as metallic, luminary, organic, thematic, structural, verbal, textual, etc. They are by definition intratextual, for analogies occur and recur within the *Conte del Graal* itself—for example, in certain of the Gawain Adventures as rewritings of specific segments of the Perceval Section, or *vice versa* perhaps, although this is not a case that I intend to argue here. Moreover, as we shall soon see in the Introduction, Chrétien broaches the very subject of specularity in opening the *Conte del Graal* with spectacular displays of intertextuality that are repeated and imitated throughout the romance.

Before continuing, I must express my sincerest thanks to my daughter-in-law, Martha Danek, for her extraordinary image of Perceval

Preface

in the snow, which decorates the cover, and the beautiful drawings that appear throughout the book.

I am also grateful to two colleagues whose invitations to speak at their universities and meet with students in their medieval literature seminars stimulated the thinking that informs this book: Sarah-Jane Murray of Baylor University (November 2008) and Caroline Jewers of the University of Kansas (May 2010). They will recognize material from different parts of the first chapter, as may colleagues who attended the International Medieval Congress (Kalamazoo) in May 2010 and heard a paper on Perceval as mediator and translator. Those present at the Annual Meeting of the South Central Modern Language Association in San Antonio in November 2012 ("Thinking about Greoreas") and at Kalamazoo in May 2013 ("Perceval and the Book of Sirach") may also recall papers drawn from parts of Chapters 2 and 3.

My thanks also to the gracious staff at the Keeneland Library in Lexington, Kentucky, for their generosity in helping me with research on medieval horses.

Introduction

The Prologue: "Through a glass, darkly"

It is fitting to start at the beginning. The ways in which dark mirrors, enigmatic reflectors of mysteries, are pertinent to the *Conte del Graal*, Chrétien's last, unfinished romance, first come to light in his highly complex Prologue, of which the following offers a concise and necessarily incomplete reading.

The opening is an exemplary embodiment of the seminal word topos:

> Qui petit seme petit quialt,
> Et qui auques recoillir vialt
> An tel leu sa semance espande
> Que fruit a cent dobles li rande;
> Car an terre qui rien ne vaut
> Bone semance seche et faut.
> Crestïens seme et fet semance
> D'un romans que il ancomance,
> Et si le seme an si bon leu
> Qu'il ne puet estre sanz grant preu ...
> [1–10].

(He who sows little reaps little, but he who wishes to reap plentifully casts his seeds on ground that will increase his fruit a hundredfold, for good seed withers and dies in worthless soil. Chrétien sows and casts the seed of a romance he begins here, and he sows it in such a good place that it cannot fail to be bountiful.)

At the outset Chrétien quotes one of St. Paul's best-known sayings, which had become proverbial in France by the end of the twelfth century: "Hoc autem dico: Qui parce seminat, parce et metet" (II Corinthians 9:6) (He who soweth sparingly, shall also reap sparingly) (1–4).[1] His

Introduction

narrator then links the proverb to Christ's Parable of the Sower[2] and thus creates a dual intertextual relationship between his prologue and certain passages in the New Testament (5–10).[3]

Intertextuality

Well over a half-century ago, Nathan Edelman demonstrated in a ground-breaking article that a mere half-verse quote from Psalm 108/109 in François Villon's *Testament* implicates the entirety of the Psalm as intertext.[4] Similarly, all of II Corinthians 9 has bearing on Chrétien's prologue and indeed all of the romance, as does the whole of the Parable of the Sower along with Christ's explanation of its hidden meanings shared only with an elite segment of the audience who has heard the story. On the one hand, in the immediate context of II Corinthians 9:6, Paul exhorts his Greek readers to contribute financially with utmost generosity to the ministry to the saints (9:1), that is, the church in far-away Jerusalem.[5] God loves cheerful givers and will provide the church at Corinth with abundant means to exercise munificence (9:7–9). On the other hand, Chrétien metaphorically sows the seed of his romance in good soil, which is the mind, heart, and soul of his patron, Phillip of Alsace, count of Flanders (11–13),[6] and he anticipates reaping a bountiful harvest from his investment (61–68).

The relevance of beneficent largesse to Chrétien's last romance goes deeper than a dependent writer's appeal to his patron.[7] He continues by asserting that Philip is infinitely superior to Alexander the Great, who, in a series of French *Romances of Alexander* written after 1150, is hailed as the highest model of noble liberality. He is regarded as such in Chrétien's two earliest romances to survive,[8] but, in the *Conte del Graal*, the emperor of Hellenic Antiquity is hyperbolically counted as worthless in comparison with Philip, a Christian vassal of both the King of France (implicitly) and the German emperor of the modern Roman empire (13). The difference is that the Ancient pagan did not know or understand charity, which governs Philip's life and his rule.[9] In charity, Philip is grieved by crude, sarcastic, or proud language (21–24); he loves true justice, feudal loyalty, and Holy Church, hates dishonorable behavior (25–27)—and he practices liberal giving, *largesse*, which is the greatest of noble virtues (28).

The Prologue: Through a glass, darkly

Chrétien then comments on Christ's injunction, "Te autem faciente eleemosynam, nesciat sinistra tua quid faciat dextera tua" (Matthew 6:3) (But when thou dost alms, let not thy left hand know what thy right hand doth).[10] The left hand denotes vainglory, which comes from hypocrisy, but the right hand signifies charity, which does not boast of its good deeds. Here he quotes from I Corinthians 13:4, where charity is personified: "Charité ... de sa bone oevre / Pas ne se vante" (44) (Charity ... does not boast of its good deed), cf. "Charitas non aemulatur ... non inflator" (charity envieth not, is not puffed up). Unlike Alexander, Philip of Flanders gives in secret[11]; like Charity, he hides his good works (43–44), "Que nus ne le set que cil non / Qui Dex et Charité a non ..." (so that only He whose name is God and Charity knows of [them]) (45–46). "Dex est Charité," he continues, translating I John 4:16, "et qui vit / An charité ... / Il maint an Deu et Dex en lui" (47–50) (God is Charity, and he who abides in charity abides in God and God in him).[12] In referring to I Corinthians, Chrétien creates a nexus linking the whole of ch. 13 to his text, and he strengthens the connection as he emphatically—and erroneously—attributes the passage from I John to Paul.[13] Unlike some scholars,[14] I believe that Chrétien is too smart and too learned to misconstrue I John as a Pauline epistle, although I concede that he may have done so because of the close thematic associations. In any case, given the context of the Prologue, both I John and I Corinthians are in perfect harmony with it and with each other.

How is I Corinthians 13 reflected in Chrétien's prologue in particular and in the *Conte del Graal* generally? In the attributes of charity, to be sure: its theological pre-eminence, its selfless concern for others, its faithfulness, its love of truth and justice, its sincerity, its devotion to service, its kindheartedness, its humility, its readiness to forgive. Such are traits that Chrétien specifically ascribes to Philip of Flanders (21–28, 51–56), and they are qualities that are extolled throughout the romance.[15] But there is also a significant link with the romance in the mirror of vs. 12. Paul's *speculum* is the glass through which we see darkly, and the kinds of specularity it implies—mirrors and ways of mirroring: reflection, distortion, refraction, perception, and speculation—abound in the *Conte del Graal*.

Our understanding of the romance is further enhanced by Paul's three-fold paradigm of human growth in charity and in the experience of charity:

Introduction

Cum essem parvulus, loquebar ut parvulus, sapiebam ut parvulus, cogitabam ut parvulus. Quando autem factus sum vir, evacuavi quae erant parvuli. Videmus nunc per speculum in aenigmate: tunc autem facie ad faciem. Nunc cognosco exparte: tunc autem cognoscam sicut et cognitus sum. Nunc autem manent fides, spes, charitas: tria haec; maior autem horum est charitas [I Corinthians 13:11–13].

(When I was a child, I spoke as a child, I understood as a child, I thought as a child. But, when I became a man, I put away the things of a child. We see now through a glass in a dark manner; but then face to face. Now I know in part; but then I shall know even as I am known. And now there remain faith, hope, and charity, these three: but the greatest of these is charity.)

The child (then, in the past) has grown into a man (now, in the present), and human adulthood shall give way to a state of perfection (then, in the future) when darkness is dispersed and all is bright and clear. The paradigm is reflected in ancient and medieval theories of translation, such as Chrétien undertakes in the *Conte del Graal*. At least from St. Augustine of Hippo to Chrétien's older contemporary Bernard of Clairvaux, charity as described in the Pauline paradigm was also seen to lie at the heart of both literal and figurative readings of the Bible and other texts.[16]

Mirrors Ancient and Medieval

It is worthwhile at this point to consider the nature of mirrors in pre-modern times.[17] In Antiquity, highly polished metals were used as mirrors, bronze at first, then silver and even gold. Glass mirrors with gold or silver applied to the back were also known. We cannot know which kind of mirrors St. Paul has in mind, although the reference in I Corinthians 13 indeed suggests a distorted or blurred unpolished image. We do know, however, that the manufacture of glass mirrors was to decline in the fifth century. Isidore of Seville mentions glass mirrors at the turn of the next century,[18] but they were virtually unknown during later years in medieval Western Europe before the late twelfth century, the very period when Chrétien de Troyes was writing. Chrétien was certainly familiar with metal mirrors, burnished silver or tempered steel, and he might also have seen the German novelty of a glass mirror silvered with mercury. In all events, medieval glass mirrors would have been quite inferior to their classical prototypes and certainly would fall far short of today's standards. Nothing like crystal-clear glass existed in the high Middle Ages. Not only was glass invariably colored, as in stained-glass windows, but the surfaces also tended to be wavy and full of indentations, protrusions, streaks, pits, and air bubbles. In the Galloway Section of the *Conte del Graal*,[19] five hundred glazed windows adorn the clerestory in the great hall at the Roche de Champguin. The windows are *clere[s]* (7679, B7721) (clear), but Chrétien qualifies the description when he remarks that anyone who looks through it must concentrate in order to make out the people below.[20] The glass is also stained in a variety of colors; even unsilvered, as it must be for observers to see through it, it would have reflective qualities, but the mirrors would be "dark."

Aside from these clerestory windows, it is burnished metals for the most part that function as mirrors in the *Conte del Graal*. Chrétien's last romance sparkles with myriad reflective points, including the windows at the Roche de Champguin, scattered from beginning to end, and every one of them is connected to another one or many others. The present volume will consider the most spectacular examples. Metaphorical mirrors, however, are perhaps even more compelling.

1

Speculary and Reflective Sequences

Reflections in the Waste Forest and Beyond

The opening scenes of the Waste Forest episode (69–616, B69–634) initiate several important instances of literal and figurative reflective sequences that run throughout the text. The first reference to mirrors after St. Paul's implicit *speculum* in the Prologue occurs within the first fifty verses of narration, where the young Perceval rides his hunting horse into his mother's woods and begins to practice throwing his javelins. He is suddenly frightened by a loud, outlandish clanking of metal, but when its source appears, he is literally bedazzled by what he takes to be a band of angels led by God the Father. Sunlight reflected by these beings' weapons and polished body armor makes them gleam all over, and they emit flashes of red, green, gold, blue, and silver.[1] The gleaming beings turn out of course to be humans, "ordinary" knights from King Arthur's court, though the boy's mother will warn him later that they are devils and not angels. The fact remains that it is the knights' shining beauty that awakens Perceval to his destiny and inspires him to become one of them. It is also significant that, in Perceval's eyes, beauty and rank are gauged by the light's intensity, for it is the knights' captain who shines the most brightly.[2] Mirrors and spectacular displays of reflected light recur subsequently in the Tent Maiden episode, at the Grail Castle, at the Roche de Champguin in Galloway, and, softly diffused, when Perceval loses himself in rapturous contemplation of blood drops diffused in new-fallen snow.

Meanwhile, another dimension of specularity emerges when Arthur's knights repeatedly ask Perceval about a party of knights and maidens who they believe have come this way (184–86, 208–11, 254–57, 278–80, 291–94). After deflecting their questions for some time in order to ask his own concerning their nature and their armor, Perceval finally responds that he has not in fact seen them. Instead he points to a group of his mother's serfs who are harrowing oats in a high field near a mountain pass and suggests that they may know about them (295–303). The knights insist that he accompany them (304–06), and so he rides with them up to the field (cf. 311–22). Perceval asks the field hands the visitors' question: Have you seen knights and maidens? He hears their answer: Just today they have ridden through these forests. And he conveys that information to the captain: They have just passed through these woods.[3] The knights' reluctance to approach the field hands by themselves signals that they need an interpreter in order to communicate with them. The knights' language is most certainly courtly French,[4] the laborers speak uncouth Welsh. Perceval's redundant repetition of their response, which the knights are close enough to hear for themselves, but must not understand, implies an act of translation. Unlike the knights whom he seeks to emulate, Perceval is bilingual—and bicultural.

The setting of the event, a productive field tended by laborers who have just sown and are now harrowing oats, covering the seed with soil so that they will take root and thrive,[5] concretizes the metaphorical imagery at the beginning of the Prologue, where Chrétien exploits the topos of the seminal word by connecting the Parable of the Sower with Pauline and Johanine discourses on charity and by describing his clerkly enterprise of writing as "sowing his romance," which purports to be a translation.[6] Perceval's act of translation and interpreting constitutes a *mise en abyme*, a specular incident in the narrative that reflects the work of the author/narrator and the production of his text.[7] Perceval is bilingual, and the cultural clash between the Welsh manor and the francophone court, which is made explicit in the remark one of the Francophone knights makes about the uncivilized Welsh,[8] haunts him throughout the romance.

The incident is complex with respect to specularity because at least two reflective sequences emanate from it, each one of which is sustained throughout the romance independently, yet always with a degree of inter-referentiality. On the one hand, instances of interrogation, which have already illuminated Perceval's incipient acquisition of knowledge about knighthood (his persistent questions, the captain's patient

1. Specularity and Reflective Sequences

responses, 174–230, 260–94), are reintroduced (1) in the instructions Perceval's mother gives him before he leaves her (549–76, B529–56); (2) in his unfinished apprenticeship with Gornemant de Gohort (1347–99, B1367–1419; 1436–42, B1356–62; 1475–84, B1495–1504; etc.); (3) at the Grail Castle—negatively, when Perceval *fails* to ask questions (3156–78, B3190–3212; 3206–19, B3240–53); (4) in his display of total recall the next day as his cousin, the Weeping Maiden, cross-examines him about what he witnessed at the Grail Castle (3514–43, B3548–77); and (5) twice in the Hermitage episode (6220–80, B6254–6314, and, in a series of indirect questions, 6334–55, B6367–89).

On the other hand, the specular power of Perceval's translation and transmission of information is amplified many times over when knights he has defeated tell Arthur and his court, in "contes de Perceval," how valiantly he has fought, just as Chrétien boasts (perhaps uncharitably, for Charity does not boast but hides her good works), that his *Conte del Graal* (Story of the Grail) with Perceval as a first and perhaps primary protagonist, is the best *conte* that can be told in a royal court (61–68). Prominent among these avatars of Chrétien are (1) the squire Yonet, who recounts to Arthur Perceval's combat with the Red Knight and his acquisition of arms (1187–1231, B1207–51); (2–3) Anguigneron, seneschal of Clamadeus of the Islands, who has besieged Blanchefleur's castle and relates Perceval's exploits in a story twice told, once implicitly in reference to himself (2714–29, B2734–53) and again explicitly with respect to Clamadeus (2730–50, B2764–84); (4) the Orgueilleus de la Lande and the Tent Maiden, whom Perceval reconciles after offending both of them and avenging the knight's self-centered and systematic mistreatment of his lover and lack of trust in her faithfulness (3961–4024, B3995–4058); (5) King Arthur himself, who tells Gawain about Perceval's arrival at Carlisle (4043–4106, B4077–4142); (6) the Hideous Damsel, whose "conte de Perceval," as prototype of Chrétien's romance, is the first "conte del Graal" ever told in a royal court (4612–49, B4646–83); and, not least of all, Perceval's own confessions: (7–8) to Gornemant de Gohort (1560–74, B1594–1618), and implicitly to Blanchefleur and her subjects (cf. 2886–98, B2920–32), about his mother's grief and fall at his departure from her manor in the Waste Forest; (9) to the Weeping Maiden about his experiences at the Grail Castle (3462–72, B3496–3506; 3500–10, B3534–44; 3630–38, B3664–72); (10) to the Tent Maiden about his "inno-

Perceval and Gawain in Dark Mirrors

cent" abuse of her (3761–72, B3795–3806) and (11) to the Orgueilleus de la Lande about his intrusion into his tent and attempts to woo his lady (3865–76, B3899–3920); and, finally, (12) to the Hermit about his despair and its causes (6338–52, B6372–86).

In reflection of the Prologue's idealized reception of Chrétien's romance by the lord who commissioned him to translate it, all such "contes de Perceval" bear fruit in varying degrees. The first three, one by Yonet and two by Anguigneron, remind Arthur about Kay's unjust, discourteous, and uncharitable treatment of Perceval and about how much he misses the brash young knight. Even more significantly, the Orgueilleus de la Lande's account moves Arthur to make a progress to look for Perceval, thereby precipitating his reunion with the court on an incongruous snowy day in Whitsuntide (4107–4568, B4073–4534) which is celebrated in the crucial second Carlion episode (4569–4762, B4535–4724). Meanwhile, Arthur's own embellished and somewhat self-serving "conte de Perceval" allows Gawain to recognize him after Perceval emerges from his trance induced when drops of blood in the snow remind him of his lady, Blanchefleur. The Hideous Damsel, whose monstrous appearance betokens her oracular powers,[9] re-energizes the narrative action at Arthur's second Carlion court at a time when Perceval seems to have forgotten the most important stories about himself. She berates him for his failure at the Grail Castle, goads him into a quest to return there, and proposes adventures for Arthur's other knights. Finally the sequence of Perceval's interrogations and confessions ultimately leads him to rehabilitation and redemption at the Hermitage.

The sequence of secondary "contes" extends into the Gawain Adventures, but in refracted distortions of Perceval's encounters: unheroic "contes de Gauvain" are told publicly, nearly always to his detriment, in royal and noble courts and in other courtly settings (1) at Carlion by Guiganbresil, who accuses him of murder (4721–61, B4755–95); (2) at Tintagel, after the Pucelle aus Manches Petites (the Maiden with the Small Sleeves) defends him (5036–45, B5070–5119), by her elder sister's friends (e.g., 5020–35, B5054–69); (3–4) in Escavalon by a vavassor, a holder of a fief from the king, as he excoriates the king's sister (5806–31, B5839–65) and then exhorts the townspeople against him (5879–99, B5913–33); and (5) on the Galloway frontier by Greoreas, who accuses Gawain of judicial harassment within earshot of his lady and

1. Specularity and Reflective Sequences

the Malevolent Maiden of Logres (7067–75, B7109–15).[10] Denigrating specular accounts of Gawain are addressed to him privately at Orqueneles by Guiromelant, who, like Guiganbresil, accuses him of murder (8709–48, B8757–96), and in the scathing verbal assaults of the Malevolent Maiden before her own confession and "redemption" (8869–8930, B8917–78).[11]

Specular Encounter

To return to the Waste Forest opening, Chrétien also introduces there a similarly complex sequence involving what Donald Maddox terms specular encounters, that is, highly charged moments when protagonists learn their life-stories and receive, sometimes clearly, sometimes darkly, foreknowledge of their destinies.[12] While Perceval exercises with his javelin, he hears, then sees beautiful knights in gleaming armor whom he believes at first to be angels, and at that very moment he discovers his true nature and his destiny. Moreover, in a concretized reflection of that vision, his mother later explains to him why she has raised him in ignorance of knighthood in order to protect him against its evils. She informs him of his noble genealogy on both sides and relates incidents in a devastating war following the death of Utherpendragon, Arthur's father: the downfall of noble families such as theirs, the wounding of Perceval's father in the thigh, their family's impoverishment, their escape to their Waste Forest manor, the knightly service of two elder brothers whom he was too young to know, their gruesome deaths, and his father's mortal grief (389–470, B407–88). As Perceval is destined to do, his brothers had served in royal courts: the elder in that of the king of Escavalon (445–46, B485–86), while the younger was sent to Ban of Gormeret (448–49, B488–89). We shall see how Escavalon looms large in the career of Gawain and serves as a link between Gawain and Perceval or, more specifically, his family; King Ban is not mentioned again.[13]

Perceval's mother has striven to keep her son safe from the dangers of serving as a knight in troubled times. She has also wished to preserve him for herself as her only comfort in grief. Perceval's destiny lies in his genealogy—in his genes—and, once he is awakened to chivalry, she recognizes that she is powerless to prevent him from going to Arthur to be knighted. She is certain that Arthur will grant him arms despite his utter lack of experience, which indeed soon happens at Carlisle, but she is fearful and unsure about what lies ahead for him after that (492–508, B510–26).

The war following Utherpendragon's death is closely bound to Perceval's genealogy and his own life's story, but, as demonstrated in the example of his act of translation, it is possible to isolate and define certain sequences. In one strand, the war that provides context for the establishment of the Waste Forest community also figures in the founding of the Roche de Champguin and its community of women and unknighted squires of all ages. Ygraine (Igerne), Utherpendragon's queen and Arthur's dead mother, has invested her treasure to build her castle after her husband's death, and a rich man who has lost a leg, perhaps a veteran of that war, guards the great hall there. Older ladies there are bereft of their husbands and exiled from their lands, while younger women have been orphaned (7477–7562, B7591–7604; 8691–8719, B8739–76). The two communities, in the Waste Forest manor and at the Roche de Champguin, along with the Hermitage, are in fact major focal points of multiple reflective sequences. According to the Weeping Maiden and the Hideous Damsel, moreover, the Grail kingdom and the Grail King's castle are currently involved in warfare.

Meanwhile, as Perceval approaches Carlisle to ask for arms, he learns from a charcoal burner in the forest that Arthur is celebrating because has recently defeated Ryon, king of the Islands (830–33, B850–53). At the same time, Arthur is sorrowful because his castle is filled with knights wounded in battle and those who are healthy have retired to their own estates, where they are better off than at Carlisle (834–38, B854–58). If we read the *Conte del Graal* alongside Wace's *Brut*, which transmits an important legendary history of Arthur's reign amplifying that of Geoffrey of Monmouth,[14] we learn that, in order to consolidate his rule, young King Arthur conquers such major outlying islands as Ireland and Iceland. In response, kings of other maritime territories (Orkney, Gotland, and Baltic lands of the Wends) fear that Arthur will ravage their own islands along with "tuz les isles" (*Brut*, 9714) (all the islands). They peacefully surrender their lands to him and receive them back as fiefs (*Brut*, 9659–9730).[15] The subjugation of the islands and Arthur's establishment of the Round Table usher in a twelve-year period

1. Specularity and Reflective Sequences

of peace, the *pax arthuriana*, during which many chivalric adventures are said to have occurred, including those recounted in Chrétien's romances (*Brut*, 9731–98).

In the *Conte del Graal*, the court jester, Arthur's Fool, announces at Carlisle the onset of such adventures (1236–39, B1256–59),[16] some of which the Hideous Damsel specifies at Carlion (4612–4712, B4646–4746). When Perceval arrives at Biaurepaire, Blanchefleur's castle is being besieged in fact by King Clamadeus of the Islands, who is perhaps meant to be King Ryon's successor, and those few of her people who are left in her castle are on the verge of starvation. Meanwhile, their fellow citizens have been killed in the siege or, like hostages from Logres in *Le Chevalier de la Charrete* before Lancelot frees them, are imprisoned in the invader's foreign castle (1979–92, B1999–2012). Likewise, Perceval becomes their defender and liberator in his first service as a knight after his partial education and training by Gornemant de Gohort (1301–1678, B1335–1712). In light of traditional history, the attack by Clamadeus appears to be a vengeful flare-up after the Saxon wars have ended.

The Fisher King suffers from the same kind of debilitating thigh-wound as Perceval's father. Moreover, according to the Hideous Damsel, war continues to rage in the quasi-invisible world of the Grail kingdom,[17] despite an apparent peace in Arthur's own realm, and, as in the case of the women at the Roche de Champguin (7521–39, B7563–81), ladies will lose their husbands and maidens will be orphaned because so many knights are doomed to death (4612–49, B4646–88). In her view, Perceval's failure at the Grail Castle makes him responsible for not putting an end to a war that afflicts the castle's dependents as well as their king. Similarly, Gawain is directly and indirectly responsible for conflicts in the realm of the Two Queens at the Roche de Champguin and perhaps as well in Orkney.

While the first specular encounter in the story of Perceval's life is concerned with warfare and genealogy, the second turns to what lies in the future. His mother predicts early on that Arthur will grant him arms despite his ineptitude (494–508, B512–26), although she has some details wrong (it is Kay who "grants" arms to Perceval; technically Gornemant de Gohort, not Arthur, makes her son a knight), but then her mirror darkens altogether. At Carlisle Perceval finds a knight in red armor outside the castle, and he is determined that the armor will be his (879–1186, B899–1206). When he rides into the great hall, Arthur tells him that the Red Knight from the Forest of Quinqueroy (930–31, B950–81) has insulted him and the queen, a crime of *lèse-majesté* that in fact poses a threat to the whole kingdom (869–77, B889–97), but Perceval thinks only of demanding the invader's arms. Before Arthur can respond, Kay sarcastically gives Perceval permission to take the armor for himself. Whereupon the young aspirant goes out and kills the Red Knight with his javelin and lays claim to his horse as well as his armor. With Yonet's much-needed help, Perceval arms himself and rides away to seek adventure. Much later, in the first Carlion episode, Arthur tells Gawain, not without prevarication, that he promised Perceval a suit of more valuable golden armor when he first came to court because he was so handsome and agreeable (4062–75, B4096–4109, compare with 955–80, B975–1000). But red, not gold, was destined to be Perceval's color.

Perceval's mother cannot see beyond a bestowal of arms in Arthur's court, but she attempts to equip her son for that shadowy future by making him new, rough clothing in the Welsh style (480–86, B498–504; 584–86, B604–06). Lest he appear too Welsh (587–93, B607–13), however, she allows him and to take just one of his three signature javelins, and he will wield it when he attacks the Red Knight. She also arms him with advice first about serving ladies and establishing relationships with them, then about seeking the company of worthy men and asking them their name or surname, and, finally, about practicing religion (509–80, B529–600). Perceval's clothing, javelin, and horse betray the land of his upbringing; they are tokens that reflect his childhood. He gradually expends them or exchanges them against emblems of courtesy and chivalry when he kills the Red Knight and takes his horse and armor (1061–1186, B1081–1206) and later when he is tutored by Gornemant de Gohort and receives from him his spurs and refined clothing. As he sheds signs of his Welsh origins, Perceval also gradually abandons his mother's advice, which informs his own childish speech and his garrulous questioning, in favor of Gornemant's lessons and his manly reticence (1577–1678, B1599–1698).[18]

Yet the words of Perceval's mother shape his destiny from his first encounter with adventure until Chrétien mentions him for the last time.

1. Specularity and Reflective Sequences

Her advice at first generates comedy as Perceval mistakes a tent for a church, and her words about *fin' amors* wrongly make him feel free to attempt a violent seduction of the Tent Maiden, to take her food and wine uninvited, and, in his savagely childish ignorance, to expose her to her lover's pathological anger (617–812, B637–832). He meets no worthy men at Carlisle, only a sadly depressed king, a sullen, discourteous, uncharitable Kay, and a hall full of knights wounded in the recent war with King Ryon, and so he asks no one his name—he does not ask Arthur's name because he sees that he is king. Comedy is gradually dispelled from the moment Perceval arrives at Gornemant's castle, where he accepts instruction from a noble knight, whose name he seeks to know (1281–1678, B1301–1698), and then as he moves out to Biaurepaire, where his innate chivalric aptitudes as well as his training serve his love for Blanchefleur and win him her castle and her lands (1679–2674, B1699–2708; 2876–2941, B2910–72). Also in response to his mother's words, he relinquishes marriage and lordship, in intention perhaps only temporarily, when recurring memories of her and his ruthless abandonment of her spur him to leave his lady,[19] but the way home leads him to the Grail Castle. Meanwhile, religious observance and an adult's knowledge of God, which may or may not have been available to him at Biaurepaire and the Grail Castle, remain unknown to him until, at the Hermitage, he hears the Good Friday offices, makes his confession, and receives communion on Easter Sunday.

Also entwined with Perceval's destiny are two interrelated strands involving the Laughing Maiden, or rather the Smiling Maiden,[20] and the Fool, Arthur's court jester (1014–42, B1034–62). As Perceval leaves the castle at Carlisle to confront the Red Knight, he greets a maiden who returns his salutation with a smile. He again encounters his destiny when she tells him in no uncertain terms that, if he lives long enough, there will never be a better knight in the whole world than he. She has not smiled in over six years, a period of dreadful warfare, and the Fool has often predicted that she will not smile again until she sees the man who shall win all lordship in knighthood. Uncharitable Kay slaps her, knocking her to the floor for having smiled not at him, but a crude, naïve country bumpkin. He then kicks the Fool into the roaring fireplace because it was he who had issued the propitious prophesy.

Perceval and Gawain in Dark Mirrors

Figure 1. Equestrian Propriety: *Destrier* **(Charger).**

Perceval rides after the Red Knight and wins his identity and along with his armor and his horse, his *destrier* (1166, B1182) (charger) (Figure 1). After giving Yonet his Welsh hunter (Figure 2), which he no longer needs, he charges the squire to return the king's goblet, which the intruder had snatched from his hands, and to tell the Smiling Maiden that he swears to set aright the injustice Kay has committed against her: "Li cuit je si bien metre cuire / Que por vangiee se tandra" (1182–83, B1216–17) (I hope to cook her such a dish that she'll consider herself well avenged). When Yonet reports Perceval's words, Arthur berates his seneschal for having driven such a promising the youth from the court with his evil tongue. Then in one breath the jester announces Arthur's coming adventures (1236–39, B1270–73) and foretells Kay's punishment for kicking him and striking the maiden which Perceval himself is destined to inflict (1240–54, B1274–88, cf. 4240–85, B4274–4319). Meanwhile, Perceval will begin making good on his oath to the Smiling Maiden by sending to Arthur's court for imprisonment defeated knights

1. Specularity and Reflective Sequences

Figure 2. Equestrian Propriety: Hunter.

who will transmit his greetings to her: Anguigneron (2732–46, B2766–82), Clamadeus des Isles (2793–2842, B2813–62), and the Orgueilleus de la Lande, 3969–4037, B4003–71).

Perceval's specular encounter with the Smiling Maiden is refracted and distorted in the comic mirror of the Tintagel episode in the Gawain adventures (4852–6164, B4886–6197). News of a tournament has distracted Gawain from his mission to Escavalon to face charges of murder, but he dares not participate for fear of an injury that might prevent him from arriving in time to defend himself. Accordingly, he sets up camp well away from the action, but within sight of the spectators at the tournament. Among them is a young lady, elder daughter of lord Tiebaut of Tintagel, whose lover has challenged her father, his vassal (4799–13, B4833–47; 4857–59, B4893–95). She and her friends are intrigued by the strange man camping outside the castle walls who openly displays multiple sets of armor. Because he does not fight, they conclude that he

Perceval and Gawain in Dark Mirrors

is either a cowardly knight or a merchant. This lady, like Kay, is adept at *ramprosnes*—crude insulting, sarcastic speech that Philip of Flanders finds intolerably discourteous and uncharitable, as does King Arthur (e.g., 988–91, B1008–11). But her younger sister defends Gawain by predicting that he will prove to be a better knight than the elder's lover. In jealous anger, again like Kay, the elder sister slaps the perspicacious and truthful maiden. Later the little girl wheedles Gawain into agreeing to fight her sister's lover as her champion, and he obligingly avenges her by humiliating his opponent.

Another specular encounter is rich in promise that is never realized in Chrétien's unfinished romance. As the Fisher King's first act of hospitality to Perceval inside the Grail Castle, he endows him with a magnificent sword which he received from his blonde niece or granddaughter (3112, B3146: *niece*), the last its smith will ever forge (3096–3150, B3130–94). The sword can never be broken except in a single circumstance known only to the smith. Finally, the Fisher King informs Perceval that "… ceste espee / Vos fu jugiee et destine[e], / E je voel mout que vos l'aiez" (3133–35, B3167–69) (this sword was ordained and destined for you, and I am eager for you to have it). The Weeping Maiden tells Perceval later how the sword may be repaired if he breaks it (3639–51, B3673–85), but it is Chrétien's Continuators, not the master, who bring the sword's potential to fruition.[21]

Reflections in a Snowy Mirror

A brilliantly complex variant of the mirror occurs as Perceval is about to be reunited with Arthur's court. After failing at the Grail Castle and learning that his mother has died, he renews his wanderings and again encounters the Tent Maiden, whom he shamed when he took her ring and foolishly attempted to seduce her (3657–3960, B3691–3994, cf. 649–812, B667–830). In belated expiation of the wrongs he has caused her, he fights and defeats her lover, the Orgueilleus de la Lande, who has savagely punished her, and orders him to take her to Arthur's court after he cares for her and restores her to health and beauty. At Carlion, the Orgueilleus tells yet another "conte de Perceval" (3978–4002, B4002–36) in honor of the Smiling Maiden. King Arthur is so inspired by the

1. Specularity and Reflective Sequences

latest story that he moves his court lock, stock, and barrel out into the countryside to search for Perceval.

Early one morning, Perceval rises early, as is now his habit, in order to continue his quest for "Avanture et chevalerie" (4133, B4267) (chivalric adventures), and rides into a snow-covered field near the court's encampment (4126–78, B4160–4212).[22] A falcon, perhaps one belonging to the king himself, frightens a flock of wild geese blinded by the dazzling snow, and they fly up in panic. The falcon strikes and wounds one of the geese, which falls to the ground, and, before it recovers and flies to safety, it leaves three drops of blood in the snow where it had lain. Transfixed, Perceval watches the blood drops as they spread into the snow. He leans on his lance, gazing at them as into a mirror, and perceives the face of his beloved Blanchefleur: "li sans et la nois ansanble / La fresche color li resanble / Qui ert an la face s'amie" (4165–67, B4199–4202) (the blood mingled with the snow [resembles] the [fresh] rosy tint of his lady's cheeks). He is lost in contemplation for hours, slowly regaining consciousness only as the sun gradually melts the snow and the spots fade away. Later he describes his experience to Gawain, adding one significant detail: the drops of fresh blood "*anluminoient* le blanc" (4418, B4452, my emphasis) (made the white snow *sparkle*).[23]

The image reflects Chrétien's description of Blanchefleur over 2,000 lines earlier: "Et mialz avenoit en son vis / Li vermauz sor le blanc asis / Que li sinoples sor l'argent" (1803–05, B1823–25) (the rosiness of [her] cheeks on her white face was more pleasing than vermilion on silver). The simile likens the lady's visage to an *objet d'art* fashioned by a skilled silversmith. In fact, Chrétien surpasses himself in his description of her great beauty as he brings to life a uniquely beautiful woman who is also extraordinarily well-dressed. Her looks belie the deprivations she and her people suffer in her ruined surroundings,[24] and she stands in sharp contrast to the "pucele meigre et pale" (1704, B1724) (thin and pale maiden) who comes to the great hall's windows at Biaurepaire when Perceval bangs on the gates. Perceval's self-effacing contemplation of his beloved in the snowy mirror is an exquisite expression of *fin' amors*, and indeed Gawain judges that this *panser*, that is, Perceval's oblivious contemplation of his beloved, "n'estoit pas vilains, / Einz estoit mout cortois et dolz" (4424–25, B4458–59) (was no vulgar thought, but a most sweet and courtly one).

29

Perceval and Gawain in Dark Mirrors

Chrétien boasts of the particularity and superiority of his description of Blanchefleur:

> ...se je onques fis devise
> An biauté que Dex eüst mise
> An cors de fame ne an face,
> Or me replest que une an face
> Ou ge ne mantirai de mot
> [1785–89, B1805–09].

(if ever before I have described the beauty God [stamped] in a woman's face and body, I would like to try another [kind of] description that would never vary from the truth).

She is not, of course, the only lady whom Chrétien's narrator describes in terms of her white and rosy complexion.

An important aspect of originality amid conventionality is recognizable in Chrétien's artistry here, for the references in the Biaurepaire and Blood-Drops episodes also introduce a specular sequence by anticipating two descriptions in the Galloway Section. Gawain's sister, Clarissant, is endowed with similar traits: "La face ot blanche, et par desus / L'ot *anluminee* Nature / D'une color vermeille et pure" (7862–64, B7904–06, my emphasis) (her face was white, and Nature had *highlighted* it with a pure and rosy tint). Meanwhile, the "face" and "gole" (neck) of the Malevolent Maiden are "plus ... blanche que nois" (6637, B6677) (whiter than snow),[25] but she seems to lack the rosy luster that brightens her two sisters. As if to underscore how specularity functions in his descriptions of such beauty, Chrétien bestows the Malevolent Maiden with a mirror[26] into which she gazes attentively from the time Gawain first sees her in her garden until they leave the castle together. Her mirror, like that of Oiseuse (Indolence) in the *Romance of the Rose*, suggests idle self-absorption as well as vanity, but the Malevolent Maiden also manages a taunting seductiveness when, still looking at her image in the mirror, she drops her mantle and wimple so that anyone watching her, and Gawain in particular in this instance, may admire her (6790–93, B6832–33).[27] Neither Clarissant nor the Malevolent Maiden can match Blanchefleur's complexion, however, for in her face Nature has produced a unique combination of red on white: a "color novele" (4175, B4209) (new [unique] color).

1. Specularity and Reflective Sequences

The luminosity of Blanchefleur's and Clarissant's faces is hideously distorted in the mirror of Chrétien's disorganized description (i.e., not from head to toe) of the monstrous Hideous Damsel who comes to Arthur's court to denounce Perceval (4580–4603, B4614–37): her skin is not white, but the color of wrought iron, and the only red she displays appears as stain on her yellowed teeth.[28]

As for the Tent Maiden, the other prominent beauty in the romance, Chrétien's narrator does not describe her in conventional detail, but again he provides a remarkable negative description of her after she has suffered from the Orgueilleus de la Lande's abuse for quite a long time.[29] Perceval sees her riding atop her emaciated palfrey, which has borne the same mistreatment as she:

>Une sanbue sor le dos
>Et un lorain ot en la teste,
>Tel convint a itel beste,
>Et une pucele ot desus.
>Einz si chestive ne vit nus,
>Neporquant bele et gente fust
>Assez, se bien li esteüst,
>Mes si malement li estoit
>Qu'an la robe qu'ele vestoit
>N'avoit plainne paume de sain,
>Einz li sailloient hors del sain
>Les mameles par les rotures.
>A neuz et a grosses costures
>De leus an leus ert atachiee,
>Et sa char paroit dehachiee
>Ausi con s'il fust fait de jarse,
>Que ele l'ot crevee et arse
>De chaut, de halle et de gelee.
>Deslïee et desafublee
>Estoit, si li paroit la face
>Ou il ot mainte leide trace,
>Que ses lermes sanz prendre fin
>I avoi[en]t fet maint chemin,
>Que jus qu'au sein li avaloient
>Et par desor sa robe aloient
>Jus que sor les genolz colant.
>Assez pooit avoir dolant
>Le cuer qui tant meseise avoit
>[3678–3705, B3711–39].

Perceval and Gawain in Dark Mirrors

(The lady's saddle on its back and the bridle on its head mirrored its own pitiful state. Upon it was riding the most wretched girl anyone had ever seen. Yet she would have been fair and noble enough had she had better fortune, but she was in such a bad state that there was not a palm's breadth of good material in the dress she wore, and her breasts fell out through the rips. The dress was held together here and there with knots and crude stitches, and her skin looked lacerated as though it had been torn by lancets, and it was pocked and burned by heat and [sunburn] and frost. Her hair was loose and she wore no hood, so that her face showed, with many an ugly trace left by tears rolling ceaselessly down her cheeks; they flowed across her breasts and out over her dress down to her knees. Anyone in such affliction might well have a very heavy heart.)

This exceptional description is, in its way, as disorganized as that of the Hideous Damsel. Chrétien's narrator first draws attention to the general appearance of the pathetic horse and the poor state of its tack, then offers a general view of the lady who rides it, finally focusing on her person: her tattered dress and how its rips and tears expose her breasts and her skin in general, which is damaged by exposure to heat and cold. Only at the conclusion is the conventional head-to-toe order achieved in a depiction of the lady's hair and face, which suffer from the lack of a hood, and the tears that fall from her eyes, down across her cheeks and breasts, and on to her knees. Yet the quality of her beauty either before she was abused or after she is healed is never specified even in the most conventional of terms.

To return to Perceval's "courtly trance," the mirror in which he sees his lady's face also reflects a knight's armor and lances as well as Welsh javelins. Perceval, whose arms are red, leans on his lance as he looks into the mirror and dreams of Blanchefleur. Does his armor not gleam in the sunlight, which melts the snow to create a unique color to match that of Blanchefleur's cheeks, just like that of the knights who first awaken him to his destiny? Perceval remembers his lady, but he does not discern all that the mirror reflects. He seems not to recall that, just days before, he also saw a red-on-white lance leading the Grail Procession when it passed before him at the Fisher King's castle, and he knew the red to be blood:

> Uns vaslez d'une chambre vint
> Qui une blanche lance tint
> Anpoigniee par le milieu,

1. Specularity and Reflective Sequences

> Si passa par entre le feu
> Et ces qui el lit se seoient,
> Et tuit cil de leanz veoient
> La lance blanche et le fer blanc,
> S'issoit une gote de sanc
> Del fer de la lance an somet
> Et jus qu'a la main au vaslet
> Coloit cete gote vermoille
> [3157–67, B3191–3201].

(A squire came forth from a chamber gripping a white lance by the middle of its shaft; he passed between the fire and those seated upon the bed, and everyone in the hall saw the white lance with its white point [from which] oozed a drop of blood, and this red drop flowed down to the squire's hands.)

Yet he remembered the procession in every detail the following morning when the Weeping Maiden interrogated him about it (3512–36, B3546–70).

He will have to be reminded again of the Bleeding Lance—and the Grail—when the Hideous Damsel (4618–27, B4652–61) castigates him and he vows to quest for them (4693–4706, B4727–40), but then he will forget them yet again. Matters seem to shift later when the fiasco involving Gawain with the king of Escavalon's sister is temporarily resolved. The Bleeding Lance, which threatens Arthur's kingdom of Logres with destruction, will become the special object of an independent quest by Gawain (6074–84, B6108–18; 6122–37, B6156–71). Finally, it may be possible that King Lot's—or Gawain's—city of Orkney (Orquenie) suffers the devastation wreaked by the Bleeding Lance on Arthur's kingdom as depicted in the last words Chrétien was ever to write (9105–84, B9155–9234).[30]

The fall of the wounded goose whose blood has seeped into the snow also recalls once again the very opening of the romance when Perceval exercises his skills in javelin-throwing in the Waste Forest (69–99).[31] He hurls his javelins in all directions, sometimes high into the air and sometimes low just above the ground. When he meets the five knights from Arthur's court and begins learning about their armor, he is amazed to be told that a lance is not cast like a javelin, as its name suggests to him (Old French *lancier*, to throw), but is tightly grasped as it is thrust at an opponent (188–201). Perceval judges that his javelins are superior to lances because they are better adapted for hunting: "…

quan que je vuel an oci," he boasts, "Oisiax et bestes a besoing, / Et si les oci de si loing / Con l'an porroit un bozon trere" (204–07) (I can kill as many birds and beasts as I want or need, and I can kill them from as far away as one can shoot a bolt [from a crossbow]). Perceval kills wild game, and the exuberant, inexperienced boy with his Welsh javelin is reflected as the shadow of the man leaning on his lance falls close to the mirror on a snowy day when a wild goose is wounded by a noble falcon.

In this romance the javelin is the Welsh weapon *par excellence*. When Perceval leaves home, he is ostentatiously dressed in Welsh clothing by his mother, yet he must yield two of his three javelins to her lest he look *too much* like a Welshman (584–93, B602–11). At Carlisle, the Red Knight waits outside the gate as Perceval goes into the castle (845–77, B865–97), and, in response to Kay's sarcastic bestowal of the Red Knight's armor (982–87, B1002–07),[32] he comes back out to challenge him (1044–46, B1064–66). The Red Knight strikes at him with his lance held in both hands, but Perceval parries the thrust and kills him by driving his javelin right through eye-slit of his helmet and into his brain (1082–99, B1102–1219). Perceval wins arms, a warhorse, and a new self-identity as a knight, the Red Knight, by wielding a Welsh javelin, but he leaves it behind along with his own mount taken from his mother's stable as he rides away in search of adventure. Thus begins of the gradual process of discarding the tokens of his childhood that we have already observed in another reflective sequence at Gornemant's castle.[33] The strand eventually re-emerges in the mirror of the Blood Drops episode. Intersections with other strands occur elsewhere—in two phases of Perceval's life's story, for example, for both his father (417–19, B435–57) and the Fisher King (3473–81, B3507–15) have suffered identical thigh wounds from javelins—blood on white skin—in the wars after Utherpendragon's death.

The lance and the javelin recur in the Gawain Adventures. While Perceval has touted the superiority of his javelins for hunting, Gawain chases a white doe with his lance in a portentous chase (5622–51, B5656–85) that is reminiscent in many ways of Guigemar's specular encounter in the eponymous *lai* by Marie de France, where the hunter's arrow mortally wounds a magical white doe and returns to wound him in the thigh.[34] We recall in this context that when Perceval meets the five

1. Specularity and Reflective Sequences

knights, he seizes upon the true etymology of the word *lance* when he asks if lances are thrown despite the fact, as he learns, that they are not (197–207).[35] Gawain charges after his quarry grasping his lance (5630–51, B5664–85), which indicates that, in order to kill it, he must catch up with it and strike at it as he rides alongside. When he ineptly trusts his lance over the deer's neck, however, it bolts away. He must be holding his lance overhanded,[36] otherwise he could not manage the lateral thrust. As he tries it a second time, his horse throws a shoe, a bad omen, and the hunt comes to naught, but the rare deer has in fact led Gawain, as is his destiny, to Escavalon, where he is meets only frustration. There his knightly valor comes into question, he is prevented from defending his honor in the anticipated murder trial by combat, and he must begin a new quest for the Bleeding Lance (see Saly, "Beaurepaire et Escavalon").

Ultimately, while the maturing Perceval defeats his opponents with both lance and sword—Anguigneron (2178–2208, B2198–2242) and Clamadeus (2628–47, B2662–81) before Biaurepaire and later the Orgueilleus de la Lande (3884–95, B3918–29)—, it is with the lance alone that Gawain overpowers those against whom he jousts, for he unhorses all of them on the first pass before swords are drawn: Meliant de Liz in Tintagel (5479–85, B5513–19) and, at the landing opposite the Roche de Champguin, both Greoreas's nephew (7311–15, B7353–57) and the Orgueilleus de la Roche a l'Estroite Voie (named 8350–55, B8393–97) (Proud Knight of the Stone at the Narrow Pass). Ironically, on the other hand, the javelin as missile, more particularly than the lance, is featured in the great hall at the Roche de Champguin when Gawain submits to the supreme test of the Perilous Bed (7775–7830, B7817–62), a spectacular simulacrum of warfare contrived by art and magic (7502–16, B7544–58) in which, like Perceval in actual hand-to-hand battle, he wins lordship of a castle (7634–7842, B7676–84).

As in diffraction, javelins reshaped into arrows and bolts mirror, in Gawain's triumph, both the adolescent Perceval's prowess at hurling javelins, which he compares to shooting bolts with crossbows (202–07), and his military prowess displayed at Biaurepaire. As Gawain sits down on the Perilous Bed, the colored clerestory windows high above him suddenly fly open. Amid a great din, hundreds of projectiles shot by as many invisible archers and crossbowmen begin to rain down on him.

Many of them he fends off with his shield, but by the time the barrage is over, he has received more than 500 wounds, one per window and one per marksman. Like the javelin, the bow and the crossbow are not a knight's weapons in the twelfth century. After being softened up, as it were, by the infantry, such as the foot soldiers in the Bayeux Tapestry, Gawain faces in single combat the semblance of a noble adversary in the form of a big, ravenous lion that leaves its claws stuck in his shield before, for the first and only time in combat in the *Conte del Graal*, he brings it down with his sword—undoubtedly Excalibur, which he drew earlier in his parodic battle against peasants and townsmen in Escavalon (cf. 5868, B5902). This shield with the lion's severed paws is the badge of a new *chevalier au lion* that later convinces Guiromelant of the truth in Gawain's tale of victory at the Roche de Champguin (8622–67, B8670–8715).

Finally, the Blood Drops mirror intersects with the sequence of Perceval's protracted specular encounter with his destiny (4177–4568). Knights in Arthur's court observe him as he gazes at Blanchefleur's reflection, and all but Gawain are offended by his failure to acknowledge them and greet them. First Sagremor rides out from the camp to confront him, berating him for his "discourtesy" as he attacks him with his lance, but Perceval, Gawain-like, meets him and unhorses him with his lance before returning to the mirror. Next, enflamed by his unbounded anger, Kay attacks, but Perceval again successfully defends himself and resumes his gazing. In fulfillment of the Fool's prediction at Carlisle (1236–54, B1216–34), Kay breaks his arm when Perceval brings him down, and thus Perceval completes his vengeance of the Smiling Maiden. In the end, Gawain's proverbial courtesy wins Perceval over, and he rejoins Arthur's court; but the joyful celebration of his pre-eminence is dampened by the Hideous Damsel's disruptive arrival.

The Amorous Couple

The Blood Drops episode is linked above all with a reflective sequence of the amorous couple, which it epitomizes. Like other major sequences, it is generated in Chrétien's text by the words of Perceval's mother, or rather by his selective memory of them, as she gingerly

1. Specularity and Reflective Sequences

instructs him in chivalric service to noble women and the rudiments of *fin' amors*. He must serve and respect all ladies and maidens, for, as a knight, honor will come to him by coming to their aid:

> ...totes enors i afierent.
> Qui as dames enor ne porte,
> La soe enors doit estre morte:
> Dames et puceles servez,
> Si seroiz par tot enorez;
> Et se vos aucune an proiez,
> Gardez que ne li enuiez
> De nule rien qui li despleise.
> De pucele a mout qui la beise:
> S'ele le beisier vos consant,
> Le soreplus vos an defant,
> Se lessier le volez por moi.
> Mes s'ele a enel an son doi
> Ou a sa ceinture aumosniere,
> Se par amor ou par proiere
> Le vos done, bon m'iert et bel
> Que vos an portoiz son anel.
> De l'anel prandre vos doin gié
> Et de l'aumosniere congié
> [520–38, B538–56].

(it is the most honorable thing to do. He who fails to honor ladies finds his own honor dead within. Serve ladies and maidens and you'll be honored everywhere. And if you ask any for her love, be careful not to annoy her by doing anything to displease her. He who kisses a maiden gains much [from her]; if she grants you a kiss, I forbid you to go any further, if you will stop for my sake. But if she has a ring on her finger, or [a ...] purse at her belt, and if she gives it to you for love or the asking, I'll not object to your wearing the ring. I give you leave to take the ring and the purse.)

In addition to her discourse on honoring and serving ladies and noble maidens, which faintly alludes at the same time to the operations of charity and to the Custom of Logres, Perceval's mother introduces into the *Conte del Graal* the classical topos of the *gradus amoris*, the steps of love, of which five are generally listed by scholars[37]: (1) *visus* (sight) or *intuitus* (looking), (2) *alloquium* or *colloquium* (conversation), (3) *contactus* (touching), (4) *basia* (kisses), (5) *coitus* and *congressio* (intercourse) or *factum* (the deed).[38] Perceval's mother specifies consensual kissing, which she allows him, and *le soreplus*, the "rest" that conven-

37

tionally follows kissing, in which she will not permit him to engage (529–30, B547–48). Significantly, she offers the exchange of love tokens, customary expressions of commitment to one's beloved, as an acceptable alternative to the forbidden steps in the paradigm, *coitus, congressio*, or *factum*—provided that the gift is voluntary: "Se par amor ou par proiere / Le vos done" (if she gives it for love or the asking) (534–35, B552–53). Perceval does not comprehend that kissing or that, *a fortiari*, *le soreplus* must be consensual: he retains "De pucele a mout qui la beise" (528, B546) (He who kisses a maiden gains much [from her]), but not "se vos aucune an proiez, / Gardez que ne li enuiez / De nule rien qui li despleise" (525–27, B543–45) (And if you ask any [maiden] for her love, be careful not to annoy her by doing anything to displease her). It is also noteworthy that Perceval's mother does not condone the "rights" given knights in certain circumstances, as we shall see, by the Custom of Logres.

Perceval has kissed his mother's chambermaids,[39] but her words—rather, his misinterpretation of them—determine the boorish way he treats the Tent Maiden, a woman of noble birth. Ignoring his mother's caution that his engagement in the permitted *gradus amoris* as she defines it is subject to his partner's consent, he kisses the maiden against her will, forcing her as well into other unwanted forms of *contactus* (682–91, B700–09). That he does not obtain the forbidden *soreplus* (530, B548)[40] may be due less to the lady's resistance or his own self-restraint than to his ignorance of what the *soreplus* is, although he has lived in a manor with farm animals and wild game and has had *contactus* and enjoyed *basia* with peasant girls. In any case, he settles instead for what he thinks his mother might approve of when he catches sight of the maiden's luminous ring: "un anel an son doi vit / A une emeraude mout clere" (he saw a ring on her finger set with a shining emerald) (692–93, B710–11), which he literally extorts from her by forcibly straightening her clinched finger and twisting it off (682–704, B700–22).

At Biaurepaire, Blanchefleur's desperate audacity induces Perceval to experience less violent and more refined forms of *fin' amors*[41] that are informed in greater detail by the *gradus amoris*. Chrétien's description of her is by far the most elaborate devoted to any woman in the *Conte del Graal*, and, as we have seen, his narrator asserts that it is the best wrought of any he has ever written (1775–1809, B1795–1829),[42] for she is indeed a woman of exceptional beauty. Perceval sees her and greets

1. Specularity and Reflective Sequences

her (1810–11, B1830–31) in the great hall (*visus*), but the several knights and ladies with whom they withdraw into a more private room observe them sitting together (Matthieu de Vendôme's *accessus*) in total silence. They find the couple to be perfectly matched physically, but they fear that Perceval, who is apparently guided by Gornemant de Gohort's exhortation not to speak too much in courtly society, may be mute (1843, B1863). As they remark to one another:

> "Mout avient bien delez ma dame,
> Et ma dame ausi delez lui.
> S'il ne fussent muël andui,
> Tant est cil biax et cele bele
> C'onques chevaliers ne pucele
> Si bien n'avindrent mes ansanble,
> Que de l'un et de l'autre sanble
> Que Dex l'un por l'autre feïst
> Por ce qu'ansanble les meïst"
> [1846–54, B1866–67].

(… how good he looks beside my lady, and she, too, at his side. If they were not both silent, he is so handsome and she so beautiful that no knight or lady was ever more suited for the other, for it appears that the two of them were destined by God for each other.)

Only the absence of courteous speech (*alloquium*) mars this vision of perfection, and the maiden, after politely waiting in vain for Perceval to initiate the conversation, finally breaks the ice herself when she asks him from where he has ridden that day (1863, B1883).

When Perceval retires after a meager meal, servants outdo themselves to make him comfortable in his bed:

> Trestot l'eise et tot le delit
> Qu'an sache deviser an lit
> Ot li chevaliers cele nuit,
> Fors que solemant le deduit
> De pucele, se li pleüst,
> Ou de dame, se li leüst.
> Mes il n'an savoit nule rien,
> N'il n'i pansoit ne po ne bien …
> [1915–22, B1935–42].

(That night the knight had all the comfort and delight one could hope for in a bed, except the pleasure of a maiden's company, if he pleased, or a lady's, had it been permitted.)

The "deduit de pucele ou de dame" is precisely the *soreplus* forbidden by Perceval's mother, but Blanchefleur, who lies awake in her chamber worrying about an imminent attack on her castle, is determined to go to her guest's bed in order to persuade him to come to her aid (1961–2017, B1981–2037). She needs a champion to protect her from Clamadeus (named 1984, B2004: "he who rails against God"), king of the Islands, who is an aspirant for her hand in marriage (2009, B1029). His seneschal, Anguigneron, has besieged her castle for nearly a year.

It is a challenge that Perceval feels compelled to accept, and he invites her into his bed not necessarily as a reward, but in order to relieve her distress:

> …Et cil la beisoit
> Qui an ses braz la tenoit prise,
> Si l'a soz le covertor mise
> Tot soavet et tot a eise,
> Et cele suefre qu'il la beise,
> Ne cuit pas qu'il li enuit.
> Ensi jurent tote la nuit,
> Li uns lez l'autre, boche a boche,
> Jus qu'au main que li jorz aproche.
> Tant li fist la nuit de solaz
> Que boche a boche, braz a braz
> Dormirent tant qu'il ajorna
> [2038–49, B2058–69].

(And he kissed her and held her tightly in his arms. He placed her gently and comfortably beneath the coverlet, and she let him kiss her, and I do not believe it displeased her. Thus they lay side by side and mouth to mouth all night long, until morning came and day was dawning. He brought her so much comfort that night that they slept mouth to mouth and arm in arm until day broke.)

Their *alloquium* has quickly led to caressing and kissing.

Scholars once debated *ad nauseam* the question of the couple's virginity at this dawning—and, indeed, throughout the whole of Perceval's sojourn at Biaurepaire.[43] More recently, commentary has focused on the four Continuators of Chrétien's romance. Lori Walters defers resolution of the question of the lovers' virginity, stressing instead the richly enigmatic nature of Chrétien's narration that led the Second Continuator and Manessier to differing portrayals of the lovers' relationship ("Image of Blanchefleur," pp. 439–45). Matilda Bruckner, for her part, likewise

1. Specularity and Reflective Sequences

alludes to Chrétien's and the Second Continuator's "innuendoes" and observes that Manessier, who, like Gerbert de Montreuil, was influenced above all by the monkish ethos of the *Quest del Saint Graal*, is unequivocal concerning Perceval's remaining a virgin. Unlike Gerbert, however, Manessier dismisses Blanchefleur and goes on to invent an alluring demonic semblance of her that Perceval dispels with the sign of the cross before he can fall into sin (*Chrétien Continued*, pp. 56, 89–90).

In any case, Perceval and Blanchefleur behave in the morning as though the comment made by Chrétien's narrator about the absence of "deduit de pucele ou de dame" in Perceval's bed before Blanchefleur's visit applies as well to their night-long embrace. Perceval tells her that if he succeeds in defeating or killing Anguigneron, he will ask for only one reward: "Vostre druërie requier / An guerredon qu'el[e] soit moie" (in recompense I ask that your love be given to me) (2084–85, B2104–05). The expression "vostre druërie"—where has he learned the courtly language of love other than from his mother, who does not use this term for affection?—denotes a personal commitment that is only Blanchefleur's to grant, an approximation of his mother's notion of the gift of a ring or a purse, but it often implies its physical expression as well—*le soreplus*. The point to stress at this juncture, however, is that Perceval would hardly hope for it if it had already been granted.

Blanchefleur's subtly complex response is of interest for other reasons:

> *Sire, mout m'avez or requise*
> *De povre chose et de petite;*
> *Mes s'ele vos ert contredite,*
> *Vos le tanreiez a orgueil,*
> *Por ce veher ne la vos vuel.*
> *Et neporquant ne dites mie*
> *Que je deveigne vostre amie*
> *Par tel covant ne par tel loi*
> *Que vos alliez morir por moi,*
> *Que ce seroit trop granz domaiges,*
> *Que vostre cors ne vostre aaiges*
> *N'est tex, ce sachiez de seür,*
> *Que vos a chevalier si dur*
> *Ne a si fors ne a si grant*
> *Com est cil qui la hors atant*
> *Vos poïssiez contretenir*

Perceval and Gawain in Dark Mirrors

> *N'estor ne bataille sofrir*
> [2088–2104, B2108–24, my emphasis].

(Sir, you've just requested [of me] a pitiful thing of little value. But if it were denied you, you'd think me proud, so therefore I don't wish to refuse you. *And yet don't say that you'd go forth to die for me on condition that I become your ladylove, as that would be most unfortunate; you are not strong or old enough, I assure you, to hold your own in skirmish or battle against a knight so strong and tall and so hardened by combat as the one awaiting you out there.*)

To which Perceval answers, "Ce verroiz vos … ancui, / Que conbatre m'irai a lui, / Ja nel leirai por nul chasti" (2105–07, B2125–27) (This very day you'll see if that is so …, for I'll go forth to fight with him. No words of yours can stop me).

Chrétien's narrator comments on the second part of Blanchefleur's response (italics above), which is what elicits Perceval's bold, confident reply:

> Tel plait li a cele basti
> Qu'ele li blasme, et si le vialt;
> Mes sovant avient que l'an sialt
> Escondire sa volanté,
> Qant an voit bien antalanté
> Home de fere son talant,
> Por ce que mialz l'en atalant.
> Ausin fet ele come sage,
> Qu'ele li a mis en corage
> Ce qu'ele li blasme mout fort
> [2108–17, B2128–37].

(She pretended by her words [*literally*: she constructed such a speech] to discourage him, though she wished him to fight; but it often happens that one hides one's true desires, upon seeing a man keen to do one's will, in order to increase his desire to do it. And thus she acted cleverly, by discouraging him from doing what she put it in his heart to do.)

In her use of antiphrasis, an ironic figure of speech, she argues that Perceval is too weak and inexperienced to face the battle-hardened Anguigneron, but her hidden intent is to convey the opposite meaning as a challenge in order to bend him to her will: he must do what she has suggested he should not attempt to do. "Clever" (2115, B2135: *sage*) Blanchefleur's use of antiphrastic irony stands in opposition to Kay's discourteous and uncharitable sarcasm, a base form of irony, which Perceval mistook for the truth at Carlisle. This time an apparently more

1. Specularity and Reflective Sequences

urbane knight shows that he has understood Blanchefleur's meaning. He does not contradict her, but proffers instead an earnest acceptance of her unspoken wish.[44]

The narrator's commentary on antiphrasis applies just as well to the first part of Blanchefleur's response and reveals the meaning hidden in her overly modest assessment of the *druërie* she has to offer. On the contrary, her love is *not* a thing of little worth, but something she values very much, and Perceval must respect it in his turn. After he defeats Anguigneron, she appears to grant what Perceval hopes for when she invites him to her own bedchamber and offers him no haughty resistance (2325, B2359: *dongier*; cf. 2090–92, B2110–12 above): "An leu de boivre et de mangier, / Joënt et beisent et acolent / Et debonerement parolent" (In lieu of food and drink they sported, kissed, caressed, and spoke together pleasantly) (2326–28, B2360–62).[45] Not just their "pleasant" talk, but indeed the elegant (*debonere*) speech that becomes their very sustenance corrects the single imperfection Blanchefleur's knights and ladies found when they first observed the couple sitting together the evening before: *alloquium*. Again, however, Chrétien's narrator leaves open the question of the *soreplus* to which their kissing and caressing might lead.

On the day when Clamadeus himself comes to renew the siege, Perceval singlehandedly slays twenty of his knights, and the starving inhabitants of Biaurepaire are reprovisioned with food and wine by merchants whose ship is miraculously blown off course. Chrétien's narrator presents the order of subsequent events as follows: (1) cooks prepare the evening meal (2537–39, B2571–73); (2) Perceval and Blanchefleur are together:

> Or se puet li vaslez deduire
> Delez s'amie tot a eise:
> Cele l'acole et il la beise,
> Si fet li uns de l'autre joie
> [2540–43, B2574–77].

(Now the young knight could dally beside his sweetheart at his ease. She embraced him and he kissed her, and each brought joy to the other);

(3) the great hall fills with people, all eat and disperse (2544–51, B2578–85); (4) attention shifts to Clamadeus's camp where word spreads of the castle's good fortune and Clamadeus sends a message challenging the

Red Knight (2552–65, B2586–99); (5) Perceval accepts the challenge, all in the castle are saddened, especially Blanchefleur, but he persists (2566–90, B2600–22); (6) Blanchefleur spends the whole night trying to "dissuade" him from fighting Clamadeus (2591–2607, B25–2641). Of interest at present are the second and the sixth segments.

The second occurs in a series of three brief scenes inside the castle that resemble a cross-cutting montage in cinema, an exquisite example of interlace in miniature. Perceval and Blanchefleur's "heavy petting"[46] appears to be going on simultaneously with the preparations in the kitchen, which lead directly into the third segment. Chrétien's narrator does not specify whether the lovers join the celebration in the great hall or continue their verbal meal in private elsewhere, but, in all events, they are present with the crowd to receive Clamadeus's messenger. Meanwhile, the camp scene appears to be simultaneous with the parallel events inside the castle. The two streams merge with the arrival of the messenger, and the chronology continues in order with the fifth and sixth segments, which are situated inside the castle walls.[47] Significantly, unlike the events that transpire in the kitchen and great hall, the scenes with the lovers are not precisely situated within the castle. Do they take place in a closed space such as Blanchefleur's bedchamber, where a previous amorous encounter has transpired? Or are they in a semi-private room like the *chanbre celee* (1827, B1847) to which they withdraw when Perceval first arrives and are soon joined by a small group of knights and ladies—and where, presumably, Perceval's bed is set up? Chrétien's narrator is just as ambivalent concerning the lovers' discretion as he is with regard to their virginity.

While the meal is being prepared, the lovers hug and kiss: "Cele l'acole et il la beise, / Si fet li uns de l'autre joie" (2543–44, B2577–78) (She embraced him and he kissed her, and each brought joy to the other). *Si* is ambiguous because it may either function as a coordinating conjunction (and) or express cause and effect (so). *Joie* (enjoyment, delight) is also ambiguous because in erotic courtly writing it may signify delight in general (including "heavy petting") or specify sexual gratification (*le soreplus*). The couplet in fact seems to abbreviate the celebrated passage in the *Charrete* in which Chrétien's reticent narrator comments on the consummation of Lancelot and the Queen's love from the knight's point of view:

1. Specularity and Reflective Sequences

> Or a Lanceloz quanqu'il vialt,
> Quant la reïne an gré requialt
> Sa conpaignie et son solaz,
> Quant il la tient antre ses braz
> Et ele lui antre les suens.
> Tant li est ses jeus dolz et buens
> Et del beisier et del santir
> Qu'il lor avint sanz mantir
> Une joie et une mervoille
> Tel c'onques ancor sa paroille
> Ne fu oïe ne seüe,
> Mes toz jorz iert par moi teüe.[48]
> Des joies fu la plus eslite
> Et la plus delitable celle
> Que li contes nos test et cele.
> Molt ot de joie et de deduit
> Lanceloz tote cele nuit[49]
> [4669–86, my emphasis].

(Now Lancelot has all he desires, since the Queen gladly seeks his company and his comfort and he holds her in his arms and she holds him in hers. So sweet and delightful was the sport to him from their kissing and touching that they experienced an amazing joy such as has never since been heard of or known, but I shall forever refrain from describing it, for such a thing must never be said in a romance. It was the most perfect and exquisite of all joys, the one the story suppresses and hides from us. Lancelot had much joy and delight that night.)

Here the steps of the *gradus amoris* paradigm clearly advance from access—kissing and touching—to *factum*. In the *Conte del Graal*, however, Chrétien's narrator is much more circumspect about the quality of the *joie* shared by the couple.

In the absence of an explicit *factum*, the "heavy petting" in which Perceval and Blanchefleur engage reflects Andreas Capellanus's definition of *amor purus*:

qui omnimoda dilectionis affectione duorum amantium corda coniungit. Hic autem in mentis contemplatione cordisque consistit affectu; procedit autem usque ad oris osculum lacertique amplexum et verecundum amantis nudae contactum, extremo solatio; nam illud pure amare volentibus exercere non licet [ed. Walsh, 1.6.470–71, p. 180].

(that which joins the hearts of two lovers with universal feelings of affection. It embraces the contemplation of the mind and the feeling of the heart. It goes as far as kissing on the mouth, embracing with the arms, and chaste contact with the unclothed lover, but the final consolation is avoided, for this practice is not permitted for those who wish to love chastely. [trans. Walsh])

The mirror in the snow, however, raises this manifestation of *amor purus* to a quasi–Platonic level.

In all events, the people of Blanchefleur's castle take it for granted that Perceval and their lady are betrothed, and they already recognize him as their lord when he prepares to fight Clamadeus the next morning: "de lor seignor mout lor grieve" (2588, B2622) (they grieve for their … lord) because they cannot find words to dissuade him from accepting the invader's challenge. Nor can Blanchefleur, who this time maintains, again antiphrastically, that her enemy is no longer a danger to them (2593–94, B2627–28):

> Si li avoit la nuit s'amie
> Mout prië qu'il n'i alast mie
> A la bataille, einz fust an pes,
> Que il n'avoient garde mes
> De Clamadeu ne de sa gent.
> Mes tot ce ne valut neant,
> Et si fu ce mervoille estrange,
> Que il avoit an la losange
> Grant dolçor qu'ele li feisoit,
> Car a chascun mot le beisoit
> Si dolcement et si soëf
> Que ele li metoit le clef
> D'amor an la serre del cuer;
> N'onques ne pot estre a nul fuer
> Que ele l'an poïst retrere
> Que la bataille n'alast fere,
> Einz a ses armes demandees
> [2591–2608, B2625–42].

(All night long his sweetheart begged him not to go do battle, but to stay in peace, for Clamadeus and his men were no longer any threat to them. But all her pleadings were in vain, and that is a strange thing, for there was much sweetness in her blandishments, since with every word she kissed him so sweetly and softly that she slipped the key of love into the lock of his heart. Yet she was totally incapable of persuading him not to go into battle; instead, he asked for his arms.)

Much kissing and caressing instills love in Perceval's heart, and this is without doubt what he remembers later as he gazes into the Blood

1. Specularity and Reflective Sequences

Drops mirror, but there is no *joie* this night, for Perceval is so adamant in his desire for battle that, despite his love for Blanchefleur, he acknowledges no conflicting emotions. His eventual departure from Biaurepaire to return to his mother, a crucial event to which we shall return in Chapter 2, involves a further degree of distancing between him and his beloved.

All other amorous couples in the *Conte del Graal* are more or less pale reflections of Perceval and Blanchefleur. As we shall see, Meliant de Liz and Tiebaut de Tintagel's daughter are parodic by comparison, as are the flirtatious Gawain and the all too willing sister of the king of Escavalon. Guiromelant and Clarissant, who love from afar, are also problematic both because of the enmity between their families and because she has caught him in a lie. Meanwhile, the Two Queens, unaware of who the liberator of their castle is, fondly dream of pairing their daughter and granddaughter Clarissant with her brother. The most noteworthy of the couples opposed to Perceval and Blanchefleur are in fact the Tent Maiden and the Orgueilleus de la Lande, whose twists of fate are, for good and ill, intimately entwined with the trajectory of Perceval's destiny, and, as we shall see in Chapter 3, Greoreas and his lady, who treacherously implicate Gawain in the adventures of Galloway, as well as the Malevolent Maiden and her string of "protectors," who include Guiromelant and Gawain himself.

Mirrors of Gold and Silver

Returning to the mirror in the literal sense of highly polished metals like the five knights' shining armor, we must take into account yet another essential reflective sequence initiated by Perceval's encounter with them that includes the Grail itself. Their armor, gleaming in the morning sunlight, awakens Perceval to the world outside the Waste Forest. His first meaningful experience away from his mother's manor is also bathed in a spectacular reflected light. Chrétien stresses the parallel between the two incidents when, after Perceval spends the night in a dark wood (612, B640), he again awakens to the singing of birds (616–17, B634–35; cf. 71–72). As though in anticipation of the Blood Drops episode as well, he then rides into an open meadow and marvels at a world bathed in golden light (615–48, B643–66). Beams from the rising sun are caught by a gilded eagle atop a luxurious tent, and golden light is reflected upon the whole landscape. Perceval exclaims in awe:

> Dex, ci voi ge vostre meison!
> Or feroie je mesprison
> Se aorer ne vos aloie.
> Voir dist ma mere tote voie,
> Qui me dist que mostiers estoit
> La plus bele chose qui soit,
> Et me dist que je ne trovasse
> Mostier qu'aorer n'i alasse
> Le Crïator an cui je croi
> [637–45, B655–63].

(My God, here I behold your house! I would do wrong not to go in and worship you. My mother spoke the truth when she said to me that a church is the most beautiful thing there is, and told me never to pass a church without going to worship the Creator in whom I believe.)

The ecstatic vision is closely linked to his earlier sighting of "angels" and "God the Father" himself wearing gleaming armor, which is informed by his mother's own description of beautiful heavenly creatures. His reaction to the luminous splendor of the "church" is similarly determined by his mother's words of advice to her son. Just as the "angels" are knights and "God the Father" is their captain, so, when Perceval goes into the tent to pray as his mother says he must, he does not see God or much that has to do with God, but finds instead a beautiful lady lying asleep on a bed. Despite the darkly comic aspects of the ensuing "adventure," Perceval's awakening in the woods and his ride to the nearby meadow mark his rebirth in a new world of knighthood, courtliness, and *fin' amors*. The rising sun's golden reflection is reiterated in the dazzling snow in which Perceval beholds Blanchefleur's image after he has awakened in yet another forest and ridden into another meadow.

Light—shining light, glowing light, reflected light—also fills the great hall of the Grail Castle in the midst of which a fire burns brightly on an immense hearth beneath a chimney supported by thick, surely highly polished brass columns (3151–67, B3185–3201; 3146–3208, B3180–3242). The hall is further lit by a profusion of candles. The squire bearing the Bleeding Lance is followed by two others who carry "chandeliers …

1. Specularity and Reflective Sequences

/ De fin or, ovrez a neel" (3180–81, B3214–15) (candelabra of pure gold, worked with enamel inlays), each holding ten more candles. As a climax, when a maiden comes in with "un graal" (3186, B3220) (a grail), "Une si granz clartez i vint / Qu'ausi perdirent les chandoiles / lor clarté come les estoiles / Quant li solauz lieve ou la lune" (3191–94, B3225–28) (the room was so brightly illuminated that the candles lost their brilliance like stars when the sun rises, or the moon). The Grail itself gleams with "fin or esmeré" (3199, B3233) (fine pure gold), and it is studded with sparkling "Pierres precïeuses ... / Des plus riches et des plus chieres / Qui an mer ne an terre soient" (3200–03, B3234–37) (precious stones, the best and costliest to be found in earth or sea). Finally, another maiden enters carrying a silver carving platter. Chrétien's description emphasizes the strength of light in the hall at various moments, but we cannot doubt that light intensifies as it is reflected by the gold of the Grail, the candelabra, the wine goblets (3249, B3282), and the polished silver of the carving platter.

Most of the luminous elements of the Grail Castle are refracted, magnified, and dispersed also to spectacular effect throughout the Roche de Champguin's great hall (7634–87, B7676–7729). The multi-colored stained-glass windows in the clerestory (7683–85, B7725–27), through which the castle's ladies and maidens watch undoubtedly distorted images of Gawain and his host (7742–44, B7784–86), are anticipated in the Grail Castle as mirrors in the brightly burnished surfaces of the carving platter, the candelabra, perhaps the brass surfaces, and the Grail itself; the windows' colored glass also recall the shimmering colors—green, vermilion, gold, blue, silver (133–35)—of the five knights' armor in the Waste Forest. The double doors into the Roche de Champguin's great hall, one of ivory and the other of ebony, reflect the ivory-and-ebony table where Perceval and the Fisher King dine.[50] The doors are adorned with hardware of pure gold and carved panels highlighted in gold leaf as well as precious stones endowed with supernatural powers. The floor's stone pavings of green, red, indigo, black (7648, B7690) are also highly polished. More significantly, no wood can be found in the *Lit de la Merveille* (7763, B7805) (Bed of Marvels), which stands in the middle of the hall (7650–51, B7692–93). Entering the Grail Castle, Perceval sees the great fireplace and before it a more ordinary *lit* (3051, B3085) of burled oak (3053, B3087) on which he and the Fisher King are to sit at as they dine at the magnificent irony table supported by ebony trestles, but Gawain's Bed of Marvels is made of solid gold and silver. The bed alone where Gawain earns his lordship of the Roche de Champguin replaces focal points of light at the Grail Castle, notably the cutting platter and the Grail itself. On each of the bedposts, moreover, is mounted a mythical precious stone, the carbuncle, which glows from within and casts as much light as four candles. We recall that the intensity of light in the Grail Castle is also described in terms of candlepower. All the splendors of the great hall at the Roche de Champguin reflect the polished gold and silver, the precious gems, and the light that illuminate the Grail Procession.

In another trick of refraction, the Grail Procession is also reflected in the prosthesis of the peg-legged man (*eschacier*) who is the hall's guardian (7606–33, B7648–75).[51] This imposing figure is immensely rich, and, like the Ferryman, he is a retainer of the castle. No doubt he is a veteran of the conflicts in the aftermath of Utherpendragon's death, but he is no knight, for there are none at the Roche de Champguin before Gawain arrives. His amputation specifically recalls the thigh-wounds suffered by Perceval's father and the Fisher King in those wars and, more recently, the wounds Greoreas suffers in Galloway.[52] In reflection of the opening and central episodes in the Perceval section, warriors with leg and thigh wounds are prominent at the beginning and in the crowning episode in Gawain's Galloway Adventures. Of the latter, Gawain heals one and the other sports a spectacular replacement.

Implicitly, the peg-legged man is a threat to Gawain, perhaps as guardian of the great hall who customarily warns away any knight who comes seeking the adventure. As the Ferryman and Gawain approach the hall, they find him sitting on a bundle of reeds at the bottom of the steps, whittling or polishing (*doler*) a stick of ash. The Ferryman tells Gawain that he would hear disturbing things from the veteran if he were not his guide,[53] but for now, in eerie reflection of Perceval, he remains silent. At its core, his artificial leg is of pure silver, but, like many other luminous surfaces described by Chrétien, it is completely covered in gold leaf. From top to bottom are alternating bands of gold and precious gems mounted in the leaf. Reflected by the peg-legged man are images of knights and warriors in general, the silver cutting platter, the golden, jewel-incrusted Grail—and also the Bleeding Lance and javelins, for the

1. Specularity and Reflective Sequences

stick of wood he is working is the very ash from which lances and spears are made.[54]

Fortified Spaces

The Grail Castle and the Roche de Champguin are highlighted features in a long reflective sequence of castles that begins with Carlisle and concludes with Orkney. Arthur's Carlisle (Carduel), Disnadaron, and Carlion are centers of royal domains, as are the Grail Castle and the Roche de Champguin, but the latter two stand outside the sphere of Logres. The fortified manor in the Waste Forest prefigures all of them, in its humble way, and most especially the Grail Castle, which is also reflected in the Hermitage dynastically and in terms of religious implications. The castle of Gornemant de Gohort, the name of which Perceval does not know, although he remembers it in great detail (1864–72, B1884–92), and Blanchefleur's city of Biaurepaire, which also constitute a subset because of family ties, likewise partake in the sequence: Blanchefleur is Gornemant's granddaughter.[55] Biaurepaire, furthermore, mirrors the Hermitage in particular because the city boasts the only other (barely) functioning churches depicted in the Perceval Adventures, while in the Gawain Adventures there are more prosperous churches in both Tintagel and Escavalon. Biaurepaire and the Hermitage are linked as well to the Grail Castle, for God's presence is manifest literally in all three: in the consecrated Host served in the Grail, in the rites performed by the Hermit and his brother priest, and in the miraculous arrival of a ship blown off course that supplies the starving inhabitants of Biaurepaire with abundant food and drink.[56] As we shall see in Chapter 4, Biaurepaire also serves as an apposite model for the castle at Orkney.

In a very different mode, the Orgueilleus de la Lande's shining tent in a meadow near a forest's edge brilliantly serves as an inversion of all these castles and holy places: an oafish Perceval barges in the belief that it is a church, and he finds there a tempting lady and a meal of pasties (encased in bread) and wine. Similarly, Gawain unexpectedly encounters another lady, the Malevolent Maiden, in a garden at the border guardian's castle. As noted before, the Orgueilleus's tent and the pavilions in Arthur's encampment in the snowy meadow are transitory centers of civilization and culture in the wilds, while the castle just inside Galloway demarcates two very different regions, Arthur's Logres and a land populated in part by exiles from Arthur's kingdom and its dependencies including two long-dead Queens who await a protector.

Meanwhile, the Waste Forest manor, the Grail Castle, and Biaurepaire are related in the fact that Chrétien's narrator focuses attention on their drawbridges. Perceval's mother falls at one such bridge, undoubtedly the most significant, as he recalls at Gornemant's castle, at Biaurepaire, and in the forest near the Grail Castle, where he learns that she has died; he remembers the bridge as well at the Hermitage. The second bridge, which is emblematic of ruin at besieged Biaurepaire, is so dilapidated that Perceval must cross it with great care in order to reach the gate without crashing through it (1692–97, B1712–17). Finally, the third is raised so quickly when Perceval rides out of a seemingly empty Grail Castle that his horse must jump to safety to avoid falling into the moat (3368–75, B3402–09).

Castles that are fortified cities, like Biaurepaire and those belonging to Arthur in the Perceval Section, are centers in the two conventionally-structured episodes in the Gawain Adventures: Tintagel, which is "besieged" by Meliant de Lis after he has challenged its lord, his vassal Tiebaut, to face him and his men in a tournament, and Escavalon, which teems with bankers, merchants, artisans, and ordinary townspeople, and whose former king Gawain is accused of having murdered. At Tintagel Gawain delays his journey to Escavalon because he cannot miss a chance to witness an exciting tournament. There he finds that a strong postern, the only entrance into the city that has not been walled up to keep out Meliant and his allies,[57] is shut and barred. He spends his first day outside the walls in an enclosed meadow abutting them (4857–87, B4891–4921). There he suffers the humiliating taunts of ladies watching from above who take him for a cowardly knight, a merchant, or a money-changer (5018–56, B5052–90). When he follows Tiebaut's men into the castle after the fighting is temporarily suspended, a wise and courteous vavassor offers him lodging in his house. When Tiebaut and his younger daughter come to visit, Gawain agrees, with charm and courtesy, to champion the little girl, the Pucele aus Manches Petites (The Maiden of the Narrow Sleeves), the next day, when in fact he will meet and defeat Meliant de Lis, suitor of her naïvely self-centered and irascible sister

1. Specularity and Reflective Sequences

(5297–5350, B5331–84). After Gawain leaves Tintagel, his horse throws a shoe as he approaches Escavalon (5646–57, B5680–85). He comes to little good there, and, after a series of serio-comic misadventures, he is forced to undertake a quest for the Bleeding Lance that he seems ill-equipped to see through to completion.

In the Galloway Section, two castles apparently of secondary importance stand, as it were, in shadow of the Roche de Champguin. Guiromelant is the lord of one, Orqueneles, which is visible from Ygraine's stronghold a short ride away; he owes homage, he says, to none but God for his vast domain (8570–78, B8618–26), which is to say that he does not recognize Ygraine—a relative newcomer?—as his suzerain. His castle is of interest because the gorge of the Perilous Ford lies nearby and more especially because the combat in which Gawain must defend himself before Arthur against Guiromelant, who accuses him and his father, King Lot, of murder, is to be fought on the plain beneath it. Furthermore, Guiromelant claims to be in love with Clarissant, daughter of the Young Queen and sister of Gawain, a lady whom he loves from afar.

The Perilous Ford is noteworthy as a blurry reflection of the bridge motif that links the Waste Forest manor, Biaurepaire, and the Grail Castle. According to most manuscripts, in fact, a well-constructed bridge spans the river that flows through the gorge (B8903: *pont*), or else there is a landing with a ferry (8855: *port*). In any case, when Gawain first crosses the gorge, he knows nothing of the safe way across the river (cf. 8440–43, B8486–89; 8854–58, B8902–06). Prodded by the Malevolent Maiden, he attempts to jump his horse Gringalet (or Le Gringalet: 6175, B6209, etc.) over the gorge from rim to rim. The jump fails, and man and beast plunge into the middle of the river. Literally, but unbecomingly, they meet the test's basic requirement of crossing the ford when they swim to the other side and scramble up the steep embankment (8452–74, B8498–8520). Later, their return is almost comically anticlimactic as they accomplish the leap with no difficulty whatsoever (8866–68, B8914–16).

Earlier, when Gawain leaves Escavalon and crosses the Galloway frontier, the Bone or Borne de Galvoie (6562; B6602: *Bosne*), he finds that the borderland is guarded by a castle that is a counterpoise to the Roche de Champguin. Its name is implicit in that of its lord, who, as Gawain learns much later, is called "... li Orgueilleus / De la Roche a

53

l'Estroite Voie" (8698–99, B8646–47) (the Proud Knight of the Stone at the Narrow Way). Chrétien's narrator initially imparts knowledge of the frontier in an enigmatic episode of great complexity as Gawain comes upon on an *angarde* (6483, B6532), an artificial mound serving as a defensive outpost, and sees a lady beneath an oak tree (6484, B6524) weeping over the inert body of a knight who apparently has suffered wounds in a battle ending with an attempt to decapitate him (6512–14, B6552–64).

The entry into Galloway inaugurates a narrative extravaganza that is unlike anything Chrétien has undertaken before. The Gawain Adventures themselves begin with discrete episodes, Tintagel and Escavalon, which are comparable in length and structure with the constituent episodes of the Perceval adventures that precede them: segments defined by arrivals at and/or departures from places where hospitality is offered or demanded.[58] By contrast, adventures in the Galloway Section (6479–9136, B6519–9188), which are not necessarily organized with respect to hospitality, are hugely amplified and amorphous. We shall return to the Galloway Section in Chapters 3 and 4. Another distinctive feature of the Galloway Section, however, is that it is illuminated by the extraordinary Hermitage episode that precedes it. The Hermitage episode likewise casts light retrospectively on the Perceval Adventures that come before it.

2

The Hermitage: "He that abideth in charity"

Reflections of Hope and Despair

Perceval's encounter with penitents in the Hermitage episode (6183–6472, B6217–6506) and his subsequent confession of failure at the Grail Castle and recognition of the sin that caused him to keep silent prompt the first explicit references to charity in the *Conte del Graal* outside the Prologue.[1] Implicitly, however, Gornemant de Gohort's counsel, which mirrors that of Perceval's own mother, and his pupil's execution of it most certainly exemplify charitable impulses: sparing defeated adversaries (1619–27, B1639–47) and praying in church to "Celui qui tot a fait / Que de vostre ame merci ait" (Him who made all to have mercy on your soul), just as Perceval must show mercy to others,[2] "Et qu'an cest siegle terrïen / Vos gart come son crestïen"[3] (1647–50, B1667–70) (and keep you [as his] true Christian in this earthly life). Gornemant continues his instruction by linking a knight's courtly discretion with the imperative to come to the aid of disconsolate men and women (1636–42, B1656–62).[4] Henceforth Perceval does not kill defeated adversaries, contrary to his treatment of the Red Knight whose identity he has assumed—and contrary to Gawain, perhaps, and certainly to the Orgueilleus de la Lande and, as we shall see, the proud guardian of Galloway. Beyond that, Perceval's exercise of charity is manifest in his service to Blanchefleur and her people, which, for some reason, her grandfather, Gornemant,[5] is unable or unwilling to perform, just as it is in his atonement for his mistreatment of the Tent Maiden and its consequences, in his vindication of the Smiling Maiden, whom he has championed, and in his justification of the Fool.

Gornemant's twin precepts bearing on charity are intertwined with similarly related instructions to curb forms of immature behavior that are attributable to Perceval's upbringing in the Waste Forest: to practice reticence in place of garrulousness (1628–42, B1648–64) and to refrain from mentioning what his mother has taught him (1655–64, B1675–86). The last of Gornemant's instructions is in fact prompted by Perceval's naïvely enthusiastic response to his command to pray in church: "autel oï ma mere dire" (1654, B1674) (I heard my mother say the same thing). In effect, Gornemant's *parole* (3213, B3247) henceforth replaces that of Perceval's mother in all matters[6]:

> Or ne dites ja mais, biau[s] frere,
> Fet li prodom, que vostre mere
> Vos ait apris et anseignié....
>
> —Et que dirai ge donc, biau[s] sire?
> —Li vavasors, ce poëz dire,
> Qui vostre esperon vos chauça
> Le vos aprist et anseigna"
> [1655–57, B1675–77; 1665–68, B1685–88].

("Now never again say, dear brother," continued the gentleman, "that your mother taught or instructed you...." "Then what shall I say, fair sir?" "You can say that the vavassor who attached your spur taught and instructed you [*or* showed you the way].")

Perceval certainly remembers much of his mentor's teachings, as he does his mother's, but aspects of the very chivalric values that underpin his precepts ultimately prove to be his undoing.

Perceval's irresistible desire to return to the Waste Forest and find his stricken mother (1560–72, B1680–92; 2883–87, B2917–21), which consumes him more than continuing his training in knighthood under Gornemant's tutelage or marrying Blanchefleur and ruling her lands, may also be ascribed to a selfless, charitable motivation born of remorse. Yet, when he learns that his mother is dead (3557–91, B3591–3625), its power to motivate him dissipates as suddenly as it overwhelmed him at Gornemant's castle despite his pledges to find her dead or alive (2892–98, B2926–32; 2928–37, B2962–71). He fails to perceive, and will not begin to comprehend until he confesses at the Hermitage, his own fault, his rejection of charity, in refusing to turn back when he saw his mother fall in a faint as he rode away from her manor (602–12, B620–30). At

2. The Hermitage: "He that abideth in charity"

the moment, he is despondent that he no longer has a reason to look for her and sets out on a path that leads him away from the Grail Castle (3584–91, B3617–25) and, eventually, back to Arthur's court.

Despite differences in tone and terminology, the Waste Forest, the scene of Perceval's first introduction to knighthood, and the Hermitage, the site of his re-education in charity, are similar in so many ways that one episode reads like a permutation of the other, that is, a reflection with variations, even with reversed images at times, as in a mirror.[7] The Waste Forest, the domain Perceval's mother has inherited from her dead husband,[8] is ironically named. It is isolated and parts of it may well be untended, but it is by no means a wasteland,[9] for the manor within it, which is the center of Chrétien's interest, is a thriving demesne, an orderly community sustained by agriculture on a large scale[10] as well as hunting. As Perceval approaches the Hermitage, he rides through another kind of "waste" land (*desert*, 6205, B6239),[11] a term that reflects his state of mind and soul more accurately than it describes the landscape in which he comes upon a party of penitents. In fact they meet in a forest, "an *ceste* forest" (in *this* forest) (6270, B6301, my emphasis), and one reaches the Hermitage by passing through a thick woods within the forest—"Par *cest* bois" (through *this* woods) (6290, B6324, my emphasis)—on a path the penitents have marked by weaving together branches in the trees (6291–96, B6325–30).[12] Not unlike the widow's manor, though in quite another sense, the Hermitage is a center of culture inside a forest where a small community of hermit, priest, and clerk (6309–10, B6275–76) lead a simple life in voluntary solitude, subsisting on what the forest provides, yet willingly receiving and serving visitors and perhaps even engaging in commercial transactions.[13]

Moreover, in the Waste Forest, the adolescent Perceval, who has never seen a knight, encounters a band of five of them (100–02) searching for a party of five other knights accompanying three maidens (184–85). If they succeed in their quest, the combined group will number thirteen, ten men and three women, but at the moment they are dispersed. In the *desert* near the Hermitage, Perceval meets a party of three knights and ten ladies (6208–09, B6242–43). Unlike their antecedents, however, these knights are unarmed, and the whole group of thirteen wear sackcloth and hoods and walk barefoot. This time, it is Perceval whose appearance in armor—in gleaming red armor, if he has maintained it well—is extraordinary. His re-education and rehabilitation also begin, like his early chivalric education in the Waste Forest, in a disorderly interrogatory exchange. Knight: Aren't you an unbeliever? (6220–23, B6254–57). Perceval: What day is this? (6230, B6264). Where have you been, looking so strange? (6267, B6301). What did you do at the Hermitage? (6273, B6307). Knight: How can you ask that? (6275, B6309). There are thirteen penitents, like the potential conjoining of knights and ladies in the beginning, but these are inverse reflections. The first knights wear radiant armor flashing in a variety of colors, and we may well imagine that the ladies they pursue are clothed in fashionable courtly attire like the Tent Maiden at first, like Blanchefleur, and like the Malevolent Maiden. By contrast, the knights and ladies leaving the Hermitage are dressed down, dull and somber-looking. The proportions of women and men are of course reversed: three to ten in the Waste Forest, where the sparkling men dominate, ten to three near the Hermitage, where men are outnumbered, although in any case the outward signs of gender distinction are interestingly muted by the common penitential garb.

The discourse that furthers Perceval's re-education reflects and amplifies the religious aspect of the *san* (509; B527: *sens*) (wise counsel) that Perceval's mother gives him as he sets off in search of King Arthur which Gornemant de Gohort renews and reframes in part when Perceval receives his knightly spurs.[14] Go to church and pray God to give you honor and a good end (549–54, B567–72). What is a church? (555, B573). A place where "an fet le servise" (556, B574) (people [honor their obligations] to the Creator) (556–58, B574–76), a beautiful, most holy building with saints' relics and treasures where the body of Jesus Christ is sacrificed in commemoration of His Passion, Crucifixion, and Harrowing of Hell (559–73, B577–91), a place where Perceval should go to hear Masses and matins and to worship God (573–80, B591–98). As does the penitent knight at the Hermitage, Perceval's mother emphasizes events before Easter and leaves the Resurrection implicit; she also implies a degree of Jewish guilt for the suffering of Christ, "cui Gïeu firent honte mainte" (whom the Jews greatly defiled) (564, B582).

I Corinthians 13 informs the Hermitage episode as it does the Prologue, especially vs. 13: "Nunc autem manent fides, spes, charitas: tria haec; maior autem horum est charitas" (And now there remain faith, hope, and charity, these three: but the greatest of these is charity)—

2. The Hermitage: "He that abideth in charity"

implicitly and darkly, at first, in the nature of Perceval's lapsed state (6183–6352, B6217–6386), and then more overtly as the intertext re-emerges in his redemption (6353–6478, B6387–6414). For five years, since his departure from Arthur's second court at Carlion in response to the Hideous Damsel's challenge, Perceval has been on a senseless, elusive quest.

In his wanderings, he has defeated sixty knights, twelve per year, and has sent them all to King Arthur as has been his custom since his tutelage under Gornemant de Gohort. The court has doubtless heard sixty more "contes de Perceval," but they have proved pointless and unproductive, as, apparently, no one, insofar as Chrétien reports, has bewailed his absence or gone forth in quest of him. Indeed, as we shall see in Chapter 4, the court at Orkney is currently obsessed with the absence of Gawain. Even more disastrously, Perceval "A si perdue la memoire / Que de Deu ne li sovient mais" ([has] lost his memory so totally that he no longer remember[s] God) (6184–85, B6218–19). Chrétien's narrator: "Cinc fois passa avrix et mais / … / Einz que il antrast an mostier / Ne Deu ne sa croiz n'aora" (Five times April and May [have] passed … since he … entered a church or adored God or his cross) (6186–89, B6220–23)[15]; Perceval: "Damedeu an oblïai, / Ne puis merci ne li crïai" (I forgot Almighty God [because of it, i.e., his failure at the Grail Castle], and never implored him for mercy) (6349–50, B6383–84).

Forgetting God constitutes a lapse of faith (*fides*), a *de-fi*-al and a *de-fi*-ance of God. Loss of faith is not only a matter of unbelief, but, more importantly in a medieval context, a disavowal of one's sworn obligations to God,[16] the least of which, as both Perceval's mother and his mentor taught him in his days of innocence, is to go to Mass (549–80, B567–98; 1643–50, B1663–70). In losing his memory of God, Perceval has also lost his sense of time and has fallen into a state of what a modern psychologists might call depression. Chrétien's narrator: "cil … n'avoit nul espans / De jor ne d'ore ne de tans, / Tant avoit an son cuer enui" (6227–29, B6251–53) ([had no care for what] day, [what] hour, or [what season it was, so troubled was he in his heart]); Perceval to the Hermit: "bien a cinc anz / Que je ne soi ou ge me fui" (6330–31, B6364–65) (for five years I have not known where I was going), "*S'an* ai puis eü si grant duel / *Que morz eüsse esté mon vuel*" (6348–49, B6382–83, my emphasis) (I've suffered such affliction [*because of my failure*] that I would rather have died).

Perceval and Gawain in Dark Mirrors

Perceval's depression is in fact reflected later, in another register, in that of Gawain when he realizes that he is a prisoner at the Roche de Champguin, the castle he has won. Chrétien's narrator: "*il voldroit estre morz*, ce cuit, / Qu'il n'ot rien qui ne li enuit" (8043–44, B8085–86, my emphasis) (*He would like to be dead*, I believe, for there [is] nothing that does not trouble him); Gawain to Ygraine: "Ne me chaloit que ge feïsse, / *Tant estoie maz et dolanz*" (8160–61, B8202–03, my emphasis) (I did not care what I did, I was so sad and dejected). Gawain's depression is quickly alleviated by courtly banter with his grandmother (8072–8163, B8114–8205), but in Perceval's case, as he confesses to the Hermit, it has thrown him into a state of despair, a profound loss of hope (*spes*): "Ne Deu n'aimai ne ne le crui, / N'onques puis ne fis se mal non" (6332–33, B6366–67) (I have not loved God or believed in him, and all I have done has been evil).

Perceval's mental and spiritual anguish is profound and resembles *tristitia*, a debilitating state of grief (cf. *duel* [sorrow], 6330, B6364) associated with *acedia* (ennui), which is a gateway to the capital sin of sloth.[17] Absent in his exploits in his five years of faithlessness and desperation is any shred of the *caritas* implied in his earlier displays of mercy to others which might reflect the mercy he would have God bestow on him again. Loving God and loving one's fellows as oneself are the exemplary human expression of *caritas*.[18] For five years, however, Perceval's acts of "mercy" come not from a consciousness of charity, but from a mindless force of habit.

The penitent knights and ladies wonder at Perceval's appearance, for they see him fully armed on Good Friday (6215–18, B6249–51). One knight asks him, "Don ne creez vos Jhesu Crist / Qui la novele loi escrist / Et la dona as crestïens?" (6221–23, B6355–57) (don't you believe in Jesus Christ, who set forth [wrote] the New Law and gave it to Christians?). Here Perceval hears again (in Chrétien's name) what Gornemant de Gohort would have him be, but he is puzzled in turn by his interlocutor: "Et don venez vos or ensi?" (6267, B6301) (And where are you coming from dressed like this?). The penitent responds:

> Sire, de ci,
> D'un boen home, d'un saint hermite
> Qui an ceste forest abite,
> Ne vit, tant par est sainz hon,

2. The Hermitage: "He that abideth in charity"

> Se de la gloire de Deu non
> [6268–72, B63042–06].
>
> (Sir, from over here, from a good man, a holy hermit who lives in this forest, and who is such a holy man that he lives solely by the glory of God.)

Thus Perceval's re-education, like his initiation into knighthood, begins with a series of questions in a "wasteland," but this time the subject is not the *lex militiae* (the law of knighthood),[19] but the *lex caritatis* (the Law of Charity), which is the law of Christ.[20] One of the knights tells him that, instead of bearing arms, instead of looking like the unrepentant knight that he is, he should be in church on Good Friday. One's duty is to "aorer la croiz" ([observe the customary Adoration of the Cross]) and "ses pechiez plorer" (6233–34, B6267–68) (and weep for one's sins), that is, confess one's sins and receive absolution, as the penitents have just done. The knight then shifts to a seamless, creed-like narration, which echoes and amplifies that of Perceval's mother (549–76, B567–94), to explain his counsel in terms of what Good Friday commemorates: God's purpose in the Incarnation (6237–51, B6271–85), the Crucifixion (6235–36, B6269–70; 6252–53, B6286–87), and the Harrowing of Hell (6254–57, B6288–91). He then embarks upon a disquisition on Jewish guilt (6258–64, B6292–98) with a virulence epitomizing what only lies implicit in the muted remark of Perceval's mother, a common view among medieval Christians that continues to haunt certain manifestations of the Grail narratives down to our own day[21]:

> Li fel Gïu par lor anvie,
> Qu'an devroit tuër come chiens,
> Firent lor mal et nos granz biens
> Qant il an la croiz le leverent:
> Aus perdirent et nos salverent
> [6258–62, B6292–96].
>
> (The wicked Jews, whom we should kill like dogs, in their spite hurt themselves and did us great good when they raised Him on the Cross: they damned themselves and saved us.)

It is in such a context that the knight refers to I Corinthians 13: anyone who does not believe in Christ's Incarnation "ja an la face nel verra" (will never see Him face to face [in Paradise]) (6248, B6282), cf. "Videmus ... tunc autem facie ad faciem" (we see [God] ... then face to face) (vs. 12). Non-believers thus exist outside the realm of charity.

What Perceval hears reawakens his consciousness of his own condition and its apparent cause, and it moves him to retrace the penitents' path in order to confess and receive absolution. He reads the signs they have left in the boughs of the trees and finds the Hermitage (Figure 4).[22] After pointedly removing his armor, Perceval enters the chapel and falls to his knees. The Hermit, who is apparently a priest in his own right,[23] another priest, and a clerk have begun "le servise / Le plus grant qui an sainte Eglise / Puisse estre fez, et li plus dolz" (the highest and sweetest service that can be said in Holy Church) (6311–13, B6345–47): the Good Friday liturgy prescribed in the Easter Triduum which includes intercessory collects, the Adoration of the Cross,[24] and the Mass of the Presanctified using the oblation reserved from Maundy Thursday.[25] The Hermit, apparently distracted by Perceval's entrance, calls to him and invites him make his confession (6314–55, B6358–89). Should we not imagine that the Hermit leaves his brethren in the chancel to continue their reading and/or chanting while he and Perceval confer elsewhere in the chapel? After confession, in any case, Perceval finally turns his attention to the Adoration of the Cross (6457–60, B6391–94).

Fearing the sins he has committed against God, Perceval asks the Hermit for counsel and confesses his loss of faith, his despair, and his neglect of religious duties (6320–33, B6354–67). In so doing, he opens yet another interrogatory sequence, but this time, in contrast to exchanges with knights in the Waste Forest, with penitents in the "desert," or with Gornemant de Gohort (1347–99, B1367–1419) and the Weeping Maiden (3514–37, B3548–71), here Chrétien's narrator phrases the questions indirectly. The Hermit's response to Perceval's confession is "Di moi por coi tu as ce fait" (Tell me why you acted in this manner) (6335, B6369), and Perceval answers with another "conte du Graal"—his second, after the one prompted by the Weeping Maiden: once he went to the Fisher King's castle, saw the Bleeding Lance and asked nothing about it, and he saw the Grail and did find out whom it served (6338–46, B6372–80). "Or me di comant tu as non" (Now tell me your name) (6354, B6388), asks the Hermit, as has the Weeping Maiden, though by now he must already know: simply Perceval (6355, B6389), this time without his ambivalent surname.

Throughout the romance, Perceval's identity—his name and his

2. The Hermitage: "He that abideth in charity"

surname as signs of who he is and what he has achieved in Arthur's kingdom—is inextricably linked to his misadventure at the Grail Castle.[26] When the Weeping Maiden berates him for his failure, she, like the Hermit, her uncle (?), asks his name. He has never thought about his name,[27] and he guesses that it is "Percevax li Galois" (3541, B3575) (Perceval the Welshman); but she changes it to "Percevax li chetis" (3548, B3582) (Perceval the Unlucky [Wretched *or* Prisoner]). The Hideous Damsel's excoriation recalls and reinforces this *renaming* by the Weeping Maiden: "Ce est tu li *maleüreus* / Qui veïs qu'il fu tans et leus / De parler et si te taüs!" (4631-33, B4665-67, my emphasis) (you are that *wretched man* who [saw] that it was time and place to speak, yet kept your silence!), and indeed Perceval's own account at the Hermitage of his Grail adventure mirrors that of the Hideous Damsel (4618-30, B4652-74) more than any other. Perceval may not yet have been conscious of his sin, but at least he remembers *her* words. This monstrous seer cares nothing about the cause of his failure, however, except to berate him for not grasping Fortune when he had the chance. She is primarily concerned with its consequences: the Fisher King's on-going physical distress amidst prolonged warfare (4635-49, B3669-83).

The Peccatum Matris: *Filial Piety*

The Weeping Maiden has already spoken of these disasters. If Perceval had asked the right questions, the Fisher King's wound would have been healed and his lands would have been restored to him (3550-56, B3584-90). In addition, she also claims to know *why* Perceval was so "mesavantureus" (3550, B3584) (unfortunate [ill-fated]): "Por le pechié, ce saches tu, / De ta mere t'est avenu, / Qu'ele est morte de duel de toi" (3559-61, B3593-95) ([ill fortune] befell you, understand, [because of a sin concerning your mother, for she] has died of grief on your account). Scholars have often commented on the ambiguity of her expression "Por le pechié … de ta mere," which may be read as "because of *your mother's* sin" or "because of a sin committed against your mother."[28] As above, a causative clause in some manuscripts may seem to resolve any confusion. On the one hand, Perceval has committed a sin *because* his mother died of grief when he did not turn back after seeing her fall in a faint.

Perceval and Gawain in Dark Mirrors

On the other hand, in half of the manuscripts, the relative pronoun *qui* (who) replaces the conjunction of conclusion *que* (for) (3561, B3595),[29] which leaves open the possibility, but not the certainty, of his mother's guilt: ill fortune befell Perceval *because of* the sin of his mother, who died of grief for him. Her alleged guilt has been attributed to despair[30] when her son, her only source of joy, abandons her, and to incest,[31] which assumes that, because both Perceval's father and the Fisher King, who is his mother's nephew (6381–85, B6415–19), have suffered the same debilitating wound, they must be one and the same. Moreover, in the late 12th century, Old French *peschiere* (fisherman) and *pechiere* (sinner) are homophonic or nearly so: Perceval's host at the Grail Castle could be, though not certainly, the "Sinner King."[32]

The Hermit reintroduces sin, and not solely Perceval's failure to seize the moment, as a cause of his nephew's failure, and his reformulation of the Weeping Maiden's declaration may or may not clarify the ambiguity in her account. Significant details vary in the two encounters. The Weeping Maiden interrogates her cousin in a forest, for example, while the Hermit counsels him in a church, and she is the lover of a murdered knight, while he is an ordained confessor. What the woman and the priest have in common, on the other hand, is that Perceval is their kinsman and that both have knowledge of Perceval's family as well as the Grail mysteries. It is of interest that the structures of Perceval's verbal encounters with them are basically identical: Perceval relates his Grail visit and his failure; his interlocutors ask him his name; he gives it, and, having recognized who he is, they blame his failure on a sin. However, the Hermit's response to Perceval's disclosures, which contain a final recapitulation of his departure from the Waste Forest, is by far the more detailed thorough of the two:

> Et dit: "Frere, mout t'a neü
> Uns pechiez don tu ne sez mot,
> Ce fut *li diax que ta mere ot*
> *De toi quant tu partis de li,*
> Que pasmee a terre cheï
> Au chef del pont devant la porte,
> Et de *ce[st] duel* fu ele morte.
> Por le pechié que tu *an* as
> T'avint que tu ne demandas
> De la lance ne del graal,

2. The Hermitage: "He that abideth in charity"

> Si t'*an* sont avenu maint mal.
> Et n'eüsses pas tant duré
> S'ele ne t'eüst comandé
> A Damedeu, ce saches tu,
> Mes sa parole ot tel vertu
> Que Dex por li t'a regardé,
> De mort et de prison gardé.
> Pechiez ta lengue trancha"
> [6358–75, B6394–6411, my emphasis].

(and [he] said, "Brother, a sin of which you are unaware has caused you much hardship: it is *the sorrow* your mother felt for you when you departed from her, for she fell in a faint on the ground at the head of the bridge before the gate, and she died of *this sorrow*. Because of [the] sin [you have *from this*] it came about that you did not ask about the lance or the grail, and much hardship has resulted for you [*from it*]. And understand that you would not have lasted until now had she not commended you to God; but her prayer was so powerful that God watched over you for her sake and kept you from death and imprisonment. Sin [cut off] your tongue.")

The Hermit's perspective is also broader than that of the Weeping Maiden. Not only is he an experienced confessor, but, more significantly, he is also heard Perceval's account of his despair and is in a position to explore the cause of his despondency.

At first, the opening of the Hermit's explanation (6358–68, B6394–6404) seems to concretize the ambiguity inherent in "le pechié ... de ta mere." On the one hand, the sin is the grief (*diax/duel*) Perceval's mother felt when he left her (6358–64, B6392–98), that is, it appears to be "his mother's sin" that caused her to die—something approaching the despair and *tristitia* that some readers of the *Conte del Graal* have attributed to her.[33] On the other hand, "his mother's sin" is one in which Perceval has a share that is his own sin (6365, B6399): it is not her sin, but *his* that lay at the root of his failure to ask the appropriate questions and triggered the many ills he has suffered (6376–80, B6410–14). Ultimately, however, the Hermit apparently resolves the contradiction with perfect lucidity.

In his discourse the Hermit mixes events he may have witnessed personally or heard about in "contes de Perceval"—including the fall and death of Perceval's mother as well as her prayer to God on his behalf (6362–64, B6496–98, cf. 604–07, B624–27; 6370–71, B6404–05, cf. 596–

601, B616–621)—with matters of belief: that sin was involved in Perceval's failure (6358–59, B6494–95) and that his mother's prayer for him before her fall has been efficacious (6372–74, B6403–05). The sum of all of them affirms, for him, the truth in what he relays to Perceval. In this light, ambiguity is dispersed in the second part of his account (6372–74, B6406–08), for he clearly regards Perceval's mother as an exemplar of saintliness whose prayer—her *parole*, her word (6372; B6406: *proiere*)[34]—has had such power that, in spite of Perceval's five years of despair and faithlessness, God has kept him safe from imprisonment and death. Unless it could be argued convincingly that the Hermit knows nothing about his closest relatives or that, according to standards of the late twelfth century, he is either deluded or a liar (as are at times the Orgueilleus de la Lande, Greoreas, Guiromelant, and the Malevolent Maiden), it would be irrational to suggest that he could ascribe such sanctity to a woman so laden with sin, be it incest, despair, or "smother love," that her son yet suffers its effects. On the contrary, the guilt for his failure is entirely Perceval's, and he alone is responsible for the pain he caused his mother when he left her. The plausibly verifiable efficacy of her prayer prompts a retrospective review of the whole of Perceval's military career—the repetitive combats during his recent five years' absence from Arthur's court, to be sure, but more especially the sequence of formative adventures beginning with his departure from home and his first encounter with the Tent Maiden, when her lover returns too late to challenge the "knight" who assaulted her, through the inevitable battle when he avenges her by defeating and converting her "protector" and, thanks to them, his ultimate reunion with the court in the snowy meadow near Carlion and its aftermath.

Or can the *pechié* be at once Perceval's and his mother's?

As we have already seen, and we shall explore the question further, one of the extraordinary features of the *Conte del Graal*, by contrast with Chrétien's other romances, is the ways in which an abundance of biblical and liturgical references are woven into its narrative fabric: the variety of biblical texts quoted in the Prologue and elsewhere, the occurrences of the term *charité* and its frequent reflections, the rites at the Hermitage, the credo Perceval recites when he beholds the shining knights and others' creed-like statements, and so forth. "Le pechié … de ta mere," read

2. The Hermitage: "He that abideth in charity"

most simply as "your mother's sin," is another such reference, and it constitutes a minor biblical theme of the *peccatum matris* (sin of the mother).

The term occurs in Psalm 108/109,[35] a prayer for an enemy's destruction that is a litany of imprecations, one of which is "In memoriam redeat iniquitas patrum eius in conspectu Domini, et *peccatum matris* eius non deleatur" (vs. 14, my emphasis) (May the iniquity of his fathers be remembered in the sight of the Lord: and let not the sin of his mother be blotted out).[36] According to the commentary of St. Augustine of Hippo, this is a reference to Original Sin, that is, sin transmitted by Adam and Eve to their descendants, and exculpation from it is achieved in conversion to the law of God. Its effects are retained, however, when sinners disavow or scorn God.[37] Other readings of Psalm 108/109:14 are certainly possible,[38] but the notion of any genealogical sin or curse passed from mother to son other than Original Sin is irrelevant in the *Conte del Graal*. Indeed, the pertinence of the *peccatum matris* to Perceval even as Original Sin does not lie in any specific matrilineal curse, but in the condition he and his mother share with all of humankind. The *peccatum matris* as the cause of his failure at the Grail Castle is another matter altogether.

An occurrence of the *peccatum matris* more germane to the *Conte del Graal* appears in the deuterocanonical Book of Sirach, a text in the Wisdom tradition. The term occurs in Sirach 3:14–17 in a passage addressed by a father to his son:

14 Fili, suscipe senectam patris tui, et non contristes eum in vita illius. 15 Et si defecerit sensu, veniam da, et ne spernans eum in virtute tua; eleemosyna enim patris non erit in oblivione. 16 Nam pro *peccato matris* restituetur tibi bonum; 17 et in justitia aedificabitur tibi, et in die tribulationis commemorabitur tui, et sicut in sereno glacies, solventur *peccata tua* [my emphasis].

(14 Son, support the old age of thy father, and grieve him not in his life; 15 and if his understanding fail, have patience with him, and despise him not when thou art in thy strength: for the relieving of the father shall not be forgotten. 16 For good shall be repaid to thee for *the sin of thy mother*; 17 and in justice thou shalt be built up, and in the day of affliction thou shalt be remembered: and *thy sins* shall melt away as the ice in the fair warm weather.)

The meaning of *peccatum matris* in vs. 16 of the Vulgate, as determined by its context, can by no means be that of Psalm 108/109:14, nor has it anything to do with the concept of Original Sin.

Perceval and Gawain in Dark Mirrors

The subject of Sirach 3:1–18, the context in which the *peccatum matris* is situated, is filial piety. In his commentary on the book, Rabanus Maurus explicitly links this passage to the Fourth Commandment: "Honora patrem tuum et matrem tuam, ut sis longaevus super terram, quam Dominus Deus tibi dedit" (Honour thy father and thy mother, that thou mayest be longlived upon the land which the Lord thy God will give thee) (Exodus 20:12).[39] God will not forget a son's *eleemosyna* (alms) towards his elderly father—it is a question not of literally giving him alms, of course, but of the spirit that prompts the son to support him and to comfort him: mercy born of charity. Meanwhile, *in lieu of* his mother's sin (*pro peccato matris*), that is, instead of its falling to the son as the Psalmist prays will happen to his enemy, credit is built up with God to redeem the son.

Rabanus Maurus is at pains to probe the nature of the *peccatum matris* more deeply. Quoting vss. 15–16, beginning at "eleemosyna enim patris," he comments:

> Misericordiae ergo affectus cum pietatis operibus, nunquam oblivioni tradetur. Unde Dominus ait: "Beati misericordes, quoniam ipsi misericordiam consequentur (*Matth.* v)." Et in Proverbis: "Foeneratur, inquit, Domino, qui miseretur pauperis, et vicissitudinem suam reddet ei (*Prov.* xix)." *Quod autem dicit: "Pro peccato matris restituetur tibi bonum." Peccatum hic tropica locutione ipsam eleemosynam nuncupat, quae delet peccata.* Sicut et alibi hostiam quae pro peccato offertur, peccatum vocat. Ut est illud: "Ponat manum suam super caput peccati sui, et sic eam Domino offerat." Qui ergo in parentibus et caeteris indigentibus misericordiae exercet opera sine dubio justiciae suae recipiet praemium, et peccatis absolutus mercedem vitae possidebit aeternae [col. 779, my emphasis].
>
> (Thus a disposition towards mercy in acts of piety is never forgotten, which is why the Lord says, "Blessed are the merciful: for they shall obtain mercy" [Matthew 5:7]. And in Proverbs [19:17]: "He that hath mercy on the poor, lendeth to the Lord: and he will repay him." *When it says, "For good shall be repaid to thee for the sin of thy mother," here sin means, in a figure of speech, the very charitable act that takes the sin away,* as in "He shall put his hand on the head of his sin, and so he shall offer it to the Lord." Therefore, one who does works of mercy for his parents and others in need will without a doubt be repaid for his righteousness, and, as one absolved of his sins, will have the heavenly reward of everlasting life.)

The phrase "Ponat manum suam super caput peccati sui, et sic eam Domino offerat" (He shall put his hand on the head of his sin, and so

2. The Hermitage: "He that abideth in charity"

he shall offer it to the Lord) is an allusion to, or perhaps a misremembered citation of, Leviticus 4:3:

> Si sacerdos, qui unctus est, peccaverit, delinquere faciens populum, *offeret pro peccato suo vitulum immaculatum Domino*: et adducet illum ad ostium tabernaculi testimonii coram Domino, *ponetque manum suum super caput eius, et immolabit eum Domino*[40] [my emphasis].
>
> (If the priest that is anointed shall sin, making the people to offend, *he shall offer to the Lord for his sin a calf without blemish*. And he shall bring it to the door of the testimony before the Lord, and *shall put his hand upon the head thereof, and shall sacrifice it to the Lord*.)

Or else, Rabanus Maurus is himself playing with language and inserts into the passage from Leviticus the metonym "sin" for the "calf," the offering made as a propitiation for the sin, in order to suggest that it is *as if* God had said to Moses that the calf, the *hostia* (sacrificial victim), takes on the sin, and thus in a sense *becomes* the sin which is erased when it is offered up in sacrifice. Exegetically, this passage and others like it in the Old Testament foreshadow the very fulfillment of the *lex caritatis*, the *lex Christi*, in the events of which Perceval is once again reminded, certainly in greater depth than before, on Good Friday.

The exegete evokes a process of expiation through sacrifice, but he never provides the term replaced by the metonym *peccatum matris*: the mother is not literally a sacrificial victim. Other readings suggest that *peccatum* may function metaphorically. In the context of Sirach 3:1–18, vs. 15 introduces the matter of the father's approaching senility: "si defecerit sensu" (if his understanding fail), which the son is exhorted to bear with charitable indulgence—"da veniam" (have patience, be merciful)—and not to scorn—"ne spernas eum in virtute tua" (despise him not when thou art in thy strength). Thus, the mother's "sin" in vs. 16 can be nothing other than an analogous infirmity afflicting her that the dutiful son must also endure with longsuffering. George Leo Haydock's popular commentary on Douay-Rheims suggests, not without a spark of humor, that the *peccatum matris* is the mother's "ill-nature" in her old age.[41] On the other hand, it is noteworthy that the Vulgate offers a version of the passage at hand that deviates from that of its source, the Septuagint, where the clauses are arranged so as to suggest that the promise of vs. 17, that on the Day of Judgment the son's credit will be redeemed and his own sins will melt away, pertains not at all to tolerance of his father's senility, but solely to bearing the burden of his ageing mother with loving patience: *eleemosyna* as *caritas*.[42]

In deflecting charity toward the father and foregrounding the mother as the parent whose "sin" must be borne as a way to redemption, the Vulgate portends the very predicament in which the adolescent Perceval finds himself in the *Conte del Graal*. He is a fatherless son who brings grief to his mother in order to realize his destiny: the *peccatum matris* as the circumstances of a mother in need that prompt a child's charitable impulses toward her. Consequently, instead of investing in his own eventual redemption (the *peccatum matris* as *hostia*), Perceval brings disaster to himself and to others. Failure to recognize the eschatological dimensions of the *peccatum matris* also results in his personal *peccatum matris*, the "pechié ... de ta mere" as the sin committed against his mother.

It is Perceval's mother herself who introduces the matter of filial piety into Chrétien's text. Mirroring a major strategy in Sirach that recurs in the Gornemant de Gohort episode, she means to educate her son in his genealogy and gives him, along with other family stories, an account of his two elder brothers' careers as young knights. They served two different kings and were knighted on the same day in different places; they died the same day in battle as they were making their separate ways home in order to perform acts of filial devotion: "... joie me voloient faire / Et lor pere" (454–55, B472–73) (they wanted to bring happiness to me and to their father). Even the gruesome detail she adds concerning her elder son's eyes, which may not at first seem to be pertinent, contains a hidden reference to filial piety: "De l'ainz né avindrent mervoiles, / Que li corbel et les cornoilles / Anbedus les ialz li creverent" (459–61, B487–89) (A strange thing happened to the elder: the crows and rooks pecked out both his eyes). The image reflects Proverbs 30:17 (my emphasis): "Oculum *qui subsannat patrem, et qui despicit partum matris suae,* effodiant eum corvi de torrentibus, et comedant eum fillii aquilae!" (The eye *that mocketh at his father, and that despiseth the labour of his mother in bearing him,* let the ravens of the brooks pick it out, and the young eagles eat it.) The weight of the rebuke against those who behave uncharitably toward their parents does not fall retrospectively on Perceval's brother, however, but points prospectively to Perceval himself. The son whom she seeks to educate about herself, his father, their families, and

2. The Hermitage: "He that abideth in charity"

Figure 3. The Waste Forest and the Hermitage: Perceval Astride a Hunter Leaving His Mother.

his brothers, abruptly cuts her short: "'A mangier, fet il, me donez. / Ne sai de coi m'aresonez'" (473–74, B491–92) ("Give me something to eat," he said, "I don't understand your words"). At this point he is obsessed only with finding Arthur, "the king who makes knights" (476, B494). The consequences are far-reaching.

As Perceval rides away from his mother's manor (Figure 3), Chrétien's narrator recounts in an elegant, yet coldly detached manner the acts that epitomize his lack of *eleemosyna* and *caritas* toward his mother

Figure 4. The Waste Forest and the Hermitage: Perceval on a *Destrier* Approaching the Hermitage.

(602–12, B622–32). We shall return to the details of his departure in due course,[43] but, for the moment, the point of interest is the fact that when Perceval leaves his mother, who has fallen in a faint and looks as though she is dead, he cannot know that he is destined to mirror the example set by his two brothers. Something in his experience with Gornemant

2. The Hermitage: "He that abideth in charity"

de Gohort initiates a developing sense of filial piety, and, after being knighted by his mentor, he decides to leave him prematurely and heads for home. The trail leads him instead to Biaurepaire, where a more profound sense of his obligations as a son spurs him to abandon the lady to whom he is betrothed and the lands he has won on her behalf and to return to his mother. Yet again his plan is frustrated, for the pathway again leads him not homeward, but to the Grail Castle, where he has his greatest adventure and suffers his greatest failure. Eventually he learns that, just as his brothers' exercise of filial piety led them to their deaths, so his own efforts result not in redemption, but insanity. Like his elder brothers, he never reaches his goal—except in the figurative sense that he finds reflections of his home at the Hermitage.

Meanwhile, in the Hermit's partial disclosure of the Grail mysteries are mirrored both an affirmative image of a parental figure sustained through acts of filial piety and a process of expiation (6381–97, B6415–31). The Grail King, who is the Hermit's father and Perceval's maternal uncle, has been cared for within the castle of the Fisher King, his son, for a dozen years, and he is nourished daily by a Host brought to him in the Grail. The Fisher King's acts of mercy reflect the very expiatory offering that Rabanus Maurus explicitly associates with the *peccatum matris*. Chrétien does not reveal the whereabouts of the priest who consecrates the Host. Is it the Hermit himself or else perhaps the (itinerate?) priest who recites the Good Friday liturgy with him? Can the forest-like *desert* where Perceval finds the Hermitage be so close to the Grail Castle?

The Peccatum Matris: *Killing the Mother and Undeserved Redemption*

By the time the Weeping Maiden first raises the issue of the "pechié ... de ta mere," however, Chrétien has already provided another, apparently contradictory explanation for Perceval's failure. Perceval sees the Bleeding Lance passing before him, but he does not ask how this "merveille" (3168, B3202) (marvel) can happen because

> del chasti li sovenoit
> Celui qui chevalier le fist
> Qui li anseigna et aprist

> Que de trop parler se gardast;
> Si crient, se il demandast,
> Qu'an li tenist a vilenie:
> Por ce si nel demanda mie
> [3172–78, B3206–12].

(he recalled the admonishment given by the gentleman who had knighted him, who taught ... him not to talk too much; he was afraid that if he asked they would consider him uncouth, so he did not ask.)

And again, when the Grail returns, he

> n'osa mie demander
> Del graal, cui l'an an servoit,
> Que toz jorz en son cuer avoit
> La parole au prodome sage
> [3210–13, B3244–47].

(did not dare ask who was served from the grail, for in his heart he always kept the wise gentleman's [words].)

The Grail comes back without the Bleeding Lance, but Perceval represses his desire to know about it and again holds his tongue "Por le prodome ... / Qui dolcemant le chastïa / De trop parler ..." (because of the nobleman ... [who] so gently warned him not to talk too much) (3260–62, B3294–96).[44]

Chrétien's narrator volunteers a judgment on the matter:

> Si criem que il n'i ait domage,
> Par ce que j'ai oï retraire
> Qu'*ausi bien se puet an trop taire*
> *Con trop parler, a la foiee*:
> Ou bien l'en praigne ou mal l'an chiee,
> Ne lor anquiert ne ne demande
> [3214–19, B3248–53, my emphasis].

(Yet I fear that this may lead to trouble, for I have heard it said that *at times it is just as wrong to keep too silent as to talk too much*. Whether for good or for ill, he did not ask or inquire anything of them.)

He remarks a few lines later that "plus se test qu'il ne covient" (he kept ... silent [longer] than he should) (3264, B3298). In the end, Perceval disastrously decides to wait until the next morning to ask one of the serving boys (3271–75, B3305–09)—too little, too late, for when he awakes the next morning, he finds the castle deserted and barely escapes with his life when the drawbridge suddenly rises as he leaves on horseback.

2. The Hermitage: "He that abideth in charity"

The comments of Chrétien's narrator reflect Gornemant de Gohort's advice to Perceval after he confers on him "La plus haute ordre … / Que Dex a fete et comandee: / C'est l'ordre de chevalerie" (the highest order … that God [has] set forth and ordained, … the order of knighthood) (1615–17, B1635–37). In exhorting the "new knight" (1680, B1700) to abstain from garrulousness, Gornemant paraphrases Proverbs:

> Et gardez que vos ne soiez
> Trop parlanz ne trop noveliers:
> Nus ne puet estre trop parliers
> Que sovant tel chose ne die
> Qu'an li atort a vilenie;
> Et li sages dit et retret:
> *"Qui trop parole pechié fet."*
> Por ce, biau[s] frere, vos chasti
> De trop parler …
> [1628–36, my emphasis].

(And be careful not to be too talkative or [too] prone to gossip. Anyone who is too talkative soon discovers he's said something that brings him reproach; and the wise man says and declares, *"He who talks too much commits a sin."* Therefore, young man, I forbid you to talk too much.)

As Solomon states (Proverbs 10:19), "In multiloquio non deerit peccatum" (In the multitude of words there shall not want sin), and he continues: "Qui autem moderatur labia sua prudentissimus est" (but he that refraineth his lips is most wise). Variants of the expressions are proverbial in Old French,[45] but no attested form of the saying is closer to the Vulgate text than Gornemant's version, which emphatically translates *peccatum* as *pechié* (sin, calamity, fault), but without conveying the wry litotes in "non deerit" (will not lack).[46]

The judgment of Chrétien's narrator, which is far more subtle than Gornemant's dictum from Proverbs, is likewise supported by the biblical authority again of the Book of Sirach, where caution against loquacity emphasizes discernment of the time for speaking, while the "sin" of garrulousness is the appearance of foolishness:

> Est tacens qui invenitur sapiens, et est odibilis qui procax est ad loquendum. *Est tacens non habens sensum loquaelae; est tacens sciens tempus aptum. Homo sapiens tacebit usque ad tempus aptum est.* Lascivus autem et imprudens non servabunt tempus [Sirach 20:5–7, my emphasis].[47]
> (There is one that holdeth his peace, that is found wise: and there is another

that is hateful, that is bold in speech. *There is one that holdeth his peace, because he knoweth not what to say: And there is another that holdeth his peace, knowing the proper time. A wise man will hold his peace till he see opportunity*: but a babbler, and a fool, will regard no time.)

The concept is also proverbialized in Old French in a formula that is not far from that of Chrétien's narrator (3216–17, B3250–51): "Sorparler nuit et trop se reput l'en tere"[48] (Speaking too much is harmful, but one can also keep silent for too long). In Ecclesiastes 3:7, such distinctions are summarized quite succinctly and far less richly than in Sirach and perhaps less aptly for the *Conte del Graal*: "Tempus tacendi, et tempus loquendi" (A time to keep silence, and a time to speak).[49] Chrétien's narrator reports Perceval's thoughts as he observes the Grail procession and the return of the Grail. He is in the process of assimilating Gornemant's instructions, to be sure, but the examples from Sirach illustrate how far he may be from acquiring wisdom and judgment, a matter that his mentor does not address, and thus the ability to discern the difference between the *tempus tacendi* and the *tempus loquendi*: Gornemant does not define what is excessive in "*Trop* parlanz ne *trop* noveliers" (*too* talkative or [*too*] prone to gossip) (1629, B1649, my emphasis).[50] Where Gornemant himself goes wrong in falling silent on the subject is exactly the point stressed by the Hideous Damsel when she says to Perceval that he *knew* that it was time to speak, and yet he held his tongue: "Ce est tu li maleüreus / Qui *veïs* qu'il fu tans et leus / De parler et si te taüs!" (you are that wretched man, for you *saw* that it was the time and place to speak, yet kept your silence!) (4631–33, B4665–67, my emphasis). How is Perceval's error in judgment related to the *peccatum matris*?

The scene in which Perceval witnesses his mother's fall begins a crucial specular sequence that recurs in his justifications of his hasty departures from Gornemant de Gohort and Biaurepaire and in his encounter with the Weeping Maiden. The light cast by the latter two upon Perceval's initial experience and his subsequent accounts of it may appear to end the sequence as he learns that his mother is dead and concludes that there is no need for him continue his quest for her (3568–91, B3602–25). When the sequence resurfaces at the Hermitage, however, it is clear in retrospect that it has recurred covertly in the Grail Castle episode and in the Hideous Damsel's diatribe: in both it has been evoked by synecdoche, that is, in references to Perceval's ruinous silence.

2. The Hermitage: "He that abideth in charity"

In his account of the seminal event, the diction of Chrétien's narrator is elegant, as in the syntax of the opening sestet, but it remains dispassionately neutral (cf. Figure 3):

> Plorant le beise au departir
> La mere qui mout chier l'avoit,
> Et prie Deu que il l'avoit.
> "Biax filz, fet ele, Dex vos maint.
> Joie plus qu'il ne me remaint
> Vos doinst il, ou que vos ailliez."
> Qant li vaslet fu esloigniez
> Le giet d'une pierre menue,
> Si se regarde et voit cheüe
> Sa mere au chief del pont arriere,
> Et jut pasmee an tel meniere
> Con s'ele fust cheüe morte.
> Et cil ceingle de la reorte
> Son chaceor par mi la crope,
> Et cil s'an va qui pas ne çope,
> Einz l'an porte grant aleüre
> Par mi la grant forest oscure
> [596–612, B616–32].

(His mother, who loved him dearly, kissed him tearfully as he left and begged God to [guide him]. "Fair son," she said, "God be with you. May He give you more joy than remains with me." When the boy was a short stone's throw away, he looked back and saw that his mother had fallen at the head of the bridge and was lying in a faint as if she had dropped dead. But he whipped his hunter across the crupper with his switch, and the horse bore him swiftly on without stumbling through the great dark forest.)

The emotionally stark narration following the sestet matches Perceval's chilling apathy towards his mother's suffering—towards the *peccatum matris* of Sirach 3:16, in light of which the "innocent" adolescent reveals his indifference to the ethos of filial piety. The lack of compassion—the absence of *eleemosyna*, of an impulse to charity—that Perceval displays is foreshadowed by the self-absorption in his insensitivity to his mother's grief when she recounts the deaths of Perceval's father and elder brothers:

> Li vaslez antant mout petit
> A ce que sa mere li dit.
> "A mangier, fet il, me donez.
> Ne sai de coi m'areisonez,

> Mes mout iroie volantiers
> Au roi qui fet les chevaliers,
> Et g'irai, cui qu'il en poist"
> [471-77, B489-95].

(The boy paid scarcely any attention to what his mother said to him. "Give me something to eat," he demanded. "I don't understand [what you're talking to me about], but I would gladly go to the king who makes knights, and I will go, no matter [whom it grieves].")

Throughout the Waste Forest episode, Perceval exhibits the worst and most heartless characteristics of egocentric innocence as well as the best and most appealing. The paradox is reiterated and compounded when he attempts to seduce the Tent Maiden.[51] What condemns Perceval is the determined action implicit in turning his head— turning his back on his mother—and the urgent spurring of his horse.

Higher degrees of empathetic awareness with respect to his mother emerge subsequently in his own reflective accounts of his departure. Insofar as Perceval's regard for his mother is concerned, Chrétien's narrator registers only his seeing her lying on the ground as though she were dead. Perceval's recapitulations are increasingly insightful. When he refuses to continue his training with Gornemant, he conveys an unexpected, though still limited, perception of what he witnessed and its cause.[52] He now recalls the incident as seeing her falling in a faint from grief and purposefully leaving her on the ground:

> Sire, ne sai se je sui pres
> Del manoir ou ma mere maint,
> Mes je pri Deu qu'a li me maint
> Tant qu'ancor la puise veoir,
> Que pasmee la vi cheoir
> Au chief del pont devant la porte,
> Si ne sai s'ele est vive ou morte.
> *De duel de moi quant la lessai*
> *Cheï pasmee, bien le sai,*
> Et por ce ne porroit pas estre,
> Tant que je seüsse son estre,
> Que je feïsse lonc sejor,
> Einz m'an irai demain au jor
> [1560-72, B1580-92, my emphasis].

(Sir, I don't know if I'm close to the manor where my mother lives, but I pray God to guide me there that I might behold her again, for I saw her fall

2. The Hermitage: "He that abideth in charity"

in a faint at the head of the bridge before the gate, and I don't know whether she is alive or dead. *I am well aware she fainted in grief at my departure,* and for this reason until I know how she is, I cannot tarry for long, so therefore I'll be on my way tomorrow at dawn.)

But he appears to forget his mission as he becomes ever more deeply engaged with Blanchefleur and the defense of her domain, which, unlike his formal training in knighthood, he sees through almost to the end, but lacking his return to Biaurepaire, his marriage to Blanchefleur, and his assumption of lordship.

Amidst the joy and celebration after he has defeated the invader Clamadeus des Isles and sent him to follow his seneschal, Anguigneron, to be imprisoned by Arthur, he is reminded once again of his mother "Que il vit pasmee cheoir, / S'a talant qu'il l'aille veoir / Plus grant que de nule autre chose" (2885–87, B2919–21) (whom he had seen fall in a faint, and he wanted to go to see her more than anything else). Blanchefleur and her people reluctantly grant him leave to look for her only after he swears to return with her, should he find her alive, to rule their lady's lands, or without her if she has died (2894–98, B2928–34). When they accompany him in procession as he leaves the city, he addresses them one last time and urges them not to mourn his departure:

> Ne cuidiez vos que ce soit bien
> Que je ma mere veoir vois
> Qui sole manoit an cel bois
> Qui la Gaste Forest a non?
> Je revendrai, voille ele ou non,
> Que ja por rien nel lesserai.
> Et s'ele est vive, g'en ferai
> Nonain velee an vostre eglise;
> Et s'ele est morte, le servise
> Ferez por s'ame chascun an,
> Que Dex el sain saint Abrahan
> La mete avec les pies ames
> [2922–33, B2956–67].

(Don't you think it is well that I go to see my mother who was living all alone in a woods called the Waste Forest? I shall come back, whether she wishes it or not: nothing will prevent my return. If she is alive, I'll make her a veiled nun in your church; and if she is dead, you'll sing a Mass each year for her soul, that God place it with the faithful in the bosom of Abraham.)

Perceval and Gawain in Dark Mirrors

The passage is of interest because it contains the only occurrence of the toponym *Gaste Forest* (2925, B2959) (Waste Forest) outside the narrator's exposition in the *Conte del Graal*'s opening episode.[53] More significantly, it is important because it shows that Perceval has acquired a certain skill in rhetoric, for he successfully persuades his audience to approve his decision to depart in quest of his mother, and, as well, a knowledge about religion and society beyond what Chrétien's narrator has previously reported. Perceval is familiar with the biblical image of the bosom of Abraham as a heavenly Paradise for the righteous,[54] and he hopes that his mother will also have a place there among the redeemed. Most especially, he demonstrates an unprecedented consciousness of filial piety grounded in charity that is consonant with his growing awareness of love, honor, and lordship in Blanchefleur's company. With respect to his mother, he seeks not only to visit her in her isolated manor and to bring her back with him to Biaurepaire, but also to provide for her material well-being, for he now knows that widows with means may retire to convents and lead comfortable lives there for the rest of their years. On the other hand, in an anachronistic perspective, there is no doubt room for discussion regarding the propriety of his presumptions concerning his mother's retirement, should he find her alive, for he makes commitments without consulting her and indeed foresees the possibility of acting contrary to her will. In addition, it is hard not to be aware of the tone of worldly connivance in his assurances that, whether she is alive or dead, Biaurepaire's religious houses will profit from her endowment and from Masses celebrated on her behalf. Finally, in light of the Prologue, Perceval's public declaration of his charitable intentions is tantamount to letting his left hand know what his right hand is doing. Even so, his negotiations exhibit degrees of awareness, sophistication, and charitable concern as yet unsuspected in the "valet galois" whom the Tent Maiden characterizes—rightly, at the time—as "Enuieus et vilain [et] sot" (772, B806) (uncouth, base, and naïve).

The way to the Waste Forest that Perceval follows in quest of his mother takes him to the Grail Castle, where an uncle (the Grail King himself?) bequeaths a miraculous sword to him and, as the Hermit tells him later, a cousin of his, who is infirm, cares for his own ageing father, who appears to be confined to his bed. There he witnesses an extraor-

2. The Hermitage: "He that abideth in charity"

dinary and mystifying procession that functions ceremonially to convey servings of courses at the banquet the Fisher King shares with Perceval at the high table. A grail is an elegant serving dish, but the Grail at the Fisher King's castle, which appears in the procession, serves only his father hidden within, not those dining in the great hall.[55] It is the silver cutting platter, which is carried in last place in the procession, that is used to convey the main course of peppered venison served on trenchers of bread (3250–55, B3284–89). Thanks to knowledge and experience concerning the acquisition of which Chrétien's narrator has remained silent—once again, as often before—Perceval recognizes what a grail is.[56] Regardless of whether or not his mother may actually have possessed one in the Waste Forest, has he not seen grails at the twice-disrupted banquet at Carlisle (cf. 874–947, B894–967) or during lavish meals in Gornemant's castle (cf. 1539–48, B1559–68) and, thanks to divine intervention (2490–2526, B2524–60), even at Biaurepaire (cf. 2544–51, B2578–85)? As the Hermit later tells Perceval with wry humor, however, the dish the Grail serves is not fish such as the Fisher King and his companion (his father?) in his boat might have caught or meats ordinarily brought to noble tables in grails, but a consecrated Host, the *hostia*, the bread of life.

Even lacking the miraculous information provided retrospectively, the procession is amazing in many ways. At the most fundamental level of customary behavior at banquets, Perceval is impressed by the fact that the Grail passes by the high table without serving the Fisher King and his guest and makes its way past through the great hall before disappearing into an inner room (3256–67, B3290–3301), whence it returns. Chrétien's narrator reports that the appropriate question springs immediately to Perceval's mind: it is not "What is in the grail?" Despite the overpowering light surrounding it, he has no reason to suspect that it does not contain ordinary meat or fish but hallowed bread. Instead, as is emphasized when it passes twice and the question is repeated three times, it is "Who in the castle is fed from a grail that is not brought to the high table, where Perceval and his royal host are seated, but taken into another room?": "cui l'an an servoit" (3211, B3245; 3259, B3293; cf. 3268, B3302) (who was served from [it]). Perceval could not discern the right question—the Grail question—if he did not already know about grails and how they are used to serve at opulent banquets. Similarly, he

Perceval and Gawain in Dark Mirrors

formulates the appropriate question about the Bleeding Lance because he has learned very well what a lance is: "How can a lance bleed? What makes it bleed? Why does it bleed?" But he is too polite to ask, too afraid of giving offense.

How does the *peccatum matris* function specifically at the Grail Castle, where, according to the Weeping Maiden and the Hermit, not to mention the Hideous Damsel (who does not use the term *pechié*), the effects of the sin are perhaps the most germane? The reflective sequence initiated with the fall of Perceval's mother re-emerges in the Hermitage, where it is explicitly made relevant to Perceval's Grail adventure. It is also thematically consonant with and therefore enriched by twin sequences that have already been identified in other contexts[57]: the tokens of Perceval's Welsh upbringing, articles of clothing made by his mother, his hunter, and his javelin, the power of his mother's *parole*, her advice—and, as the Hermit emphasizes, her life-sustaining prayer: "Et prie Deu que il l'avoit" (and [she] begged God to [guide] him) (598, B616; cf. 6369–74, B6403–08). The material signs of his Welsh origins are discarded in two steps as he acquires the refined trappings of knighthood: first, at Carlisle, after he kills the Red Knight with his javelin, he dons the dead knight's armor with the help of the he squire Yonet, and takes his charger (1055–1186, B1075–1206), and, second, at Gornemant's castle, when he finally accepts luxurious clothing offered by his host, who formally knights him by attaching his spurs (1577–1603, B1597–1623).[58]

His mother's speech is more significant and infinitely more durable than the clothing she has fashioned for her son: it has the power to shape both Chrétien's romance and the destiny of its primary protagonist even beyond her death. She knows that, whether for good or ill, Perceval will receive arms at Arthur's court and that he will not know how to use them. Her story about Perceval's elder brothers sets the pattern of his wanderings at least as long as he consciously seeks to return to the Waste Forest and perhaps until he reaches the Hermitage, which is in another "waste forest." Her words of advice, in the perverted ways Perceval understands them, specifically prompt him to enter the Tent Maiden's pavilion and determine his behavior once inside. They also resonate in accounts of his relationship with Blancheflor. Finally, they shape his relationship with Gornemant de Gohort, who convinces him to stop

2. The Hermitage: "He that abideth in charity"

talking so much—the irony in his translation of Solomon shines all the more clearly: "Qui trop parole pechié fet" (1634, B1654), for Perceval errs by not speaking at all—and to refrain from quoting his mother at every turn and remember and act upon only the words, the *parole* (cf. 3178, B3212), of the vavassor who has made Perceval a knight (cf. 1666–68, B1686–88). At the behest of the mentor who guides him along the path from raw adolescence toward manhood in fulfillment of a destiny that his mother both fears and determines, Perceval commits a metaphorical matricide that mirrors his fatal abandonment of her in his refusal to respond with charity to the *peccatum matris* as it is illuminated in Sirach. Aiding and abetting in this "murder" is Gornemant's last act on behalf of his pupil. Ironically, Perceval renounces his mother's *parole* just as an incipient awareness of her fall and its causes and consequences have moved him to leave his mentor, leaving his apprenticeship incomplete so that he can be reunited with her.

According to the Hermit, however, the power of his mother's *parole* as prayer has sustained him through all adversity despite his sin. Furthermore, its strength has not waned, as is denoted by the Hermit's use of the perfect: "sa parole ot tel vertu / Que Dex *por li t'a regardé*, / De mort et de prison *gardé*" (6372–74, B6408–10, my emphasis) (her prayer was so powerful [when she uttered it] that God [*has*] *watched* over you *for her sake* and [*has*] *kept* you from death and [capture]). As penance for Perceval's failure to fulfill the duties inherent in the observance of filial piety, the priest imposes, but with different emphases, the very duties required to meet the standards of noble, chivalric behavior counseled by his mother in a domestic setting and reiterated by Gornemant de Gohort in context with secular knighthood. He must attend Mass and believe, love, and worship God (6405–25, B6439–59); honor noble men and women (6426, B6460), including priests (6427–30, B6461–64), a new element that points to matters ecclesiastical and liturgical; and come to the aid of maidens, widows, and orphans who are in need of it (6431–33, B6465–67):

> Icele *almosne* iert enterine.
> Ce voel que por tes pechiez face,
> Se ravoir viax totes tes graces
> Ausi con tu avoir les siax
> [6434–37, B6468–71, my emphasis].

(This ... *penance* [is complete in itself]. I want you to do [it] for your sins if you wish to regain the graces you used to enjoy.)

Here Chrétien's unusual term *almosne* (beneficial act of mercy), which Kibler correctly translates as "penance" within the context of the confessional, clearly reflects the usage of its etymon, *eleemosyna*, in Sirach 3:14–16 and in the commentary of Rabanus Maurus.[59] It elucidates—and revitalizes—the "tot el" (4693, B4727) (different oath) that Perceval swore at Arthur's court when other knights accepted to pursue adventures proposed by the Hideous Damsel and he sets out to right the wrongs he committed at the Grail Castle.[60] That path led to failure and despair, but, redeemed, Perceval renews his quest in the light of Easter. In redemption, as Donald Maddox has so cogently argued (*Arthurian Romance*, pp. 112–13), Perceval is reoriented away from the Arthurian realm and towards the world as it envisaged by his kin—his mother, the Grail King, the Hermit—, but is it too late for him to restore it?

Perceval's redemption is sealed by his charitable "penance" and assured in his Easter communion—thematically if not biographically, for we cannot know where else Chrétien might have led him. Yet it almost seems too easy: weighty, romance-shaping sins are wiped away with so little fanfare. By this point in the *Conte del Graal*, however, a pattern of undeserved redemption has long since come to the fore—in the secular arena, to be sure—in the reflective sequence marked by acts of mercy wrought by Perceval himself, at Gornemant's behest, when he sends defeated criminals like Anguigneron, Clamadeus, and the Orgueilleus de la Lande to Arthur for assimilation into his court. The strand will re-emerge in Gawain's Galloway adventures when he forgives the Malevolent Maiden and integrates her into the Two Queens'—rather his own—court at the Roche de Champguin. The Hermitage episode, where we learn in retrospect that Perceval has been protected by his mother's *parole* no thanks to his own merits, is indeed a re-enactment of the Parable of the Prodigal Son (Luke 15:11–32).

3

Gawain in the Galloway Borderland

Greoreas

When Gawain crosses from Escavalon into Galloway, he witnesses an amazing scene at a defensive *angarde*. As he rides up the mound, he discovers a severely wounded knight lying unconscious in a lady's arms in the shade of a great oak tree (6479–6509, B6519–49). Of his body Chrétien describes only its mutilations: his face is in shreds, the back of his head bears a deep sword wound, and blood flows from both of his sides.[1] Some 600 lines later, Gawain recalls the knight's name: Greoreas (7076, B7118). Antoinette Saly ("Récurrence") evokes the iconography of the Pietà, and she demonstrates how the Greoreas scene profoundly reflects the Weeping Maiden episode, in which Perceval meets his cousin under an oak tree (3397, B3431) similarly mourning her lover, who has been beheaded by the Orgueilleus de la Lande. Greoreas's head wound results from a *failed* decapitation by another Orgueilleus, as Gawain will learn much later from Guiromelant: the "Orgueilleus / De la Roche a l'Estroite Voie[2] / Qui garde les porz de Galvoie" (8598–8600, B8646–50) (Proud Knight of the Stone at the Narrow Way, ... [who] defends the passes into Galloway). In context with the Pietà, Greoreas's head wounds may recall the crown of thorns and his bleeding sides the lance wound inflicted on Christ's right side by the Roman centurion identified in the Middle Ages as Longinus. In addition, Keith Busby draws attention in this connection to the Fisher King's sexual mutilation,[3] which also recalls that of Perceval's father.

For all the heartbreak evoked by the Pietà motif, Gawain's encounter with Greoreas is not devoid of comic touches. Gawain awakens the stricken knight, despite his lady's protests, by gently nudging his spur with the tip of his lance. Once Greoreas comes around, he thanks Gawain with excessive politeness for restoring him to consciousness, then tells him that he has been wounded by an incredibly fierce knight: "Preu et hardi et fort et fier, / Onques si vaillant ne trovai / Ne a si fort ne m'esprovai" (bold and brave and strong and proud—I've never before encountered such a bold one or tested myself against one so strong) (6570–72, B6610–12). Gawain feels compelled to seek success where Greoreas has failed, but Greoreas warns him to go no farther. No one, he says, has ever ridden beyond the outpost and lived to return except for himself (6563–68, B6600–08).

Without compunction, and characteristically ignoring Greoreas's warning, Gawain abandons the distraught couple and follows the wounded knight's path for some distance—"Par plains et par forez" (6618, B6658) (across plains and through forests)—to a walled city by the sea, presumably the castle of the Roche a l'Estroite Voie. The fortress is accessible by a drawbridge across a river surrounding it on all sides (6619–29, B6659–69). The adventure Gawain expects does not await him within, and he is destined to win only disappointment and humiliation there. He encounters not the fierce knight described by Greoreas, but a viper-tongued maiden whom he finds dallying in a garden (*prael*, 6634, B6676): the "pucele sanz merci" (8331, B8373) (merciless maiden), the "male pucele" (malevolent maiden) (8505, B8551; 8416, B8458) or "damoisele enuieuse" (8287, B 8319) ([hostile damsel])—her name is later given as the Orgueilleuse de Logres (8590–91, B8638–39) (the Proud Maiden of Logres). The portentous nature of his discovery is suggested by the garden itself, for it features a plank (6685, B6727) thrown across a stream that partakes of the reflective sequence of ominous bridges at the Waste Forest manor, at Biaurepaire, and at the Grail Castle—an omen of misfortune, as when Gawain's horse loses a shoe in the forest before Escavalon.

The maiden, who viciously taunts Gawain from the very beginning (6642–77, B6684–6719), intimates that she will leave the castle and follow him wherever he leads her, but first he must fetch her palfrey (Figure 5),[4] which grazes in the inner garden (*jardin*, 6673, B6715; also *vergier*, 6702, B6744) that is connected to her *prael* by the perilous plank.[5] Gawain hesitatingly entrusts his charger, Gringalet, to

3. Gawain in the Galloway Borderland

her because the bridge appears not to be strong enough to bear its weight, but he takes all his armor with him should anyone, perhaps the elusive knight who wounded Greoreas, challenge him for the palfrey (6699–6706, B6741–48). In the inner garden he encounters a great crowd of people who curse the Malevolent Maiden, accusing her of causing many a noble man to be beheaded (6714–15, B6756–57), and they warn Gawain against associating with her.[6] Finally, he meets a forbiddingly huge knight sitting by himself beneath an olive tree, like a pagan lord in a *chanson de geste*, who might well be taken for the dreadful guardian of the borderland, but anticipations are again deflected when, without threatening Gawain in any way, he warns him that others who have brought the palfrey to the maiden have lost their heads (6707–76, B6742–6819). Naturally, Gawain cannot suffer the shame of avoiding the adventure he has come to undergo.[7]

When he brings the palfrey across the plank, it is not the bridge itself that proves sinister, but his very gesture in taking the knight's warning as a challenge. He in fact sets a very complex adventure into motion, as Greoreas must also have done, when he retrieves the horse and then allows the maiden to ride it in his company.[8] The knight who wounded Greoreas is absent, and thus the adventure is defused at least temporarily, but Gawain's gesture results in other perils to his person and to his reputation, which, ironically, he has sought in vain to protect by undertaking this very adventure in the first place.

A number of reflective sequences already identified converge at the Borne de Galvoie—the castle, the bridge and drawbridge, the mirror, the beautiful woman, the amorous couple, and others—, but the matter of equestrian propriety, the identity of horses and their relationship with their human companions, surfaces with renewed power at the *angarde*. In the Perceval adventures, the young Welshman acquires at Carlisle a horse worthy of his new status as knight, or so he believes, when he exchanges his Welsh hunter, which he has ridden him from the Waste Forest to Arthur's castle, for the Red Knight's *destrier* (1166, B1186) (charger). Chrétien's text appears to be indifferent, however, as to whether or not Perceval is on same horse when he arrives at the Hermitage.[9]

When Perceval meets the Tent Maiden a second time, the condition of her emaciated palfrey signifies the extent to which she herself has suffered at the hands of her abusive lover. We recall that, in a jealous rage,[10] the Orgueilleus de la Lande has punished her (for Perceval's crime) by forcing her to follow him without changing her clothing and to leave her palfrey unshod, should be throw a shoe, ungroomed, and malnourished from eating grass as he may find it instead of being fed decent oats. The punishment will continue until he has avenged *himself* by beheading the Welsh intruder to whom he believes she gave her love (796–812, B816–32; cf. 3657–3712, B3691–3746, 3856–64, B3890–97). The lady's close identity with her palfrey submerges, however, as Chrétien eventually loses sight of him after Perceval defeats her lover, at which point all the attention of his narrator focuses on the couple, their reconciliation (cf. 3896–4024, B3930–4058), and their welcome at Arthur's first Carlion court.

Seeing the border outpost in Galloway for the first time, Gawain is immediately struck by an incongruity he immediately perceives in a setting fraught with narrative possibilities. In a brilliant example of Chrétien's deft experimentation with visual perspective, Gawain does not see the Pietà configuration from the bottom of the mound when he arrives, for the couple are out of sight above him and away from the slope. As he rides up, he first observes a shield hanging in the oak tree with a lance standing next to it, but he is astonished to discover a breach of equestrian propriety: with the armor he sees "Un palefroi norrois petit" (6490, B6530) (a small Norwegian palfrey) (Figure 5):

> Si li vint mout a grant merveille
> Que ce n'estoit chose paroille,
> Ne pas n'advienent, ce li sanble,
> Armes et palefroiz ansanble.
> Se li palefroiz fust chevax,
> Donc cuidast il qu'aucuns vasax
> Qui por s'enor et por son pris
> Alast errant par le païs,
> Eüst montee cele angarde
> [6491–99, B6531–39].

(and he was quite surprised, for it was most unusual, it seemed to him, to find a palfrey together with a shield and arms. Had the palfrey been a charger, he might have presumed that some [knight], who had gone off through the countryside to seek his glory and honor, had climbed this hillock.)

3. Gawain in the Galloway Borderland

A palfrey (6494, B6534) is not the horse (here *chevax*, 6495, B6535) of a knight errant, but a mount suitable for women, merchants, old men, and noblemen at leisure—appropriately, for example, Tiebaut de Tintagel rides a palfrey in the evening within his own city (5353, B5387). As Gawain climbs higher up the mound, the lady whose mount the palfrey must be comes into view, but the charger belonging to the wounded knight he sees is nowhere to be found. A knight's aversion to palfreys is played out in the walled city's inner garden when Gawain does not lead the Malevolent Maiden's horse across the plank bridge, much less ride it, but instead drives it ahead of himself (6780–83, B6822–25).

Gawain is astride Gringalet when he returns with the Malevolent Maiden to the *angarde* where he has left Greoreas and his lady, and he immediately dismounts to tend the injured knight, whom he treats with a medicinal herb he has recognized growing in a hedge (6868–6919, B6910–61). As Greoreas begins to heal, he fears that he will die before reviving sufficiently to be able to confess his sins and receive absolution, as Perceval has done in the preceding episode in a setting such as Greoreas envisages:

> Ge sai un chapelain ci pres,
> Se j'avoie sor coi monter,
> Cui g'iroie dire et conter
> Mes pechiez an confessïon,
> Et p[r]anroie comenïon
> [6930–34, B6972–76].

(I know [of] a nearby chaplain, if I had [a horse to ride], to whom I'd go and tell all my sins in confession and take communion.)

As Greoreas recovers his sight, he makes out a squire, who soon reveals himself to be excessively impertinent and unruly, approaching them riding a broken-down nag (6940, B6982: *roncin*) (Figure 6). He begs Gawain to bring him the horse to him so that he and his lady—she on her palfrey—may ride to the chapel where he may confess his sins and prepare for death (6938–56, B6980–7001). Thus the fear of death unshriven urges him to ignore chivalric propriety.

Gawain turns about and sees that the squire is extraordinarily ugly (6943–55, B6985–97). His wild hair and beard and his misshapen head and upper body in fact mirror the monstrosity of the Hideous Damsel (4578, B4612), and he is indeed as worthy of his nag as his counterpart

Perceval and Gawain in Dark Mirrors

Figure 5. Equestrian Propriety: Palfrey

is of her tawny mule (4578, B4612) (Figure 8).[11] Gawain remarks Greoreas's lack of probity in his ready willingness to ride a broken-down horse,[12] but he approaches the Unruly Squire all the same and asks him his business. His excessively discourteous reply[13] rightly (6976, B7018: "a droiture") provokes Gawain to strike him down from his saddle with an open-handed blow. Meanwhile, as Gawain and the squire quarrel (6988–98, B7030–40), Greoreas continues to gather strength. He regains full use of his voice and shouts to Gawain not to waste time arguing and to bring him the nag so that he and his lady can embark on their mission. Gawain seizes the squire's mount, but by the time he walks it back to Greoreas, hands him its reins, and turns to help the lady mount her pal-

3. Gawain in the Galloway Borderland

Figure 6. Equestrian Propriety: The Unruly Squire's Nag

frey, Greoreas's vision has returned to normal and he sees exactly who his savior is.

Matters take an unanticipated turn that is signaled when Greoreas's recognition of Gawain sends him straight to Gringalet—a striking example of "thinking on the spot," with no need of Lacanian chicanery to explain it, as described in a recent notable study as a hallmark of Chrétien's romances.[14] Greoreas mounts Gawain's charger and gambols all about the hilltop. Gawain is taken aback by what he sees, but smiles as he courteously advises Greoreas to stop such foolishness before he reopens his wounds. The response he receives is astonishing in both tone and content:

> Gauvains, tes t'an!
> Pran le roncin, si feras san,
> Que au cheval as tu failli.
> Ge l'ai a mon oés porsailli,

Perceval and Gawain in Dark Mirrors

> Si l'an manrai come le mien
> [7043–47, B7085–89].

(Hold your tongue, Gawain! You'd be smart to take the nag, for you've lost your charger. I made him prance to test him out, and now I'll take him as my own.)

Greoreas hates Gawain because he once shamed him by forcing him to eat with dogs for a whole month with his hands tied behind his back. Now it is Gawain who will be shamed (7067–76, B7109–18).

Equestrian Propriety and the Custom of Logres

Unexpectedly, these disconcerting circumstances illustrate how, in the *Conte del Graal*, equestrian propriety is intertwined with matters of the Custom of Logres so as to point to a certain definition of knighthood. When the Orgueilleus de la Lande accuses his lady of infidelity with another knight, he has grievously—and obstinately—misread all the signs of Perceval's presence to infer that she has willingly entertained a knight: hoof prints (766, B786) made by Perceval's hunter and disorder inside the tent—pasty crumbs, spilled wine—as well as the lady's disheveled appearance and her very words of explanation about the blunders of an uncouth adolescent. All signs, he persists in believing, point to her own disloyalty: "Et dist: 'Dameisele, je croi / A ces ansaignes que je voi / Que chevalier a eü ici: (767–69, B787–89) (and [he] said, "My lady, I believe by these signs that a knight was here").[15] As soon as he condemns his lady and her horse to torment and humiliation, both his words, which reflect his pathological obsessions, and his actions are seen to mirror distorted readings of the Custom of Logres, which is not explicitly evoked in the *Conte del Graal* to until Gawain and Greoreas lock horns.

In the *Chevalier de la Charrete*, the Amorous Maiden reminds Lancelot of the Custom (1295–1301) when they set out together, and Chrétien's narrator continues by explaining that throughout his kingdom of Logres (1) Arthur guarantees protection to a noble girl or maiden traveling alone, and any knight who takes her by force is forever shamed, but (2) a knight desiring a maiden accompanied by another knight may win her by challenging and defeating her protector.[16] When Perceval

3. Gawain in the Galloway Borderland

forces himself upon the Tent Maiden, he only aspires to knighthood and is not yet knight, yet he unwittingly violates the spirit of principles that are explicit in both clauses of the Custom: the lady is alone, which guarantees her safety, and she also informs him that she is protected by an absent "ami" (674, B694, etc.), against whom, according to the Custom, he should fight in order to win her. Subsequently, the Orgueilleus de la Lande claims to exercise his rights as construed in the second clause. His lady implicitly belongs to him until he is defeated by another knight, but he assumes erroneously that he has a right to "defend" her against those who he assumes may desire her even though they have not laid claim to her. Thus he fights and beheads any knight who so much as speaks to her, one of the most recent of whom is the Weeping Maiden's lover (3781–96, B3815–30). In essence, the Orgueilleus restages Perceval's earlier encounter with his lady, using her as a lure by leaving her alone to attract unsuspecting knights, who should in any case honor the Custom, and then arrives on the scene to invoke the second clause.

The Amorous Maiden in the *Charrete* wishes Lancelot to "lead" her (1297), just as the Malevolent Maiden, though on her own terms, will "follow" Gawain (6857, B6899). Both ladies thus place themselves under the protection of the Custom's second clause, as the Tent Maiden has unsuccessfully pled against an ignorant and indifferent Perceval. The Custom is implicitly at play throughout the "second *vers*" of *Erec et Enide*, although it is as a married lady, not as a maiden, that Enide literally "follows" her husband. On her wedding night "Ot perdu le non de pucele" (2103) (she had lost the name of maiden), as have in deed, if not in word, both the Tent Maiden and the Malevolent Maiden: "pucele n'est ele pas" (7413, B7455) (she's not a maiden!).

While the first clause of the Custom explicitly guarantees the security of undefended solitary maidens, the second clause reifies women who follow knights as fair game and provides sociopaths in the *Conte del Graal* like the Orgueilleus de la Lande (and, as we shall see, at least one "protector" of the Malevolent Maiden) with an excuse to murder defeated opponents without consideration of mercy. Such practices are patently contrary to Gornemant de Gohort's concept of chivalry. As abhorrent as the second clause is, however, nothing in the Custom justifies the Orgueilleus de la Lande's mistreatment of his lady and her palfrey. Moreover, in an exquisite caricature of a narrative principle that informs the *Conte del Graal* itself, which abounds in "contes de Perceval," "contes del Graal," and "contes de Gauvain," the Orgueilleus de la Lande degrades his lady further by telling knights whom he intends to slaughter an utterly fictionalized and self-justifying version of the story of her "seduction" and her "wanton submission" to an amorous Welshman—a slanderous "conte de la demoiselle" *cum* "conte de Perceval" that begins with her truthful account of events and concludes with his own distorted interpretation of it (cf. 767–812, B787–832):

> Oan el bois alez estoie
> Et ceste dameisele avoie
> Lessiee an un mien pavellon
> (Ne n'amoie rien se li non),
> Tant que par aventure avint
> Que uns valez galois i vint:
> Ne sai quex voies il ala,
> Mes tant fist que il la beisa
> Par force, si le me conut.
> ...Et s'il la baisa mau gré suen,
> N'an fist il aprés tot son buen?
> ...Fame qui sa boche abandone
> Le soreplus de legier done,[17]
> S'est qui a certes i antante,
> Et bien soit qu'ele se defande[,]
> Si set an bien sanz nul redot
> Que fame vialt vaintre par tot
> Fors qu'en cele meslee sole[.]
> ...Por ce cuit ge qu'il jut a li
> [3811–43, B3845–77].

([A year or so ago][18] I had gone off into the woods, leaving this damsel in one of my tents—and I loved no one but her; by chance came along a young Welshman. I don't know where he was headed, but he managed to force her to kiss him, so she told me.... But even if he kissed her against her will, didn't he take advantage of her afterwards? ... A woman who lets herself be kissed easily gives the rest if someone insists upon it; and even if she resists, it's a well-known fact that a woman wants to win every battle but this one.... Therefore I believe this Welshman lay with her.)

His words, which are interestingly informed by the *gradus amoris*, and the manifestations of his punishment are the inevitable realization of a sadistic vision centered in a distrust of women that is projected in his willfully twisted readings of the signs that Perceval left behind and the account his lady offers in her defense.

3. Gawain in the Galloway Borderland

After fighting a long, hard battle against Perceval, the Orgueilleus de la Lande surrenders and begs for mercy, but Perceval denies him forgiveness

> Jusque que tu l'aies de t'amie,
> Que le mal n'avoit ele mie
> Desservi ...
> Que tu li as fet andurer
> [3905–08, B3939–42].

(until you show it for your ladylove, for she never deserved the punishment you inflicted upon her.)

As a condition for granting him mercy in charity, Perceval forces him to perform an act of *eleemosyna* of his own by ordering him to care for his lady until she is restored to health; then he must dress her in her finest clothing and escort her to Arthur's court. And in truth, "tant li fist d'aeisemant / Qu'an sa biauté fu revenue" (3966–67, B4000–01) (he gave her such tender care that her beauty was ... restored). Among other requirements for his imprisonment, he must amend the false "conte de la demoiselle"/"conte de Perceval" that he has spread abroad by repeating to the Queen and her ladies the true story of his mistreatment of her. Chrétien's narrator summarizes his truthful account in indirect discourse:

> ...et li conte
> Tote la viltance et la honte
> Qu'il li avoit longuemant fete
> Et la poinne qu'ele avoit trete
> Et l'acheison por qu'il le fist;
> Trestot sanz rien celer li dist
> [4019–24, B4053–58].

(And he related to her all the wickedness and shame had had made his lady endure for so long, and the sufferings she had undergone, and why he had done this to her: he told her everything, hiding nothing.)

One may well wonder how self-critical his account really is—in what terms, for example, does he explain his reason for doing what he did (4023, B4057)? Yet his courageous acceptance of Perceval's conditions and his admission that he loves his lady and is deeply sorry for what he has done to her bespeak the sincerity of his desire for reconciliation. As difficult as it may be to comprehend fully the justice in Perceval's achievement in light of the knight's crimes and the suffering he has inflicted, Perceval's act of mercy is later mirrored in his own unmerited redemption at the Hermitage, which likewise serves as a model in Galloway.

According to Gawain, Greoreas was guilty of violating the Custom of Logres outright by raping a maiden who was travelling alone (7067–76, B7109–18)—he succeeded, as it were, where Perceval failed when he assaulted the Tent Maiden. To remind Greoreas of his guilt, Gawain paraphrases the Custom's first clause:

> an la terre le roi Artu
> Sont puceles asseürees.
> Li rois lor a trives donnees,
> Si les garde et si les conduit
> [7080–83, B7122–25].

(maidens are protected in King Arthur's land. The king has given them safe conduct, and watches over and protects them)

Moreover, he defends his bitterly harsh treatment of Greoreas as legal and appropriate under the circumstances: "gel fis por leal justise / Qui est establie et asise / Por tote la tere le roi" (7087–89, B7129–31) (I acted in accord with the law that is established and set throughout the kingdom). In light of the Amorous Maiden's summation, Greoreas fully deserves to be "honiz an totes corz" (*Charrete*, 1310) (shamed in every court).

Greoreas is familiar as well with the second clause of the Custom and has in fact displayed his knowledge of it when, as Gawain brought him out of his coma, he begs him to defend his lady in the event of his death (6601–07, B6641–47). In effect, he wishes Gawain to assume in his stead the responsibilities—and consequently the liberties—of "leading" her. His plea implicitly conveys his belief that it is easy for predatory knights to violate the first clause, as he has done himself. Moreover, if Gawain's experience inside the strange castle mirrors that of Greoreas, as seems to be the case, then Greoreas must have taken the Malevolent Maiden under his "protection" as well; but he, unlike Gawain thus far, was attacked at some point by the "fierce knight," who won her back after disabling him, even though he did not succeed in beheading him. Thus, like the Tent Maiden, the Malevolent Maiden is used—or rather, as it turns out, willingly uses herself—as bait to attract knights willing to serve as her escort; it so happens that she plays her role with far greater relish than her abused sister.[19] Let it be noted at this juncture

3. Gawain in the Galloway Borderland

that her existence and her game-playing are facts that Greoreas has hidden from Gawain. We shall return to Greoreas's plea to protect his lady,[20] for in it Chrétien's narrator attributes to his voice—somewhat ironically, in view of his morbid behavior past, present, and future—the first occurrence since the Prologue of the key word *charité* (6599, B6639).

Meanwhile, to return to the theme of equestrian propriety, Gawain is blind to Greoreas as an individual and does not recognize him by his looks, his demeanor, or his arms, which held his attention so strongly when he first considered them in the absence of a knight's charger (Figure 1). He identifies Greoreas only by means of the spiteful "conte de Gauvain" he tells about his own humiliation:

> ...grant honte me feïs.
> Ne te sovient il de celui
> Cui tu feïs si grant enui
> Que tu feïs oltre son pois
> Mangier avoec les chiens un mois,
> Mains lïees derriers le dos?
> [7068–73, B7110–15].

(you brought me great dishonor. Don't you recall the knight you tormented so and forced against his will to eat for a month with the hounds, his hands tied behind his back?)

Greoreas also suffers from blindness caused by injuries to his head and not necessarily from a lack of perspicacity. As soon as his vision is restored thanks to Gawain's ministrations, he recognizes that his healer is his enemy. At the same time, he perceives the best available strategy for taking his revenge and acts at once by appropriating Gawain's horse. As Gawain exclaims in a serio-comic lament, "Or oi je ... / Un proverbe que l'an retrait, / Que l'an dit 'De bien fet col fret' ..." (This reminds me of a proverb ... which states, "Stick out your neck for someone and he'll break it") (7056–58, B7098–7100).[21]

Thus Greoreas initiates a wicked comedy as the paragon of Arthurian knighthood suffers humiliation after humiliation. Greoreas has Gringalet in his possession, and he proudly rides away leading his lady on her palfrey (Figure 5) and leaving Gawain with only the Unruly Squire's worthless nag (Figure 6) to ride,[22] much to the Malevolent Maiden's scornful delight. She ought to be ashamed of being "led" by Gawain, but she cannot resist the pleasure of mocking him:

Perceval and Gawain in Dark Mirrors

> Bien sai que miens an est li torz
> De vos sivre, se Dex me gart!
> Ja ne torneroiz cele part
> Que trop volantiers ne vos sive!
> Et car fust or li roncins ive
> Qu'a l'escuier tolu avez:
> Ge le voldroie, ce savez,
> Por ce que plus avreiez honte!
> [7108–15, B7150–57].

(I'm perfectly aware that it's wrong of me to follow you, so help me God, but wherever you turn I'll gladly follow. I just wish that nag you took from the squire were a mare! You know why I wish that? Because it would be even more disgraceful.)

Later, across the broad river from the Roche de Champguin (7260–7321, B7302–63), Gawain is threatened by a knight who charges towards him astride Gringalet. The Malevolent Maiden identifies the rider as the nephew of Greoreas, who she says has sent him to kill Gawain and bring back his head (7260–66, B7303–09). As we shall see, this personage is an enigmatic conflation of uncle and nephew with the guardian of the borderland himself. Meanwhile, with the ladies of the castle across the river looking on (7211–15, B7253–57), Gawain courageously—and quixotically—stands his ground instead of escaping with the Malevolent Maiden in her boat, as she urges him to do.[23] Just before the knight attacks, Gawain's nag refuses to budge, and he breaks a stirrup as he rises to defend himself, leaving the beast all but impossible to control. Yet, as the treacherous attacker passes, Gawain resists his blow and takes him to the ground with his lance. Like the Tent Maiden's decrepit palfrey much earlier, the nag is forgotten as Gawain triumphantly leaps atop his own charger (7289–7317, B7331–59):

> Ceste avanture li fu bele,
> S'an ot tel joie an son coraige
> C'onques an trestot son aaige
> Ne fu si liez de tant d'afaire
> [7318–21, B7360–63].

(This good fortune pleased him: his heart was so filled with joy that never in his life had he been so happy over any such affair.)

Gawain's rehabilitation is a moment of unsurpassed achievement.

Turning back towards the landing, he looks for the Malevolent

3. Gawain in the Galloway Borderland

Maiden and is dismayed to see that she has disappeared with her boat (7322–28, B7364–70). Soon, however, a Ferryman, his future host and guide at the Roche de Champguin, makes his way across the river. He bears greetings from the ladies at the castle who have been watching him (7194–7215, B7236–57), and, he says, they bid Gawain to pay him his fee, for, by custom, the horse of any knight defeated at the landing belongs to him (7329–50, B7371–92). A dispute of Gawain's ownership of Gringalet is comically allayed, however, when the Ferryman admits that the custom allows him to take the defeated knight as his prisoner instead of his mount (7363–64, B7405–06). Gawain gladly exchanges Greoreas's nephew for Gringalet.

Gawain: Gregoreas's Secret Adventure and Beyond

The equestrian strand seems to submerge for the moment as Gawain reclaims his charger, but the Malevolent Maiden continues to be implicated in issues concerning the Custom of Logres both as perpetrator and as victim. In fact, she acquires the status of a major figure in Chrétien's narrative. At this point she has disappeared, but onstage, absent, or observed from afar, she occupies more textual space in the *Conte del Graal* as it stands than any character except the two major protagonists and Blanchefleur.[24] No sooner does Gawain hand Greoreas's nephew over to the Ferryman than he asks him who the maiden is and where she has gone. She is no maiden, the Ferryman responds, and is more evil than Satan, "Car a cest port a fet tranchier / Mainte teste de chevalier" (7415–16, B7457–58) (for she has had many a knight's head chopped off at this port). His indictment reflects that of the crowd in the inner garden at the border guardian's castle, as does Ygraine's judgment later, when, from a high turret in the castle, she and Gawain see the Malevolent Maiden with an armed knight across the river and he asks her who they are: "Ce est cele cui maz feus arde, / … / Mes de li ne vos chaille ja, / Que trop est estoute et vilainne" (May Hell fires burn her.… But don't pay any heed to her, for she is [quite deranged] and wicked) (8270–73, B8312–15). The knight, a strong, brave fighter whom Gawain would also do well to avoid (8274–80, B8316–24), turns out to be the border guardian himself.

Perceval and Gawain in Dark Mirrors

It appears at this point that two paradigms may be at issue in the guardian's defense of the Galloway border, one implied by Greoreas's account, which Gawain initially follows when he enters the castle in search of a "fierce knight" and finds the Malevolent Maiden instead, and the other, corroborated by the Ferryman, which Gawain will in fact realize when, at the landing opposite the Roche de Champguin, he engages the Orgueilleus de la Roche in a battle that mirrors the unwarranted attack on Gawain by the Greoreas's putative nephew. Ygraine knows him to be a valiant and skilled fighter because "maint chevalier a ce[st] port / A veant moi conquis et mort" (8279–80, B8321–22) (I have seen him defeat and kill many a knight at this port). So the guardian of the border, Greoreas's "fierce knight," is the same Orgueilleus de la Roche who frequently jousts at the landing opposite her castle, and he is strongly identified with the Malevolent Maiden.

Yet the apparently opposed paradigms merge into one: Gawain may well have followed Greoreas's path much farther into Galloway than it has seemed. If this is so, then, like others before him, as both the crowd in inner garden at the guardian's castle and the huge knight have explicitly warned Gawain, Greoreas too has fallen under the Malevolent Maiden's spell and fought a customary battle against the Orgueilleus de la Roche at the landing opposite Ygraine's castle and not, as Greoreas intimated, at the border guardian's own castle much nearer the outpost. Even so, contrary to the custom implied by those in the inner garden, Greoreas has escaped total decapitation. As he has bragged to Gawain, he is indeed the only knight to escape death at the defender's hands despite the fact that no witness at the Roche de Champguin mentions him. Greoreas did not tell the whole story when he informed Gawain about his adventure, but the extended version, which I propose is mirrored in Gawain's progress, seems to be substantiated by the fact that Greoreas knows exactly where to send his nephew to find Gawain and, just as significantly, by the Ferryman's custom, which casts light retrospectively upon the scene that so astonishes Gawain at the mound when he sees armor and a palfrey, but no horse fit for a knight. Greoreas returned—or, more aptly, given his wounds, was brought back—to the *angarde* without his charger because the Ferryman took possession of it, as was his customary right; Greoreas's loss of his charger and what it represents about manhood and knighthood, as exemplified in his mis-

3. Gawain in the Galloway Borderland

treatment of Gawain, are salt poured into his wounds: like his nephew, he was so badly wounded that it was not worth the Ferryman's trouble to keep him prisoner.

The means by which the debilitated and horseless Greoreas may have returned to the border are far less clear and are perhaps irrelevant. He cannot have made the trek back to the *angarde* under his own power. A plausible alternative is suggested by the boat in which the Malevolent Maiden sailed away from the landing when Gawain faced Greoreas's surrogate. She may well have taken both Greoreas and the Orgueilleus de la Roche, who was himself severely wounded (cf. 8379-91, B8421-33), back to the borderland castle in the same boat. Implicitly, when she reappears with the Orgueilleus de la Roche at the landing two days after leaving Gawain to his own devices, the couple may have come in the boat and intend to return by the same means after the Orgueilleus has defeated Gawain. If, earlier, the Ferryman did not keep an obviously dying man prisoner for ransom, neither would the border guardian, who in any case was much more interested in exterminating intruders venturing into Galloway. I find no bases for speculating about how or by whom Greoreas may have been transported from the Roche a l'Estroite Voie to the outpost and left to die. In any case, Greoreas's lady must have been waiting for him in the meantime, having been abandoned there while he "led" the Malevolent Maiden, as she would have hoped, to his encounter with death.

The Malevolent Maiden and the Orgueilleus de la Roche, a murderous couple if there ever was one, arrive at the landing the morning after Gawain undergoes the adventure of the Bed of Marvels, and they succeed in luring him out of the castle where he is the imprisoned lord. Characteristically, Gawain feels compelled to face them, and, thanks to the Ferryman's intervention, Ygraine overcomes her reluctance to expose him to danger and violates her own custom in granting him leave from the castle (8250-8329, B8292-8312). As they watch Gawain disembarking from the Ferryman's boat, the Malevolent Maiden tells her companion that he is the knight "Qui hier m'amena ceste part" (8337, B8379) (who escorted me to this place the other day[25]). The Orgueilleus de la Roche responds that the unnamed knight is just the invader for whom he has been searching, and he redundantly reminds the Maiden of his custom, just as Ygraine described it, with the exception that this time, for unexplained reasons, he seeks to take his opponent prisoner instead of decapitating him:

> Peor en ai eü mout grant
> Que il ne me fust eschapez,
> Que chevaliers de mere nez
> Ne passa les porz de Galvoie,
> Se tant avient que ge le voie,
> Et que ge devant moi le truisse,
> Que ja aillors vanter se puisse
> Qu'il soit de cest païs venuz.
> *Cist ert bien pris et retenuz,*
> *Des que Dex veoir le me lesse*
> [8340–49, B8382–91, my emphasis].

(I was very much afraid he had escaped me, for no knight born of a woman has ever crossed the frontier of Galloway, if I have seen him and found him before me, who has lived to boast anywhere that he's come back from this land. *This knight will be captured and held prisoner, since God has let me see him.*)

Greoreas has heard such a boast for himself.

Like Greoreas's purported nephew, the Orgueilleus de la Roche charges treacherously, without or warning or a challenge (8351, B8393). The matter of a challenge—a *de-fi*-ance, a breaking of faith with[26]—is of interest because the failure to break faith is precisely the basis of Guiganbresil's charge of murder against Gawain:

> …Gauvains, tu oceïs
> Mon seignor, et si le feris
> Ensi c'onques nel *desfias*.
> Honte et reproche et blasme i as,
> Si t'an apel de traïson;
> Et sachent bien tuit li baron
> Que ge n'i ai de mot failli
> [4725–31, B4779–85, my emphasis].

(Gawain, you killed my lord, and you struck him without *issuing a challenge*. For this you are disgraced and shamed. May all the barons acknowledge that I've spoken nothing but the truth.)

Even the murderous Orgueilleus de la Lande warns Perceval to be prepared to fight him (3801–05, B3835–39; 3877–81, B3911–16). In failing to defy Gawain, the border guardian is no better a knight than Greoreas's nephew.

3. Gawain in the Galloway Borderland

Gawain is not taken unaware this time, but rides against him and brings him to the ground in short order, wounding him so seriously with his lance that his strength fails him. Following the local custom, Gawain hands him over to the Ferryman, and, in accordance with the Custom of Logres, he claims the Malevolent Maiden for himself: "Ci ne vos lesserai ge mie," he tells her, "Einz vos an manrai avoec moi / Oltre cel eve ou passer doi" (8376–78, B8418–20) (I'm not going to leave you here; no, I'm taking you back with me over this river I must cross). True to her nature, she sarcastically diminishes Gawain's achievement by asserting that her companion has been weakened by old wounds (8379–91, B8421–33). This time she may indeed be telling the truth, for Greoreas may well have fought him to the point of exhaustion.

As Ygraine has made explicit, it is the Orgueilleus de la Roche's custom to engage opponents in battle across the river from her castle, and it is evident from Greoreas's experience that such is his means of defending the border of Galloway. Neither Greoreas nor Gawain is the first to follow the Malevolent Maiden to the landing or to face the guardian there, but Greoreas is undoubtedly Gawain's most recent precursor. Unlike the others, moreover, Greoreas has beaten the odds and escaped total decapitation, and Gawain follows him likewise in living to tell the tale. Greoreas seeks redemption in charity, and he will receive the grace of healing at Gawain's hands, but inwardly he is so consumed by a festering hatred that he strikes out against the one who has saved him. In this, he is the reverse image of Perceval, who suffers from a forgotten sin, rejects God, and ultimately finds redemption. But, just as Perceval and Gawain are reflections of each other, so Greoreas also mirrors Gawain and Gawain, Greoreas. Despite Gawain's sparkling role as an embodiment of Arthurian ideals, or rather, because of that role, as Norris Lacy is the first to have suggested ("Gauvain and the Crisis of Chivalry"), the *Conte del Graal* probes his dark side: he stands accused of murder by the young king of Escavalon and, as we shall see, also by Guiromelant, who indicts Gawain's father King Lot as well. Moreover, in light of the Amorous Maiden's analysis of the Custom of Logres, which imposes a moral punishment, the stigma of shame, for violations, Gawain's physical and psychological degradation of Greoreas may appear to be cruelly excessive. Finally, Greoreas, whose adventure Gawain seeks to duplicate and surpass, unknowingly leads him to the scene of his greatest achievement.

4
Apotheosis and Relapse

Gawain and Charity: Greoreas

Gawain's entry into Galloway, which is meaningfully juxtaposed with the Hermitage episode, is distinguished, among other reasons, by the fact that it manifests the first occurrence of the key word *charité* (6599, B6639) since Chrétien's Prologue, which charity deeply informs. It is also of interest that the related term *almosne* is introduced into the *Conte del Graal* in an unexpected sense shortly before, toward the end of the Hermitage episode (6434, B6468). As a matter of fact, the words *almosne* and *charité* are paired once again in the last lines ever written by Chrétien (9161, B9211). Thus these key terms thus "embrace" Chrétien's Galloway Section as it is preserved.

In the Hermitage episode, Perceval's rediscovery of God and his confession and Easter redemption constitute a harmonious sequence that is mirrored in distorted fragments at the frontier outpost. Gawain "gently" awakens a gravely wounded Greoreas and then makes to desert him in order to undertake, and, he hopes, to surpass him in the adventure in which he has been maimed. At this point, Greoreas seems by his words not to think of himself, but pleads with Gawain, should he return and find him dead, to take care of his lady "par charité / Et por la sainte Trinité" (6599–6600, B6639–40) (in charity and in the name of the Holy Trinity). For fear that "ele n'ait honte ne meseise" (6603, B6643) (she … [might] be disgraced or abused), Greoreas specifically seeks to ensure the protection of his lover by a knight, who is yet unknown to him, whom he perceives to be capable of defending her against predators—like himself, as it turns out—who would violate the Custom of Logres. The integrity of the couple's mutual love appears to be unimpeachable.[1]

4. Apotheosis and Relapse

When Gawain returns to the outpost with the Malevolent Maiden, who mercifully remains an almost silent witness to everything that subsequently transpires there, he finds Greoreas in a coma so deep that his lady fears him dead. Assuring her that he is indeed alive, Gawain begins the process of healing him by applying to his wounds a medicinal herb he has found growing in a hedgerow and binding them in strips cut from the lady's wimple. He does not move from Greoreas's side until he hears him sigh and begin to speak:

> ...mout ai grant peor eüe
> De morir sanz confessïon,
> Li deable a processïon
> M'ame estoient ja venu querre.
> Einz que mes cors soit mis an terre
> Voldroie mout estre confés.
> Ge sai un chapelain ci pres,
> Se j'avoie sor coi monter,
> Cui g'iroie dire et conter
> Mes pechiez an confessïon,
> Et p[r]anroie comenïon.
> Ja la mort n'an redoteroie
> Puis que comenïez seroie
> Et ma confesse avroie prise
> [6924–37, B6966–79].

(I was in great fear of dying without confession. The devils had come in procession to seek my soul. Before my body is buried I dearly wish to confess my sins. If I had [a horse to ride], I know [about] a nearby chaplain to whom I'd go and tell all my sins in confession and take communion; I would no longer fear death once I had made my confession.)

First and foremost, this extraordinary passage and its immediate context vividly reflect the healing of Perceval's spiritual wounds and his redemption through confession and communicating, in the dual senses of exchanging information and receiving the sacraments. Second, Greoreas seeks for himself the absolution that Perceval received at the Hermitage, and he knows of a "chapelin" (6930, B6972) whom he associates with a "chapelle petite" such as that of the Hermitage itself (6308, B6342). Third, Chrétien's text is the first to endow Gawain with exceptional powers of healing.[2] In folklore, a potent medicinal herb that can restore life, strength, or consciousness is often associated with animals that humans observe using it—serpents, weasels, etc.—and then apply it to others, as in Marie de France's *Eliduc*, 1010–68.[3] Gawain, by contrast, has a trained physician's knowledge of herbs that he has acquired by reading. Chrétien's narrator remarks that Greoreas "de mire eüst grant mestier" (6866, B6908) (was in great need of a doctor) to treat his wounds and that

> mes sire Gauvains savoit
> Plus que nus hom de garir plaie.
> Une herbe voit an une haie
> Trop bone por dolor tolir
> De plaie, et il lava coillir
> [6868–72, B6910–14].

(And my lord Gawain knew more about healing wounds than anyone. In a hedgerow he saw an herb that was excellent for relieving pain from wounds, and he went to pick it.)

His is not an empirical knowledge enshrined in folk tradition, like that acquired by Eliduc's wife Guildeluec, nor does he rely on magical salves like the Dame de Noroisson in *Yvain*.[4] On the contrary, he claims, his wisdom comes from reading an authoritative Latin text ("la letre"). As he tells Greoreas's lady,

> ...l'an ne set sor plaie metre
> Meillor herbe, ce dit la letre
> Qui tesmoigne qu'ele a tel force,
> Qui la metroit desor l'escorce
> D'un arbre qui fust antechiez,
> Mes que del tot ne fust sechiez,
> Que la racine reprandroit
> Et li arbres tex devandroit
> Qu'il porroit foillir et florir.
> N'avroit plus garde de morir,
> Ma dameisele, vostre amis,
> Qui ceste herbe li avroit mis
> Sor ses plaies et bien l'iee....
> [6893–6901, B6935–43].

(one cannot place a better herb upon a wound, according to the book, which states that its strength is such that if it is placed on the bark of a tree that's been injured, as long as it isn't completely withered, the roots will grow again and the tree will once more be able to leaf out and flower. My lady, your friend will be in no danger of dying once this herb is placed upon his wounds and bound tightly ...)

4. Apotheosis and Relapse

Salernitan pharmaceutics is naturally based in herbal treatments, primarily in decoctions, although sometimes the herbs are applied topically.[5] According to the first-century Greek physician Pedanius Dioscorides,[6] leaves, flowers, or gums from several sources will close wounds when applied directly to them, among them frankincense (Book 1, p. 86), cypress leaves (pp. 100–01), rose (p. 129), phoenix (fruit of the date palm, p. 153), mulberry (p. 158), wild fig (p. 181), wild kale (Book 2, p. 271), poppy (p. 348), rue (p. 359), and, perhaps most relevant, dragonwort (p. 328), which, like Gawain's herb, grows in shady areas near hedges in a northern European setting. Meanwhile, a decoction of dried iris leaves boiled with balsamum wood is recommended specifically for head wounds (Book 1, p. 24). Although the book cited by Gawain recommends applying the herb to injuries on trees, it functions as a panacea that, not uncommonly, reaches across biological kingdoms. Mention of the tree, incidentally, draws attention to the single oak that marks the scene in which Greoreas's healing takes place and brings to mind the fact that the oak, as an emblem of strength, is also a powerful source of herbal cures of wounds in its own right.

Finally, Gawain's care for the injured knight takes on a certain aura of the *Christus medicus*.[7] Greoreas's lover sobs to Gawain, "Or cuit ge que cist chevaliers / Est morz" (I fear that this knight is dead) (6878–89, B6922–23), but the healer finds that his pulse is strong and his mouth and cheeks are warm: "Cist chevaliers ... / Est vis" (this knight is alive) (6884–85, B6926–27).[8] With a change in gender, the dialogue recalls Christ's miraculous healing of the ruler of the synagogue's daughter, who, as Greoreas's lady fears for her lover, has also been pronounced dead: "At ille dixit: Nolite fiere, non est mortua puella, sed dormit" (But he said: Weep not. The maid is not dead, but sleepeth) (Luke 8:52; cf. Matthew 9:24, cf. Mark 5:39). After applying the herb to Greoreas's wound with the lady's help, Gawain demonstrates his concern for his charge by patiently sitting with him until he regains consciousness: "Mes sire Gauvains ne se muet / Tant que li chevaliers sospire / Et parole" (My lord Gawain did not move until the knight sighed and spoke) (6920–22, B6962–64). As Greoreas gradually emerges from his coma, his first words are a blessing:

> ...Dex li mire
> Qui la parole m'a rendue,

> Que mout ai grant peor eüe
> De mourir sans confessïon
> [6922–25, B6964–67].

(May God [reward] the one who restored my speech, for I was in great fear of dying without confession.)

Confession is foremost in his mind at this point, for in his coma he has had a vision of devils coming to drag his soul down to Hell.

One manuscript[9] transmits a meaningful, though technically ungrammatical, variant (6922, B6964) where, in a common idiom marked by a sporadic conflation of the verbs *merir* (to reward) and *mirer* (to look at),[10] one later reader understood *mire* not as a verb, but as the noun "physician": "Si parole et dist: Dex est mire ..." (And he speaks and says, "God is a physician ...").[11] The origin of the confusion undoubtedly lies in the form *li*, which has dual functions: an indirect object pronoun before a verb, as in the idiom, or a definite article before a noun. The reading of *mire* as "physician" lies in the text as a potentiality that is concretized in S^{12}: God is the physician who restored Greoreas's power of speech—and, it is to be understood, Gawain is his instrument—for he was in great fear.... As a healer, Gawain is an agent of the will of God. In all events, according to both readings of the passage, Greoreas's blessing resonates with injunctions of Sirach 38: 1–6:

> Honora medicum propter necessitatem; etenim illum creavit Altissimus. A Deo est enim omnis medela, et a rege accipiet donationem.... Altissimus creavit de terra medicamenta, et vir prudens non abhorrebit illa.... Ad agnitionem hominum virtus illorum; et dedit hominibus scientiam Altissimus, honorari in mirabilibus suis.
>
> (Honour the physician for the need thou hast of him: for the most High hath created him. For all healing is from God, and he shall receive gifts of the king.... The most High hath created medicines out of the earth, and a wise man will not abhor them.... The virtue of these things is come to the knowledge of men, and the [most] High hath given knowledge to men, that he may be honoured in his wonders.)

Gawain's medical prowess is no doubt attributable to his well-known identity with the Apollonian powers of the sun.[13] In *Yvain*, Chrétien's narrator pronounces his apotheosis, though without specific reference to medicine:

> Chil qui des chevaliers fu sire
> Et qui seur tous fu renommés

4. Apotheosis and Relapse

> Doit bien estre soleil clamés.
> Pour monseigneur Gavain le di,
> Que de lui est tout autressi
> Chevalerie enluminee
> Com li solaus la matinee
> Espant ses rais, et clarté rent
> Par tout les lieus ou il resplent
> [2400-08].

(He who was lord of knights and was celebrated above all of them must indeed be called the Sun. I say this about my lord Gawain because in him knighthood is illuminated just as the sun in the morning casts its rays and brings light everywhere it shines).

The encomium occurs in context with a perhaps ironic distinction between him and Lunette: "Et de cheli refais la lune, / Dont il ne puet estre que une, / De grant foy et de grant aÿe" (2409-11) (And in turn I speak of her as the moon of whom there can be only one of such faithfulness and devotion).[14] The passage clearly resonates with Chrétien's description of the Grail:

> Quant ele [the Grail bearer] fu leans antree
> A tot le graal qu'ele tint,
> Une si grant clartez i vint
> Qu'ausi perdirent les chandoiles
> Lor clarté come les estoiles
> Quant li solauz lieve ou la lune
> [3190-95, B3224-29].

(After she entered the hall carrying the grail, the room was so brightly illuminated that the candles lost their brilliance like stars [or the moon] when the sun rises.)

We recall that, as Perceval learns at the Hermitage, the Grail contains a Host, which by itself sustains the life of the Grail King; thus the light that accompanies the Grail—or emanates from it?—may well represent the light of Christ, who is present in the life-sustaining wafer. As a privileged healer himself and a reflection of *Christus medicus*, the Apollonian Gawain partakes of that light.

True to the rule in the Gawain Adventures, however, the healer's honor is undercut by his own behavior present and past. First he abandons Greoreas and his lady in order to pursue an adventure. Then, when he returns leading the Malevolent Maiden, he is profoundly humiliated in an unexpected reversal stemming from Greoreas's hatred, which bursts out as he recognizes the one whom he has blessed for curing him and vilifies him while prancing about on his charger:

> Gauvains, par itel mesprison,
> Que qu'il m'an deüst avenir,
> Voldroie ge ton cuer tenir
> De ton vantre antre mes deux mains....
>
> ... grant honte me feïs.
> Ne te sovient il de celui
> Cui tu feïs si grant enui
> Que tu feïs oltre son pois
> Mangier avoec les chiens un mois,
> Mains lïees derriers le dos?
> Saches que tu feïs que fos,
> Qu'orandroit grant honte i as....
>
> Gauvains, tu la preïs de moi,
> La justice, bien m'an sovient;
> S'est or ensi qu'il t'an covient
> A sofrir ce que ge ferai
> [7052-55, B7094-97; 7068-75, B7110-17; 7095-7108, B7137-40].

(Gawain, [by such treachery, i.e., appropriating Gringalet], whatever might happen to me, ... [I would gladly] rip your heart from your belly with my two hands ... you brought me great dishonor. Don't you recall the knight you tormented so and forced against his will to eat for a month with the hounds, his hands tied behind his back? Know that you acted foolishly, for now it will bring you disgrace ... Gawain, ... [you deprived me of justice], I remember it well; so now you must suffer what I choose to do.)

Gawain thus serves to expose the evil side of Greoreas's nature just as Greoreas exposes Gawain's weaknesses. Greoreas has begged him for charity's sake to protect his lady, and he is afraid to die unshriven and has sought redemption such as Perceval has attained at the Hermitage. Ultimately, however, he reveals himself to be a most unrepentant sinner. He curses and shames the divinely-ordained healer whose learning and skill have saved his life, and he manifests no sense of guilt for raping the maiden. Even as he presumably makes his way to a Hermitage-like chapel, he also sends another knight, whom the

4. Apotheosis and Relapse

Figure 7. The Goddess Fortuna and Her Wheel.

Figure 8. Equestrian Propriety: The Hideous Damsel's Mule.

Malevolent Maiden identifies as his nephew, to attack Gawain unchivalrously with orders to bring back his head as though he, and not the Orgueilleus de la Roche, were the guardian of the border (7260–68, B7302–10).

Gawain "li maleüreus"

The Greoreas episode and its aftermath portray a series of such reversals, all of which reflect the portrayal of Fortuna (Figure 7) by the Hideous Damsel astride her tawny mule (Figure 8):

> Ha! Percevax, Fortune est chauve
> Derriers et devant chevelue.

4. Apotheosis and Relapse

> Maudahez ait qui te salue
> Et qui nul bien t'ore ne prie,
> Que tu ne la retenis mie,
> Fortune, quant tu l'encontras! ...
>
> Mout est maleüreus qui voit
> Si bel tans que plus ne covaigne,
> S'atant ancor que plus biax vaigne.
> Ce est tu li maleüreus
> Qui veïs qu'il fu tans et leus
> De parler et si te teüs!
> Asez grant loisir en eüs!
> [4612-17, 4628-34; B4646-51, 4662-68].

(Ah, Perceval! Fortune is bald behind and hairy in front. Cursed be anyone who'd greet you or who'd wish you well, for you didn't catch hold of Fortune when you met her! ... Wretched is the man who sees that the propitious hour has come but waits for a still better one. And you are that wretched man, for you saw that it was the time and place to speak, yet kept your silence! You had plenty of time to ask!)

The Hideous Damsel's use of "maleüreus" (4631, B4665) (wretched) in this context clearly recalls the synonym in the Weeping Maiden's change of Perceval's surname from Perceval the Welshman to "Percevax li chetis" (3548, B3599) (Perceval the wretched).[15]

The image evoked in the Hideous Damsel's diatribe is a medieval blend of the goddess Fortuna and the Greek concept of καιρός (opportunity), which in art is personified as having a long lock of hair in front and no hair in back (Figure 7).[16] Fortuna, who is also frequently depicted as blindfolded, turns her wheel facing those who climb up, while those who fall off behind her have nothing to grab hold of. The lesson the monstrous maiden would teach Perceval is that, instead of pondering his dilemma at the Grail Castle, he ought to have seized his opportunity to act by exercising the same kind of "thinking on the spot" as Greoreas when he runs to mount Gringalet the instant he recognizes Gawain. More relevant to the Galloway Section, however, is the certainty that those whom Fortune takes to the top are subject to prolonged declines or, more tragically or comically, abrupt turns of fate.

It should come as no surprise that it is Perceval's mother who yet again initiates a reflective sequence in the theme of Fortune in the *Conte del Graal* as she implicitly evokes her wheel not without bitterness as she describes the fall of her and others' noble families including the house of Utherpendragon:

> li mellor sont *decheü*—
> S'est [bien] an plusors leus seü
> Que les *mescheances* avienent
> As prodomes qui se maintienent
> An grant enor et an proësce.
> Malvestiez, honte ne peresce
> Ne *dechiet* pas, qu'ele ne puet,
> Mes les bons *decheoir* estuet
> [409–16, B427–34, my emphasis].

(the best have *fallen* on hard times—and it is widely known that *misfortune* often comes to noble men who cultivate great honor and prowess. Cowardice, shame, and sloth can never *fall* …; it is always the good [= noble and courtly] who [must *fall*].)

In many medieval depictions of Fortuna, her wheel has four quadrants labeled *regnabo* (I shall rule) on the ascent, *regno* (I rule) at the apex, *regnavi* (I have ruled) at the descent, and *sine regno sum* (I have no realm) at the nadir. The fall of Utherpendragon's kingdom (424–28, B442–46); the simultaneous fall and exile of Perceval's paternal forebears; the deposition of the royal line of Perceval's mother, especially the Fisher King, who, according to the Hideous Damsel, has yet to regain his lands[17]; the exile of the Two Queens at the Roche de Champguin, the founding of which likewise follows Utherpendragon's death; and most certainly Arthur's decline throughout the romance culminating, as we shall see, in the scene at Orkney castle—all mirror the paradigm implicit in the vision of Fortuna imagined by Perceval's mother and the Hideous Damsel in relation to nobility, kingship, and indeed the rule of queens and particularly those whose castle falls to Gawain. In this light, Perceval's is a failure to bring about an ascendant reversal of fortune by rehabilitating his royal cousin and returning him to his throne.[18]

Also relevant in the *Conte del Graal* are reversals at other levels and in lower registers. The ascendant course of the Perceval adventures is punctuated by a succession of ambiguous turning points leading simultaneously to quick advancement and a gradual, long-term decline. The cycle begins with his departure from his mother's manor, for which he bears the mark of the *peccatum matris*, and culminates in his assimilation into the Arthurian world. His first adventure, an encounter with the Tent Maiden, results in her downfall and abuse at the hands of her "defender" and ultimately in the slaughter of countless knights until Perceval reconciles the couple and leads them to redemption. In the interim, a sudden memory of his mother's fall compels him to leave Gornemant de Gohort with inadequate training, and, after proving his mettle, a gradual realization of its possible significance moves him to forswear marriage with Blanchefleur and relinquish lordship over her lands. All the while, according to the Hermit, the sin he eventually forgets is the underlying cause of his failure in his greatest adventure. In time, the consequences of that failure, combined with his obsession with Arthur's court, doom him to insanity. He reaches the nadir of his decline on Good Friday, when pilgrims point to the pathway to redemption at the Hermitage.

In the Galloway Section, a highly erratic sequence of reversals begins with Greoreas, who prepares for death and is unexpectedly healed. He knows no gratitude toward his savior and, in the end, he proves himself a horse thief and rides away with his lady—perhaps not to the chapel he ached to visit after all, for he no longer has an immediate, pragmatic need for confession thanks to Gawain, but to a place where he can plot murder with his nephew. Gawain seeks adventure and is dishonored at the hands of both Greoreas and the seductive Malevolent Maiden, but he steadily reverses his fortune at the landing across from the Roche de Champguin and especially in the castle's great hall and at Orqueneles. He has earned acclaim as the world's greatest knight and wins lordship over his grandmother's domain, yet he is strangely imprisoned there at least until Arthur's desperate court convenes on the plain between Orqueneles and the Roche de Champguin.

Where Greoreas Has Not Trodden

The Malevolent Maiden will not meekly follow Gawain across the river to the Roche de Champguin. She mocks his victory over the Orgueilleus de la Roche, then, as a tempting challenge, she proposes yet another adventure, a feat she says her lover performed for her pleasure whenever she wished: crossing the Perilous Ford in a deep gorge nearby.

She even claims that success there brings "tot le pris del monde" (8464, B8510) ([worldwide renown]), which Guiromelant asserts is in fact true. Meanwhile, the ladies who are watching them from the Roche de Champguin have begun tearing out their hair because no knight has ever returned after attempting that test: the "evil maiden" (8416, B8462), they believe, is sending their lord to his death (8408–24, B8450–66).

Gawain's performances at the Perilous Ford have been noted.[19] Of equal, perhaps greater importance, in terms of narrative structure, is the pivotal passage embraced by his two crossings in which he and Guiromelant, lord of the region beyond the chasm, engage in illuminating exchanges of information (8488–8869, B8534–8917).[20] Guiromelant first asks Gawain how he has managed to leave that "evil maiden" (8505, B8551: *male pucele*) all by herself and what has become of her companion. He responds directly to the second question and explains that he has fought and defeated the knight who brought her there. He continues by evoking the Ferryman's custom: "Mené l'an a li notoniers, / Qu'il dist qu'il le devoit avoir" (8512–13, B8558–59) (The mariner led him away, for he told me he was to have him.). As for the first question, which Gawain dodges, the answer is implicit in the Custom of Logres, which both justifies his control over the Malevolent Maiden, for he can do with her as he will, and, theoretically, assuming that Arthur's authority is effective in Galloway, it protects her when she is alone.

Guiromelant continues by remarking that she was once his "amie" (8515, B8553) (sweetheart) despite the fact that she never showed him any affection, "Car ge l'amoie mau gré suen" (8520, B8558) (for I loved her against her will). He had taken her from her true lover in accord with the Custom of Logres: "Si l'ocis et li an menai / Et de li servir me penai" (8523–24, B8561–62) (I killed him and [led her] and strove to serve her). In less courtly terms, he committed, or attempted to commit, legalized rape. Eventually she found a way to escape from him and took the Orgueilleus de la Roche as her protector. Guiromelant's account of their "friendship" is corroborated by the Malevolent Maiden herself in her subsequent confession to Gawain (8884–97, B8932–45). In conclusion, he adds that her current lover, now imprisoned by the Ferryman, is a very bold knight, but he boasts that he never dared venture "An leu ou trover me cuidast" (8534, B8582) (anywhere he thought he might encounter me)—implicitly because the Orgueilleus de la Roche has already "won"

4. Apotheosis and Relapse

her without fighting for her or else Guiromelant was afraid to fight for her. In this context Guiromelant congratulates Gawain for being the first knight ever to leap into the Perilous Ford and come out of it alive: "Le pris del mont et le los as / Par ta grant proësce conquis" (8538-39, B8586-87) (your great prowess has won you praise as the best knight in the world). The Malevolent Maiden has in fact lied about her lover's daily exploits, and Guiromelant guesses her motive: she must have wanted Gawain to drown in the turbulent waters.

The tenor of the exchange inspires Guiromelant to propose playing a game of "Truth or Consequences" in which each one will ask a question that the other promises to answer truthfully. The game provides a means of conveying a variety of pertinent information in relatively little space, in particular with regard to the history of the castle across the river, but it is also fraught with ambiguity. Much of it corroborates and augments information provided previously by the Ferryman and others, but some of the data must be verified elsewhere, for Guiromelant proves himself to be a liar on at least one account. Gawain seeks names: of his host's nearby castle (Orqueneles), of his interlocutor (Guiromelant, lord of the castle), of the Malevolent Maiden (the Orgueilleuse de Logres,[21] a name of origin, as she was brought to Galloway as a child), of her present lover (the Orgueileus de la Roche, guardian of the passes into Galloway), of the strong and beautiful castle from which Gawain has just come down ... (8557-8604, B8605-53). At this point, Guiromelant abruptly accuses his interlocutor of breaking faith with him, for he cannot have come from there if he does not know its name (we recall that Perceval does not learn the name of Gornemant's castle). In his defense, Gawain claims to have slept there in the Bed of Marvels—which is even worse, responds Guiromelant, for now he is a *fableor* (8631, B8679) (teller of tales, a liar) and a *jogleres* (8632, B8680) (a [professional] storyteller) whom he challenges to relate his "bold deeds." And so he does in a first-person "conte de Gauvain" that finally convinces his host of his veracity when he produces conclusive evidence: the lion's paws dug into his shield (8609-77, B8657-8725).

Guiromelant now asks his first questions, which Chrétien's narrator reports in rapid-fire indirect discourse in a style resembling the Weeping Maiden's interrogation of Perceval: Did he see "la reïne chenue" (8678, B8726) (the white-haired queen) and ask her where she came from? He did not think to ask her about herself. Thus Gawain, the master of courtly banter who never asked the name of the castle where he is lord, is no more perceptive of when and where to speak or hold his tongue than the half-acculturated adolescent Perceval at the Grail Castle. Accordingly, in a passage rife with paradox and irony, Guiromelant tells him that she is the mother of King Arthur and wife of Utherpendragon (—But Arthur has not had a mother for sixty years or more!), and yet she came to this land with her treasure to build her castle on the rock. The other queen, the "Young Queen," is the wife of King Lot and mother of Gawain (—I know him well, and he has been without a mother for twenty years!), and she came to the castle pregnant with the beautiful and noble maiden who is his host's sweetheart and sister to the man he would gladly behead and rip out his heart (—You do not love as I do, for I would love and serve my lady's family) (8678–8728, B8726–76). And Gawain, who has heard himself accused of murdering Guiromelant's cousin, agrees to take his new enemy's ring to his own sister and to tell her that he loves her so much that he is certain she would rather have her brother die a bitter death than see her suitor injure his little toe (8738–51, B8786–99). The message, which reflects Guiromelant's own passions and hatred, is a blatant misrepresentation of Clarissant's true feelings, which of course he cannot know, but his exaggerated presumption betrays his character.[22] Guiromelant finally answers the question that prompted the digression on the castle and its inhabitants and informs Gawain that it is called the Roche de Champguin (8769, B8817). Finally, when he asks Gawain's name, the response—for Gawain must give his name whenever it is asked—triggers a challenge to judicial combat and an agreement to postpone the combat for a week so that Arthur and his retinue can witness it and bring all the more glory to the victor (8729–8853, B8777–8901).

When Gawain leaves Guiromelant's domain, Gringalet easily makes the more difficult jump back across the gorge. Remarkably, witnessing the adventure has changed the Malevolent Maiden's heart, and, instead of haughtily waiting for Gawain to come to her, she rides to meet him in order to "Merci crïer de son mesfet" (8877; B8925: *comme mesfaite* [as an evil-doer])[23] (to beg forgiveness for her wickedness). Her confession (8878–8915, B8926–63) rewrites and verifies Guiromelant's story

4. Apotheosis and Relapse

about her from her own point of view as an innocent victim of the Custom of Logres: he slew the only knight she has ever loved and took her for his own, but he wasted his time trying to win her affection. She managed to escape and associated herself with the Orgueilleus de la Roche, for whom she cared nothing. Driven mad by a self-destructive grief (the sin of *tristitia*),[24] she began slandering and mocking all knights, including those whom she has "followed" (necessarily including Greoreas)—many of them no doubt to their deaths at the nearby landing—in the hope that one of them would kill her for her wicked tongue—a "suicide by knight" attempted in despair. Her sins are, furthermore, compounded by her abusive use of speech in her verbal assaults. Her account in fact echoes the words of Chrétien's Prologue:

> Ai si longuement esté fole
> Et de si *estoute parole*
> Et si *vilainne* et musarde
> C'onques ne me prenoie garde
> Cui j'alasse contrarïant,
> Einz le feisoie a escïant
> [8901–06, B8949–54, my emphasis].

(I've been behaving [like a mad woman] and [have] been so rude of tongue and so wicked and foolish that I never paid any heed to whom I was insulting, but did it deliberately ...)

> Li cuens est tex que il n'escote
> *Vilain gap* ne *parole estote*,
> Et s'il ot mal dire d'autrui,
> Que ce soit, ce poise lui
> [21–24, my emphasis].

(The count does not harken to *wicked gossip* or *prideful words*, and if he hears evil spoken of another, no matter whom, it grieves him.)

The Malevolent Maiden's speech exemplifies the kind of uncharitable language that Chrétien's patron refuses to tolerate, and, aside from her own scornful denigration of Gawain, it resembles nothing in the *Conte del Graal* more closely than Kay's sarcastic bestowal of the Red Knight's arms to Perceval, which Arthur regards as *vilenie* (997, B1017) (a wicked thing),[25] or the arrogant taunts of Tiebaut de Tintagel's elder daughter, whose self-centered, "romanticized" notion of *fin' amors* (cf. 4812–40, B8946–86) recalls that of Mabonagrain's lady in *Erec et Enide* (6040–

119

6106). Gawain endures her assaults with exquisite patience and courtesy—with charity—just as he refuses to comply when she pleads with him to punish her as an example for other women who would abuse knights (8912–15, B8960–63). Arthur rebukes his seneschal, as does the Fool, but they are powerless to correct him. As for Tiebaut de Tintagel, he berates his elder daughter less for her speech than for physically tormenting her younger sister.

By eventually naming the Orgueilleuse de Logres and the Orgueilleus de la Roche, whose identities Chrétien's narrator has long withheld, Guiromelant calls attention to what they have in common with the Orgueilleus de la Lande. These murderers are aligned with Greoreas in a constellation of abusers of the Custom of Logres who exploit it for their own self-seeking purposes, and they expose thereby injustices inherent especially in the second clause. They are indeed "Proud," [26] a term implying the foremost of the capital sins that is associated with Satan: "Contritionem praecedit *superbia*, et ante ruinam exaltatur spiritus" (Proverbs 16:18, my emphasis) (*Pride* goeth before destruction and the spirit is lifted up before a fall [and an haughty spirit before a fall (AV)]). In a second reflection of the Prologue, their pride—their vainglory—is the antithesis of charity:

> L'evangile, por coi dit ele:
> "Tes biens a ta senestre cele"?
> La senestre, selonc l'estoire,
> Senefie la vainne gloire
> Qui vi[e]nt de fause ypocrisie.
> Et la destre, que senefie?
> *Charité* qui de sa bone oevre
> *Pas ne se vante*, ençois la coevre,
> Que nus ne le set se cil non
> Qui Dex et Charité a non
> [37–46, my emphasis].

(Why does the Gospel state: "Hide your good deeds from your left hand"? The left hand, according to tradition, stands for vainglory, which comes from false hypocrisy. And what does the right hand stand for? Charity, which does not boast of its good deed, but hides it.)

And, to return to the source in I Corinthians 13:

Charitas patiens est, benigna est. *Charitas* non aemulatur, non agit perperam, *non inflatur*, non est ambitiosa, non quaerit quae sua sunt, non irritatur, non cogitat malum, non gaudet super iniquitate, congaudet autem veritati; omnia suffert, omnia credit, omnia sperat, omnia sustinet [vss. 4–7, my emphasis].

(Charity is patient, is kind: *charity* envieth not, dealeth not perversely; [*vaunteth not itself* (AV),] *is not puffed up*; is not ambitious, seeketh not her own, is not provoked to anger, thinketh no evil; rejoiceth not in iniquity, but rejoiceth with the truth; beareth all things, believeth all things, hopeth all things, endureth all things.)

Yet, as in the case of the Orgueilleus de la Lande, a perverter of *fin' amors*, custom, and language who confesses first to Perceval and then to Arthur's court, the Malevolent Maiden's confessional narrative moves an exemplary knight who has been her victim to forgive her and eventually to reconcile her with a joyful royal community despite the heinous crimes in which she has played an essential role. Such examples of mercy and grace operating in secular settings both reflect and illuminate Perceval's own confession, absolution, and reconciliation at the Hermitage, where charity is manifest in a religious context for which Greoreas longs at times.

Gawain and Charity: Orkney

When Gawain succeeds at the Lit de Merveilles, dispels the magic of the great hall, and is hailed as lord of the castle (7882–86, B7924–28; 8072–75, B8114–17), he haltingly begins to assert his personal rule of his domain (for instance, in breaking for one day the custom that prohibits him from leaving his castle) and simultaneously begins actively to govern the narrative of the Galloway Section. Indeed, prior to his triumph and for a time thereafter, events are determined by the irresistible lure of adventure and by others: Greoreas, the Malevolent Maiden, the Ferryman, Guiromelant, his grandmother... His secret preparations for his combat with Guiromelant are exemplary of the trend despite the fact that Chrétien's text prematurely falls to a close before his designs can be carried out. Guiromelant, allegedly the aggrieved party, has offered him a choice between a private duel on the spot or a public trial by combat presided over by King Arthur[27]; true to his character, Gawain opts for the latter (8836–53, B8884–8901).

Guiromelant sets the parameters for the combat, which Gawain

Perceval and Gawain in Dark Mirrors

passively accepts: it will take place on the plane in seven days' time (on the Thursday after Pentecost), and Gawain, who is bound to the castle, must send a messenger to Orkney, where Arthur is holding is Pentecost court. Within such constraints, Gawain masterfully takes the initiative himself. He singles out the ablest-looking of the castle's five hundred unknighted squires,[28] whom he spots standing in the great hall, and takes him unobserved to a lower chamber, where he swears him to secrecy and explains his mission. Several details stand out:

1. Contrary to his custom, Gawain voluntarily names himself: "donc iras tu / A mon seignor le roi Artu, / Que j'ai non Gawain ses niés" (9047–49, B9097–99) (then you shall go to my lord King Arthur, for I am called Gawain, his nephew).[29] Of course, Gawain's name must be an integral part of the message. He completely trusts the squire, who swears to reveal nothing of his mission before he reaches Arthur at Orkney.
2. Gawain correctly predicts that his messenger will find Arthur "mout correcié" (9057, B9107) (very upset), presumably because of his own overlong absence from court (neither Gawain nor Arthur seems to think of Perceval at this stage) and that the king will be overjoyed when the squire greets him in Gawain's name. Tantalizingly, the text ends before the squire approaches Arthur to deliver his message.
3. Gawain stresses that Arthur's queen and all the other ladies in the court are to join the king and his knights "por la moie amor" (9084, B9134) (for love of me). He thus anticipates that the assembly gathered in the plain across from the Roche de Champguin will be a major court event.
4. In addressing the squire, Gawain repeats and embellishes the well-known joke that Chrétien's narrator cracks at the opening of *Yvain*, where Arthur holds court at Carlisle "A chele feste, qui *tant couste*, / C'on doit nommer le *Penthecouste*" (5–6, my emphasis) (on that feast day, which *costs so much* that it must be called Pentecost). Gawain's version is at the same time wittier (because his rhyme is richer) and ironically undercut (because he links the verb not to the feast day, but to a mundane financial transaction):

4. Apotheosis and Relapse

> a la cité d'Orcanie
> A li rois sa cort establie
> A tenir a la Pan*te*coste,
> Et se la voie rien *te coste*
> Jus que la, si t'an tien a moi
> [9051-55, B9101-05, my emphasis].

([the king has decided to hold his court in the city of Orkney at Pen*te*cost, and,] if the journey there *costs you* anything, I'll reimburse you.)

The reference to *Yvain* is not a gratuitous retread of an old gag. On the one hand, as we have just seen, it recalls the court scene in the romance Chrétien wrote—or completed—just before the *Conte del Graal*.[30] On the other hand, it points to a connection between the Pentecost celebration in *Yvain* and what is projected to happen in the court at Orkney. Both courts offer occasions for telling stories that function to generate narrative action—and, especially in the *Conte del Graal*, to renew it. Calogrenant's tale of failure triggers chivalric adventure in *Yvain*. Similarly, the squire's anticipated "conte de Gauvain" at Orkney has the potential to be the only affirmative secondary account of him thus far in the whole of the *Conte del Graal*, despite Guiromelant's grim accusations, because it promises to re-engage Gawain with Arthur's court and, even more intriguingly, to reunite Arthur with his mother and sister in a land of the living dead.

5. The reflective sequence of equestrian propriety resurfaces when Gawain grows unnecessarily preoccupied with choosing a mount for his messenger: "d'une chose ai grant peor, / Que tu n'aies tel chaceor / Qui tost te port an jus que la" (9085–87, B9135–37; B9136: *bon chaceor*) (Only one thing worries me: you might not have a good hunting horse to take you swiftly there). Possessing greater *sang froid* than his master, the squire leads Gawain to the castle's stables, which boast an abundance of appropriate horses. One of them, which has just been reshod, is especially well equipped for the journey.
6. Chrétien's narrator interrupts his account of the messenger's journey to relay Gawain's knighting of the squires back at the Roche de Champguin (9117–38, B9178–88). It is notable that

123

the squires range in age from adolescents to gray-headed old men, an indication of the extraordinary length of time the eldest of them have awaited a savior to knight them (7521–31, B7563–73). The scene mirrors similar ceremonies conducted by Arthur in *Cligés* (1122–40) and, with less detail, in *Erec et Enide* (6652–58). Now it is Gawain who "makes knights." The text thus underscores the fact that the faithful squire's mission ironically excludes him from the long-anticipated ceremonial event. Perhaps Gawain means to reward him by knighting him in context with the trial by combat in Arthur's presence, but the omission, like other peculiarities just mentioned, proves meaningful in terms of the final episode's reflexivity.

The fragmentary Orkney episode is a mere 46 lines long,[31] yet it is deeply poignant in its content and potential for meaningfulness. It consists of two major movements: (1) the messenger's progress through the streets of the city, which is observed by a crowd of beggars and other members of the underclass (9139–64, B9189–9214), and (2) his arrival in the great hall of the castle, where he finds a distraught King Arthur surrounded by hundreds of kings and high noblemen (9165–84, B9215–34). It is Pentecost Sunday, traditionally a major high court day in Arthur's kingdom (cf. the court at Disnadaron, 2751–2875, B2785–2909), but the mood is far from celebratory. The crowds in the street are deeply troubled, and they know that Arthur too feels "mornes et pansis" (9170, B9220) (sad and downcast).

At the opening, Chrétien's narrator displays his flair for shifting points of view: he eschews description in favor of evoking and interpreting observers' feelings and reactions to what they witness, but the sense of place reflects, more than any other city in the *Conte del Graal*, that of Biaurepaire under siege. Perceval's ride through that depressed city to Blanchefleur's castle prefigures and gives definition to the progress of Gawain's messenger through Orkney:

> un pont passer li covint
> Si foible, ainz qu'a la porte veingne,
> Qu'a poinnes cuit que le sosteingne….

4. Apotheosis and Relapse

Jus que devant la porte vint, ...

Et tantost quatre sergent vindrent....

Si ont la porte desfermee
Et dïent: "Sire, venez anz."
Se bien esteüst as sergenz,
Mout fussent bel, mes il avoient
Meseise eü tant qu'il estoient
De geüner et de vellier,
Tel qu'an s'an poïst mervellier.
Et s'il ot bien defors trovee
La terre gaste et escovee,
Dedenz rien ne li amanda,
Que par tot la ou il ala
Trova degastees les rues
Et les meisons viez decheües,
Qu'home ne fame n'i avoit.
Deus mostiers an la vile avoit
Qui estoient deus abaïes,
L'une de nonains esbaïes,
L'autre de moinnes esgarez.
Ne trova mie bien parez
Les mostiers ne bien portanduz,
Ençois vit crevez et fanduz
Les murs et les torz descovertes....

Molins n'i mialt ne n'i cuist forz
An nul leu de tot le chastel, ...

Ensi trova le chastel gaste,
Qu'il n'i avoit ne pain ne paste
Ne vin ne sidre ne cervoise.
Vers un palés covert d'atoise
L'ont li quatre sergent mené
Et descendu et desarmé
[1692–1756, B1712–76].

(he had to cross such a fragile bridge before passing to the gate that he thought it would barely hold him.... He reached the gate.... Immediately four men-at-arms came ..., unbolted the gate, and said, "Sir, come in." Had the men-at-arms been in good health, they would have been handsome indeed, but they were so weakened by famine and long vigils that they were wondrously changed. And just as he found the land wasted and impoverished outside the walls, he found things no better within, for everywhere he went he saw the streets laid waste and the houses in ruins, for there was no man or woman to be seen. There were two churches in the town, which had both been abbeys: one for distraught nuns, the other for impoverished monks. He did not find the churches well decorated or in good repair.... No mill was grinding or oven baking anywhere within the castle walls.... Thus he found the town desolate, without bread or pastry, without wine, cider, or beer. The four men-at-arms led him to a slate-roofed hall, where they helped him dismount and remove his armor.)

Biaurepaire is notable because it appears to be largely deserted except for guards at the main gate and the two abbeys plus a severely reduced population of soldiers and courtiers within the bailey, for Clamadeus, like Meleagant in the *Charrete*, has taken prisoners whom he holds in his own alien castle. Meanwhile, the streets of Orkney teem with a "wasted" populace: the poor, the needy, and the starving, who have nowhere to else to take refuge.

At the same time, as in one image superimposed upon another, Orkney reflects several aspects of the Carlisle episode. On the one hand, the messenger mirrors the young Perceval, the *valet galois* (771, B791; 1199, B1219) who purposefully rides to meet Arthur in the certainty that he will "make him a knight." As astute and accomplished as Gawain's messenger is, he is also a *valet* (9027, B9077, etc.), a young man who aspires to be made a knight, and, because of his mission, he is singled out to remain a *valet* after Gawain has knighted all his fellows at the Roche de Champguin (9123, B9173, etc.). Moreover, as Chrétien's narrator has so pointedly emphasized, this squire, like Perceval (609, B627) arriving at Carlisle, rides a hunter. On the other hand, before Perceval arrives at Arthur's great hall, he has been told by the Charcoal Burner to expect to find Arthur "lié et dolant" (825, B845) (sad and happy), happy because he has defeated King Ryon (831–32, B851–52), we recall, and sad because, except for those who have been too seriously injured in battle, all of Arthur's knights—including Gawain, as it turns out—have left him to live more comfortably in their own domains (834–36, B854–56). Arthur is indeed "pansis et muz" (891, B911) (disheartened and silent) at Carlisle, but he manifests no compensatory joy. Not only is the great hall filled with wounded knights, most prominently a surly Kay, but his person has also been assailed and his kingdom threatened

4. Apotheosis and Relapse

by the Red Knight, and there is no champion close enough or well enough to defend him. Nor is joy restored after Perceval rids the kingdom of Arthur's enemy, for the abrupt departure of his savior and Kay's animosity have redoubled the king's grief.

Among those gathered in the streets of Orkney, Chrétien's narrator singles out a group of beggars, the "contret" and the "ardant" (9143, B9193) (the crippled and mangy),[32] who observe the passage of Gawain's messenger, and he focuses attention on particular spokesmen from among them. One beggar speculates about the messenger's mission: "Je cuit qu'il aporte de loing / Estranges noveles a cort" (9146–47, B9196–97) (I think he's coming from far away with wondrous[33] news for the court); however, Arthur, whom the squire will find to be not just morose, but "mu et sort" (9148, B9198) (deaf and dumb), and whom the beggar knows to be "mout plains de duel et d'ire" (9150, B9200) (quite upset and sad), is in no state to comprehend such a message, much less to act upon it. The beggar wonders in bemusement about Arthur's competence as well as that of his courtiers: "… qui ert ore qui savra / Consoil doner quant il avra / Oï que li messages quiert?" (9151–53, B9201–03) (who will be there to offer counsel after he's heard what the messenger has to say?).

This beggar and his fellows represent a segment of the medieval social underclass whom Chrétien highlights with some frequency during the course of his last romance. Like the Charcoal Burner, Arthur's Fool, and the peasants with their farm implements and townspeople with other makeshift arms who take to the streets of Escavalon against Gawain and the king's sister, these beggars have knowledge of and express opinions about goings-on in the world of kings. Chrétien bestows the needy denizens of Orkney with intelligence and perspicacity, and without irony he endows them with an informed—and informative—point of view. In fact, they recall none with greater clarity than the serfs of Perceval's mother who tremble with fright when they see her son riding towards them in the company of knights because they know how she has raised him and why; and, like her, they fear what his nature will compel him to do once he learns more about them (311–22).[34] Similarly, Chrétien's narrator relays the messenger's progress as through the beggars' eyes: "le vaslet *vont regardant*" (9144, B9194, my emphasis) ([they *keep watching* the squire]).

Perceval and Gawain in Dark Mirrors

No less validly, other beggars express a conflicting viewpoint: "Di va, font il, a *nos* qu'afiert / A parler del consoil le roi?" (9154–55, B9204–05, my emphasis) ("Go on," they said. "What business is it of *ours* to talk of advising the king?"). The gravity of their challenge mitigates the comic potential in a dispute among the rabble that lies in the colloquial interjection and the trope of "getting above one's raising." The scoffers contend, for their part, that king and court are right to be afraid and that beggars who are concerned about affairs of state should be worried about their own condition and feel as frightened and desperate as their betters: "Vos deüssiez estre an esfroi / Et esmaié et esperdu" (9156–57, B9206–07) (You ought to be frightened and dismayed and saddened). The king's distress rises from a vision of imminent danger to his kingdom in a world without Gawain—such is the business of lords and kings. In fact, however, the court and the underclass mirror one another because they suffer from the same deprivation:

> ... nos avons celui perdu
> Qui por Deu toz nos revestoit
> Et don toz li biens nos venoit
> *Par aumosne et par charité*
> [9158–61, B9208–11, my emphasis].

([we have] lost [him] who gave us all clothing in God's name and from whom we received everything [*through almsgiving and*] in charity.)

It hardly bears repeating that, as Chrétien's Prologue affirms, *eleemosyna* (giving alms: *aumosne*) and *caritas*, divine love which impels the act of giving, are near synonyms. The bestower of charity mourned by the beggars is none other than Gawain himself: "Ensi par tote la cité / Mon seignor Gawain regretoient / Les povres genz qui mout l'amoient" (9162–64, B9212–14) (Thus throughout the city the poor people lamented the loss of my lord Gawain, whom they all loved dearly). His absence and, therefore, the ensuing failure of his charitable enterprise have riven the social fabric from top to bottom.

In the second movement, Gawain's messenger arrives at the great hall and finds Arthur presiding over a court utterly bereft of joy. The king is indeed profoundly distraught, as Gawain has predicted— "mornes et pansis" (9170, B9220) (sad and downcast), that is, afflicted with *tristitia*— precisely because his nephew is missing (9172, B9222),

4. Apotheosis and Relapse

but here, contrary to what Perceval is told to expect at Carlisle, Arthur has no compensating victory over a foreign king nor any champion to raise his spirits by expelling an intruder from the outside. Just when Gawain's squire enters, the king falls in a faint as helpless courtiers rush to his side. Meanwhile, a certain Lady Lore (Laurel), who has been sitting in a gallery, comes down in distress to the Queen, who asks her what is troubling her (9180–84, B9230–34)—whereupon Chrétien falls silent. Lady Lore has not answered the Queen's question and Arthur has not come to his senses, nor yet has the squire made his way through the crowd to announce the news to the king that Gawain believes will bring him joy.

In addition to the analogies and relationships between Orkney and the Perceval Section already discussed (Perceval at Carlisle and at Biaurepaire), the potential of that communication and Gawain's motivation in sending it mirror Arthur's Pentecost court at Disnadaron (2751–2875, B2785–2909), where Anguigneron and then Clamadeus come as Perceval's messengers to give Arthur the first news he has received about his absent champion since Yvonet's account of his first "chivalric deeds," and the first Carlion episode, not long thereafter (3968–4119, B4002–4153), where Gawain appears for the first time (4052, B4096) to witness the arrival of the Orgueilleus de la Lande and his lady with their own messages to Arthur and the Queen as dictated by Perceval. As a reflector of these incidents and consequently the events they in turn recall, the Orkney episode once again brings Perceval to mind. Despite the fact that he is not mentioned once in the last 3,000 or so lines of the *Conte del Graal*, he is never lost sight of at Tintagel (Tiebaut's younger daughter, who is slapped for telling the truth about a knight's worth, recalls the Smiling Maiden) and in Escavalon (questions about Gawain's quest for the Bleeding Lance) as well as in much of the Galloway Section (Greoreas, Orqueneles, the Roche de Champguin), but his presence is evoked even more strongly in the Orkney fragment.

The anonymous First (or Gawain) Continuator, often called Pseudo-Wauchier in order to distinguish him from the presumed author of the Second (or Perceval) Continuation, produces a plausible enactment of possibilities latent in Chrétien's unfinished court scene.[35] Very clearly, the Continuator has perceived the import of the Perceval episodes to which Chrétien refers throughout the Orkney fragment.

Like the beggars in the street, Lady Lore has observed Gawain's messenger—significantly, from a higher vantage point—as he entered the great hall. She has come down to tell the Queen the news of his arrival, and she looks worried because, once again mirroring her counterparts of lower estate, she fears that the messenger may bring astonishing (*estranges*) news. At this point, the Continuator recalls Chrétien's account of the first Carlion court (3968–4119, B4002–4153) and shapes it to the new context. Like the Orgueilleus de la Lande with his lady, the squire approaches the king, faithfully delivers his message, and restores Arthur's joy—this time specifically because Gawain has won a great castle. In addition, just as at Carlion, when the news Arthur received prompted him to move the entire court into the countryside in search of Perceval, so, rejoicing at Orkney, he now commands the court to pack up and set out to meet Gawain in Galloway; and, as before, all is ready in amazingly short order. Finally, just as Arthur and his court were encamped on a snow-covered meadow when Perceval happens upon them, so now tents are pitched and pavilions set up on the plane between the Roche de Champguin and Orqueneles. There the court awaits reunion with Gawain.

The completed Orkney fragment is the first in a series episodes in the First Continuation governed by Gawain's clash with Guiromelant. William Roach in fact designates the segment *Le Guiromelant*.[36] However, as Annie Combes points out, with the exception of the conclusion to Chrétien's Orkney episode, very little in *Le Guiromelant*, and even less in the First Continuation as a whole, exploits the full potential of Chrétien's unfinished "host romance."[37] Arthur is reunited with his nephew and they with their mothers, and Guiromelant and Clarissant marry. At Clarrisant's behest, however, the king calls a truce between Gawain and Guiromelant, and Gawain leaves in a huff to resume his quest for the Bleeding Lance, which will end in failure. Meanwhile, the First Continuator introduces much material extraneous to the *Conte del Graal*—concerning, for example, an ally of Guiromelant, Brun de Branlant, who is eventually made the center of a second series of episodes. Finally, the Continuator demystifies the otherworldly Roche de Champguin and its inhabitants.[38] Once Arthur leaves to besiege Brun's castle, the Roche de Champguin and its world disappear altogether from the annals of Grail history.[39]

4. Apotheosis and Relapse

Although Gawain is his primary protagonist, the First Contin-uator is uninterested in realizing the highly charged narrative poten-tial that remains undeveloped in the Galloway Section—matters concerning Gawain's succession as lord of the dominant castle, for example, the nature of the knighthood he has established there, the defense of Galloway after the capture of the Orgueilleus de la Roche, or yet, in a wider vision, imminent relations between Gawain's newly-won domain and Logres, on one side, and, on the other, with the Grail kingdom, whose existence, without being named, is imprinted throughout the "host romance" in reflected images. Instead, except for elements in *Le Guiromelant* already accounted for, the Continuator seeks inspiration in the *Conte del Graal* outside the Galloway Section: Escavalon (in an episode in Gawain's relaunched quest for the Bleeding Lance), the Hideous Damsel's challenges at the second Carlion court (Gawain's adventure at Montesclere, interrupted when Guiganbresil recalls him to Escavalon, cf. 4672–86, B4706–20), and the Grail Castle, which he radically transforms. Moreover, he looks so frequently for material from outside Chrétien's romance, which would include his own imagination, that, as Keith Busby notes, the Continuation ends up as a mere "repository of Arthurian tales" ("The Continuations," p. 223). Continuation for the First Continuator is a process of reshaping, renewing, and, above all, replenishing from new funds of narrative material.

His brief conclusion to the Orkney court scene advances a tripartite plan to bring about the resolution of two issues that are unsettled in Chrétien's romance: the marriage of Clarissant and Guiromelant and the restarting of Gawain's quest for the Bleeding Lance, on the one hand, and, on the other hand, within extraneous matter concerning Brun de Branlant, Arthur's re-engagement in the realm of chivalric adventure. In the end, however, the First Continuator fails to do justice to Chrétien's Orkney fragment as a whole. Other important issues are left unresolved in the re-energized plot, which soon moves beyond resources left untapped in the Galloway Section. Nevertheless, for the curious reader, the possibility of finding answers may lie in the ways Chrétien's fragment reflects the matter elsewhere in his romance that the Continuator apparently chooses to ignore. He does not take up the overarching theme of charity that dominates not only in the reprise of "aumosne et charité"

(9161, B9211), but more especially in demonstrations of its absence, nor does he account for the fact that Perceval, in whom he has no vested interest, appears throughout the episode in diffused reflections that highlight the dysfunctionality of a depressed, perhaps insane Arthur who rules in a devastated city.

Conclusion
"Hide your good deeds from your left hand"

Perceval has unwittingly pursued a mission to the Grail Castle. The Hermit confirms that its object was to heal the Fisher King by asking whom the Grail serves. The task of discovering the mystery of the Bleeding Lance has, it would appear, passed to Gawain, who has sworn to undertake a quest for it that proves inconclusive in Chrétien's text.[1] Despite the Continuators' optimism, we cannot know with absolute certainty whether, in a completed *Conte del Graal*, Perceval was destined in the end to return to the Grail Castle, perhaps to achieve his goal, or if Gawain, in his quest for the Bleeding Lance, was meant to visit the Grail Castle for the first time. A consensus among scholars is that both propositions seem plausible. Gawain's Grail Castle adventure occurs in the First Continuation, while Perceval's return, which is unsuccessful as before, develops in the Second.

Escavalon and the Bleeding Lance

Perceval's first Grail adventure and its consequences are tantalizingly recorded by Chrétien from several points of view. Of Gawain's Lance quest, only the initial impetus is known. As the serio-comic Escavalon episode unfolds, Gawain arrives in his enemy's city to settle in battle the matter of Guiganbresil's charge that he has murdered the present king's father. The young king, not recognizing who Gawain is, sends him to his castle to be entertained by his sister while he goes away to hunt with Guiganbresil (5754–6049, B5788–6083). Chaos erupts in the city when farmers and townspeople learn that the lady's guest, with

Conclusion

whom she is enjoying an afternoon of dalliance, is their most hated enemy, and they attack the castle, threatening to undermine the tower where Gawain and the very willing lady have been caught *in flagrante dilecto*. In a comic simulacrum of desperate warfare that might have occurred at Biaurepaire, the besieged couple defend themselves as the king's sister hurls outsized chessmen down at the rabble while Gawain uses the chessboard as a shield against their makeshift weapons.

The king returns from the forest and is astonished to learn that his guest is an adversary whom he must nevertheless protect because he has offered him his hospitality. He accepts advice from a Wise Vavassor, who proposes, as a way out of the dilemma, that he postpone the trial by combat for one year and that, in the meantime,

> ...[Gauvain] s'an aille
> Querre la lance don li fers
> Sainne toz jorz, ja n'iert si ters
> C'une gote de sanc n'i pande:
> Ou il cele lance vos rande
> Ou il se remete an merci
> An tel prison com il est ci
> [6078–84, B6112–18].

(Gawain go in search of the lance whose point bleeds constantly, from which the last drop can never be wiped clean. Either he brings you this lance or he must surrender himself your prisoner here as he is now [i.e., unarmed].)

Once the townspeople have been dispersed, the vavassor[2] repeats the offer to Gawain and adds a momentous prophesy concerning the Bleeding Lance:

> Et s'est escrit qu'il ert une ore
> Que toz li reaumes de Logres,
> Qui jadis fu la terre as orges,
> Sera destruiz par cele lance
> [6134–37, B6168–71].

(And it is written that it will yet come to pass that all the kingdom of Logres, which was once the land of ogres, will be destroyed by this lance.)

Despite the facile, though very rich, rhyme *Logres : ogres*, which looks suspiciously like a throw-away line, the Wise Vavassor's comment about giants in ancient times is in reality a meaningful allusion to Wace's *Brut*. In that history, Trojan exiles led by Brutus, who have migrated westward, find that Great Britain, their "promised land," is inhabited by giants whom they must expel before they can establish their colony of New Troy.[3] At his death, Brutus's kingdom of Britain is divided among his three sons, the eldest of whom, Locrinus, inherits the lion's share and founds the kingdom of Logres bearing his name that Arthur ultimately inherits from Utherpendragon. The lesser kingdoms are Wales and Scotland (1251–92).

At the same time, in a reference mirroring the Carlisle episode, the prophesy casts light on an enigmatic prediction made by Arthur's Fool that also recalls the *Brut*. When Yvonet reports to the court that Perceval has left the castle wearing the Red Knight's armor and has promised to avenge Kay's humiliation of the Smiling Maiden, the Fool dances and jumps for joy as he announces:

> …Danz rois, se Dex me saut,
> Or aprochent *voz avantures*:
> *De felenesses et de dures*
> An verroiz avenir sovent
> [1236–39, B1276–79, my emphasis].

(Sir King, so help me God, the time of your *adventures* is nearing. You will often witness *cruel and harsh ones*.)

His jubilant news recalls Wace's well-known comment concerning the twelve-year *pax arthuriana*:[4]

> En cele grant pais ke jo di,
> Ne sai si vus l'avez oï,
> Furent les merveilles pruvees
> Et les aventures truvees
> Ki d'Arthur sunt tant recuntees
> Ke a fables sunt aturnees[5]
> [9787–92].

(In that great time of peace I am speaking about, I don't know whether or not you have heard of it, were the wonders experienced and the adventures discovered [*or* written down in poetic form] that have been so often told about Arthur that they have turned into fables)

In anticipation of Perceval's ascendancy, the Fool announces just such a new age of chivalric accomplishment as Wace describes. In this case, the adjectives *felenesses* (evil) and *dures* (harsh) undoubtedly express greater degrees of difficulty and therefore worth as challenges.[6] Perceval and Gawain encounter such adventures as a matter of course in the sec-

Conclusion

tions devoted to them; the Hideous Damsel proposes many additional adventures at Carlion, and the Wise Vavassor at Escavalon proposes yet another.

The significance of Escavalon's place in Grail history must not be overestimated, however. Not only is it obscure, but also the kingdom's aspirations are not long-standing. Contrary to indications in the Perceval Section, where the Bleeding Lance accompanies the Grail in a banquet procession and Perceval undertakes a quest for the Grail and the Lance together, the Wise Vavassor of Escavalon asserts for the first time that the Lance may become the object of an independent quest. Moreover, he reports, to the surprise of one and all, that the Lance possesses a destructive power that far surpasses in intensity any salutary property that has been attributed to the Grail. The Grail conveys consecrated bread that sustains the life of one king without, however, affecting his wounded son, but, as a container, it is not necessarily life-giving in and of itself. As we have seen, on the other hand, the light of the Grail is indeed reflected in Gawain as a trained healer. In all events, the Vavassor implies an interest in acquiring the Bleeding Lance for his king precisely because it is capable of annihilating Arthur's kingdom. His requirement that Gawain undertake a quest for the Lance on behalf of the young king of Escavalon is, moreover, a devious means of luring him into a betrayal of his liege lord, King Arthur.

Gawain has come voluntarily to Escavalon to answer a charge of regicide. Perceval, by contrast, has deeper, more personal ties to the kingdom in part because his father sent his eldest son there to be knighted by the king, undoubtedly the present king's father, whom Gawain is accused of murdering. As Brigitte Cazelles justly observes, Chrétien's "allusions to this past are too evasive to provide a clear answer regarding the fate of Perceval's elder brothers,"[7] but it is nonetheless useful to consider the words of Perceval's mother on the subject:

> Quant grant furent vostre dui frere,
> Au los et au consoil lor pere
> Alerent a deus corz reax
> Por avoir armes et chevax.
> Au roi d'Escavalon ala
> Li ainz nez, et tant servi l'a
> Que chevaliers fu adobez.
> Et li autres, qui puis fu nez,

"Hide your good deeds from your left hand"

> Fu au roi Ban de Gomeret.
> An un jor andui li vaslet
> Adobé furent et chevalier furent,
> Et an un jor meïsmes murent
> Por revenir a lor repeire,
> Que joie me volurent faire
> Et lor pere qui puis nes vit,
> Qu'as armes furent desconfit.
> As armes furent mort andui,
> Don j'ai grant duel et grant enui.
> De l'ainz né avindrent mervoiles,
> Que li corbel et les cornoilles
> Anbedeus les ialz li creverent:
> Ensi la gent morz [le]⁸ troverent
> [441–62, B459–90].

(When your two brothers were grown, on the advice and counsel of their father they went to two royal courts to receive their armor and horses. The elder went to the king of Escavalon and served him until he was knighted. And the other, the younger, went to King Ban of Gomeret. Both youths were dubbed and knighted on the same day, and on the same day [some time later] set forth to return to their home, for they wanted to bring happiness to me and to their father, who never saw them again, for they were defeated in arms. Both died in combat, which brings me great grief and sadness. A strange thing happened to the elder: the crows and rooks pecked out both his eyes: this is how the people found [him] dead.)

Her account is extraordinary in many ways. For example, she portrays the brothers as thinking and acting in unison even when separated, almost as though they were linked telepathically, but she does not state how or by whom they were attacked. Meanwhile, as we have seen, she introduces into Chrétien's text the subject of filial piety, which is reflected in the poignant detail concerning the elder son's eyes (460–61, B488–89).⁹ Perceval is destined to follow much the same course as his brothers.

The context of her remarks is, of course, the period of warfare that broke out following the death of Utherpendragon and Arthur's succession to the throne of Logres. The noble families of both Perceval's mother and his father fell from positions of power and authority into utter ruin as a result of the turmoil. Apparently, warfare in the Grail kingdom and the establishment of the Roche de Champguin date from approximately the same events. While Perceval's mother does not specify his father's

Conclusion

lineage, nor does Chrétien's narrator, her own nobility is clearly identified, in specular moments later in the *Conte del Graal*, with that of the ruling dynasty of the Grail kingdom. Were it not for their fall in troubled times, Perceval's brothers might well have gone to the Fisher King or the Grail King, for that matter, for their education and training.

Why not to Arthur?[10] Chrétien provides too little information to justify a definitive explanation. He does not even specify whether Escavalon, which appears to be on the island of Great Britain,[11] is independent of Logres or one of the petty kingdoms—like Orkney, which is associated with Gawain's father Lot[12]—that are ruled by kings who have sworn fealty to Arthur. On the other hand, in the time between Arthur's succession and the establishment of the *pax arthuriana*, when the legendary adventures began, Wace's *Brut* depicts a Logres in chaos as the young king, as yet unproven, moves from battle to battle throughout Great Britain, in the lesser islands, and on the Continent in order to quell uprisings within his kingdom, to stave off invasions, and to consolidate his power. Arthur is a peripatetic warrior king who does not in fact establish a quasi-permanent *cort real* (65, cf. 443, B461) (royal court) as a center of cultural life in Carlion until his kingdom is secure (*Brut*, 9003–9730). The ostensible rejection of Arthur by Perceval's father is, furthermore, strongly mitigated by the fact that not only does his widow refer to the king as "le bon roi Artu" (428, B456) (good king Arthur), an expression in which *bon* is a laudatory term denoting high degrees of nobility and courtesy,[13] but, once she resigns herself to granting Perceval her leave, she also appears to approve his determination to seek knighthood in Arthur's own court—and this despite her doubts that, although he is to the manner born, he will know how to wield the arms he receives there.

Whatever his reasons may have been, Perceval's father chose to send one son to the court of the king of Escavalon, and the other to that of Ban of Gomeret (or Gomoret). Neither Escavalon nor its king is mentioned in Chrétien's other romances, or indeed anywhere else before the *Conte del Graal*, but King Ban attends the young couple's wedding in *Erec et Enide* (1971: Baus) as Arthur's guest. Thus there is no ill will between them at that point in Arthurian history according to Chrétien. Chrétien's narrator even takes the time to comment in some detail on Ban's extraordinary entourage of 200 very young men all carrying a variety of hunting birds perched on their wrists (1971–80).[14] King Ban of

"Hide your good deeds from your left hand"

Gomeret is also present at the quintessential Arthurian tournament at the Castle of Maidens in *Le Bel Inconnu* (5479, 5839).[15] Despite Chrétien's greater interest in the identity of King Ban, it is the kings of Escavalon—whom, ironically, his narrator does not name—and the mysterious Escavalon itself, to which Gawain is led by a white doe, that are by far the more significant in the *Conte del Graal*.

Perceval is reflected in any allusion to the Grail Castle in the Escavalon episode, but his elder brother's past allegiance to the old king does not necessarily oppose him as an Arthurian knight either to the present king of Escavalon or to Gawain, the accused in the matter of the alleged murder of his father. Even so, as long as Gawain stands accused of regicide, he is *personally* considered an enemy of Escavalon. A degree of estrangement from Arthur himself is further indicated in the fact that Guiganbresil, the young king's ambassador, contrary to Guiromelant under similar circumstances in the Galloway Section, does not request that Arthur adjudicate his case. In the end, little else in the *Conte del Graal* besides the hypothesis of Escavalon's use of the Bleeding Lance against Logres suggests that a rivalry between these two kingdoms, which is perceived as such far more strongly on the young king's side than on Arthur's, has developed or may develop into full-blown enmity. In fact, the hypothetical threat from Escavalon soon dissipates.

Much is amiss in Arthur's Logres, there can be no doubt about that. Neither is all well with the shadowy and passive young king in Escavalon, who, contrary to his own interests, errs grievously in nonchalantly extending his hospitality to Gawain. As Guiganbresil leaves Carlion, he sets the conditions for Gawain's appearance in Escavalon for trial by combat in a speech that Chrétien's narrator reports in indirect discourse, which is to say, in his own terms:

> Et cil dit qu'il l'an provera
> De traïson laide et vilaine
> Dusqu'al chief de la quarantaine
> Devant le roi d'Escavalon
> Qui est plus biax que Ausalon,
> A son san et a son avis
> [4754–59, B4788–93].

(Guiganbresil said he would prove his [Gawain's] foul and wicked treason at the end of forty days before the King of Escavalon, who, in his thoughts and opinion was more handsome than Absalom.)

Conclusion

The allusion to Absalom is more probably an ornament in the poetic discourse of Chrétien's narrator than an element of Guiganbresil's speech. In any case, the rhyme *Escavalon : Ausalon*, however rich it is phonemically, is perhaps too facile, but, as in the occurrence of another such pairing in much the same context,[16] it is fraught in signification as well. Absalom, the third son of King David, was in his time considered to be the most handsome man in all of Israel; he was known especially for his extraordinarily abundant hair (II Samuel/II Kings 14:25-26). In the person of Guiromelant Gawain will meet another exceptionally handsome knight (8496-8502, B8542-48) who also seeks restitution in a trial by combat for the murder of his father—who he charges was killed by King Lot, Gawain's father, while he holds Gawain personally guilty for the death of his cousin (8729-37, B8777-85).

The similarities between Gawain's two adversaries in anticipated trials by combat are noteworthy. Guiromelant's beautiful features hide a flawed character: he has taken advantage of the provisions of the Custom of Logres to imprison the Malevolent Maiden, thinking, in her words, that he could honor her by forcing her to love him (8884-92, B8932-40); he also foolishly exaggerates the exclusivity of the love that Gawain's sister feels for him. More importantly at present, the young king of Escavalon's resemblance to Absalom is not necessarily the compliment that the comparison seemingly intends, for it may well betray hidden secrets while it appears to express an observable fact. King David's beloved son avenges, not without stealth, the incestuous rape of his sister Tamar against his eldest brother (II Samuel/II Kings 13), but eventually he treasonously revolts against his royal father and succeeds in usurping the throne (chapters 15-18). After a final, decisive battle against his father's forces, however, Absalom flees into the Wood of Ephraim and is slain by David's general, Joab, whose men are able to track him down because his hair, the very emblem of his manly beauty, was caught in the branches of an oak tree as he rode beneath it, and he was left hanging "between the heaven and the earth" (II Samuel/II Kings 18:9).[17] David in anguish laments his son's death in a well-known *planctus* (II Samuel/II Kings 18:33).[18]

In a romance overwhelmingly concerned with the succession of fathers to sons, mothers to a daughters to sons, and uncles to nephews, the allusion to Absalom draws the Escavalon episode into the pervasive theme of filial piety as a negative example: Perceval before his conversion also reflects Absalom as the unrepentant, uncharitable son. The young king of Escavalon is as handsome as Absalom. Has he been merely an ungrateful son or, more in keeping with the simile Chrétien attributes to Guiganbresil, a traitor against his own father? If so, the young king mirrors as well the fate at Mordred's hands that awaits Arthur in the *Brut* if not also in Chrétien's world of romance. In any case, the young king appears to be all too ready to yield to the dictates of his overbearing seneschal and, as we shall see, his sophisticated advisor, the Wise Vavassor.

To return to the question of Arthurian adventure, when Chrétien's narrator repeats the words of Arthur's Fool as he summarizes Perceval's descent into insanity, the strongest possible senses of the terms *felenesses* and *dures* come to the fore in context with *estranges* (alien, weird, unearthly). Perceval has forgotten God and has not once entered a church to worship God or adore His cross (6183–87, B6216–20)—an appropriate reference to Good Friday:

> Tot ensi cinc anz demora,
> Ne por ce ne lessa il mie
> A requerre chevalerie:
> Et les *estranges avantures*,
> Les *felenesses et les dures*,
> Aloit querant
> [6190–95, B6224–29, my emphasis].

(Five years he remained so, yet for all this he never ceased pursuing deeds of chivalry; he sought out *the most difficult, treacherous and unusual adventures* ...)

It is this configuration that sheds light on the "estranges noveles"— news of "strange" adventures—that so alarms the beggars in Chrétien's Orkney fragment and, in her turn, Lady Lore early in the First Continuation. Except for the Grail mysteries, little in the *Conte del Graal* or indeed in any other of Chrétien's romances is more outlandish—more *estranges*— than the humiliations and adventures undertaken or endured by Gawain in the Galloway Section, beginning with his encounter with Greoreas.[19] Perceval's sixty combats during his years of insanity are perhaps comparable with Gawain's adventures, but Chrétien barely accounts for them at all. The dark pall cast over Orkney may also exemplify the most sinister aspects of the *estrange*. Is the Bleeding Lance part of the equation?

Conclusion

With respect to Gawain's quest, it is crucial to bear in mind the fact that at first he rejects in strong, even hyperbolic terms the king's proposal as an invitation to commit treason against Arthur:

> Certes ge me leiroie ençois,
> Fet mes sire Gauvains, ceanz
> Ou lenguir ou morir set anz
> Que ge seremant an feïsse
> Ne que ma foi vos an plevisse.
> N'ai pas de ma mort tel peor
> Que ge mialz ne voelle a enor
> La mort sofrir et andurer
> Que vivre a honte et parjurer
> [6140–48, B6174–82].

("Indeed," said my lord Gawain, "I'd rather let myself languish seven years in prison, or even die, than swear this oath to you or give you my word upon it. I'm not so afraid of death that I'd not rather suffer and die an honorable death than live in shame, having broken my word.")

The sense of his rejection might seem at first to lie in his oath at Carlion to Guiganbresil to appear for trial within forty days of his accusation (4736–62, B4660–96), but such a reading does not account for his likely cognizance of the king's burden of duty as his host. On the contrary, Gawain speaks of his allegiance to King Arthur in response to the condition that he must deliver to Escavalon a dreadfully destructive weapon to wield against Arthur's own kingdom. Gawain will not betray Arthur as Absalom did David—or as the young king may have done *his* father. Accordingly, the Wise Vavassor retreats from the certainty that Escavalon could possess such power[20] and negotiates a blatantly sophistic compromise:

> ...Il ne vos iert ja desenors,
> Ne ja, ce cuit, n'an seroiz pire
> An un sans que ge vos voel dire:
> Vos jureroiz que de la lance
> Querre feroiz vostre puissance;
> Se vos la lance ne trovez,
> An ceste tor vos remetez,
> Si seroiz del seremant quites
> [6150–57, B6184–91].

(... it will not bring you shame, and your honor will not suffer, if you formulate your oath as I propose: you will swear to do all in your power to

"Hide your good deeds from your left hand"

seek the lance; if you do not find the lance, you'll return to this tower and be absolved of your oath.)

And so Gawain swears "Que il metra tote sa painne / A querre la lance qui sainne" (6163–64, B6197–98) ([that he will] do everything in his power to seek the bleeding lance). He is bound neither to find the lance nor to surrender it to Escavalon if he does.[21] For the Vavassor, saving his king's honor and reputation for hospitality is more important in this instance than gaining possession of the Lance, which would assure him of victory against Arthur if they were enemies. In this light Escavalon looks very much like a paper tiger.

The Grail Kingdom and the Bleeding Lance

Implicit in the Wise Vavassor's remarks concerning the Bleeding Lance is the suggestion that it can be removed from the Grail Castle and taken elsewhere. Moreover, the Hermit hardly mentions the Lance in the very next episode, although Perceval confesses to failing to ask about both it and the Grail. Donald Maddox argues that, in any case, the Lance is not directly linked to the Grail and has no function with respect to the Grail Procession itself: "the lance does *not* [his emphasis] figure in the grail procession itself but precedes it."[22] An important distinction must be made, however, between the lance's preceding the Procession and being separate from it and its leading the Procession and being integral with it. Chrétien's text may seem to be ambiguous on the point, as in so much else, but it does not necessarily support a "separatist" reading despite the fact that, in the light of ordinary twelfth-century reality, a grail seems to belong in a banquet procession and a lance does not. As Chrétien describes the scene (3156–97, B3190–3231), (1) a young squire passes carrying a bleeding lance; (2) "*Atant* dui autre vaslet vindrent / Qui chandeliers an lor mains tindrent ..." (my emphasis) (*Then* [= *next in order*] two other squires [enter] holding candelabra); (3) they are followed by a maiden carrying a grail from which emanates, or around which appears, a bright light; (4) another maiden bearing a silver carving platter follows her. Later the Grail, but not the cutting platter or the candelabra, for these function to serve the banquet in the great hall, "*Tot ausi passa con la lance: / Par devant le lit passerent / Et d'une chanbre* an autre entrerent" (3206–08, B3240–42, my emphasis) ([*passes just as the lance has*]: they [*pass*] before the bed [on which Perceval and his host are seated at the high table] and into another chamber). Thus the Lance *leads* the Grail into the other room, and, paired with the Grail, it appears to be essential—symbolically if not materially—in the service of a special, sacramental meal, which, as we learn from the Hermit, the older king receives from the Grail in an inner room.

The Grail Procession proper (1–4 above) ceases to exist when the Lance and the Grail together disappear into the Grail King's chamber, leaving behind the cutting platter to serve venison in the great hall and the candelabra presumably to provide enhanced illumination. Subsequently, to be sure, the Grail alone returns—uncovered for reasons that are not explained—as courses are served from other dishes (cf. 3256–57, B3290–91). Undoubtedly, after the Fisher King's father has consumed its contents, the Grail bearer returns with it to whence she came.[23] The Bleeding Lance does not reappear and thus remains in the inner chamber, but again Chrétien's narrator proffers no explanation. Yet nothing in the events that transpire in the Grail Castle's great hall contradicts the relevant information in the Weeping Maiden's discourse, in the Hideous Damsel's diatribe, or in Perceval's own confession, according to all of which the Grail and the Bleeding Lance serve in tandem to stimulate questions that are meant to bring peace and healing—and also, we learn from the Hermit, to transport a holy meal to the invalid king.

Only the Hermit, who apparently knows the mysteries of the Grail Castle intimately, appears to ignore the link between the two by not emphasizing the Lance when he imparts the salutary truth about the Grail custom to his nephew. To anticipate subsequent discussion, may not his silence signal that the redeemed Perceval, who now possesses knowledge of the Grail and its contents, need no longer be told the mystery of the Lance because he has already understood it instinctively or regarded it in light of the Passion Gospel he may have heard on Good Friday? In all events, the Grail kingdom and its secrets are a family matter, and Perceval is a member of that royal family and the heir to its castle after his cousin, the Fisher King. As the First Continuator very well understands, the Lance is not in fact Gawain's to take possession of.

Some of the early readers of the *Conte del Graal*, in fact one of its

"Hide your good deeds from your left hand"

very first rewriters before 1200, initially identify the Grail with the cup—the "vessel"—of the Last Supper (Robert de Boron) and, somewhat later, the Bleeding Lance with the Holy Spear (the First Continuator).[24] The latter was rediscovered, as far as the Medieval West is concerned, in Antioch early in the First Crusade.[25] It was used by a Roman soldier, later identified as Longinus (Lancer), to verify Christ's death by wounding him in the side, from which flowed blood and water (John 19:31–37). In light of what Perceval learns about the Grail at the Hermitage, an aspect of the logic in a Grail Procession led by the Lance may well be that an instrument of the Passion might necessarily precede the Host borne in the Grail (6388–97, B6422–31), the priestly consecration of which commemorates Christ's suffering and death.

Moreover, in a common motif in medieval iconography (Figure 9), a young woman,

Figure 9. Synagoga (The Synagogue).

often stooped and blindfolded, holding a lance or spear, which is usually lowered or broken, represents the Synagogue (Synagoga). She is most frequently paired with the Church (Ecclesia) as represented by another young woman with an uplifted face and wearing a crown who holds a Eucharistic chalice (Figure 10). Synagoga and Ecclesia portray the dispute between Judaism and its daughter, Christianity, or the triumph of

Conclusion

the New Law over the Old, or else, ultimately, the daughter's conversion of her mother.[26] In depictions of the Crucifixion with these figures, Synagoga stands on Christ's left, while Ecclesia is situated at his right side, sometimes collecting the discharge from the lance wound in her chalice or raising it toward the wound as though in anticipation of its flowing. The sense of Synagoga's lance is ambiguous: it refers to the Holy Spear (Rowe, *The Jew, the Cathedral,* pp. 63–64), but in depictions of the Crucifixion that include Longinus with his own lance, he naturally stands at Christ's right ready to inflict the wound, while Synagoga remains on his left.[27] As a matter of fact, in representations outside the immediate context of the Crucifixion (as individually in Figures 9 and 10: paired statues, images in windows, etc.), most often Synagoga is similarly placed at "stage left" and Ecclesia at "stage right."

Despite the indisputable facts that, in the *Conte del Graal*, (1) the lance drips blood (a vestige of its use by Longinus, according to the First Continuator), (2) the lance bearer is a young man who walks upright, (3) the lance is not broken or lowered, and (4) the Grail is not a chalice but a serving dish, which happens in Chrétien's text to function perhaps as a pyx or a ciborium, it is nonetheless a certainty that informed contemporary or near-contemporary readers of Chrétien identified elements in the Grail Procession with

Figure 10. Ecclesia (The Church).

attributes ascribed to Synagoga and Ecclesia. As painful as it is for many readers, an interpretation of the motif *stricto sensu* may well seem relevant to the *Conte del Graal* in light of the penitent knight's anti-Semitic diatribe on Good Friday and, in terms of the placement of the figures in contemporary artistic representations, to Chrétien's explanation of the left and right hands of the charitable in his Prologue.

The figures are allegorical, but by no means necessarily in an exegetical sense.[28] The use of such a motif by a writer like Chrétien de Troyes is in fact essentially poetic and therefore plurivalent and susceptible to multiple readings, some of which may appear to contradict conventional interpretations. In addition to or instead of references to a theological debate, the preferment of Ecclesia over Synagoga may reflect (1) continuity in a succession of orders, which is in fact a dominant theme in the *Conte del Graal* (cf. Maddox, *Arthurian Romances*, pp. 112–18): inheritance, knighthood, letters; (2) literary history: the seed that thrives in fertile earth, buds that burst into flower, etc.; (3) successions of texts in the realm of literature: Count Philippe's Latin book updated and translated into French by Chrétien; (4) the accumulation of "contes de Perceval," "contes de Gauvain," and "contes del Graal" that grow into the *Conte del Graal*; (5) the succession of kingdoms, from murdered father to son in Escavalon, from Utherpendragon (also murdered: *Brut*, 8951–9004) to Arthur, from Arthur in Logres to Gawain as his nephew and heir, in Champguin from Ygraine to Gawain, from the Grail King or the Fisher King to Perceval as heir to his mother and the more vigorous of the Grail King's nephews; (6) the translation of Ygraine's status as queen from Logres to the Roche de Champguin and her daughter's as queen of Lothian and Orkney, as wife of King Lot, to subjection to her mother and later to her brother, Gawain; (7) the progression of ages from Antiquity to modernity, from Alexander to Philippe, from Rome to France, from Troy to Britain, from Britain to France; (8) the ages of man, as reflected by the 500 squires at the Roche de Champguin, and human growth and education from childhood to adolescence to adulthood to eternal life, from *valet galois* to the Red Knight who names himself Perceval the Welshman; (9) advancement in insight and knowledge from looking into dark mirrors to seeing face to face; (10) growth in conversion from the sinner redeemed to the old man made new....

Conclusion

Orkney and the Grail Kingdom

Yet the Bleeding Lance, it seems, can be unbound from the Grail and raised against the kingdom of Logres despite the fact that it is essential to the Grail custom. The infirmity of the Fisher King, who, with his father, is currently in possession of the Lance, is the only visible sign in the *Conte del Graal* of warfare involving the Grail kingdom in any way; Chrétien does not reveal why the Grail King is bed-ridden. War and suffering implicitly involving both the Grail kingdom and Logres are otherwise portrayed in secondary narratives by Perceval's mother (389–470, B409–90), the Weeping Maiden (3549–58, B3583–92), and the Hideous Damsel (4635–49, B4669–83) in references that are also reflected in the history of the Roche de Champguin, which originates in Logres (7477–7562, B7591–7604; 8691–8719, B8739–76). We have also seen how the city of Orkney, which teems with a diseased and wounded populace and is ruled by a grief-stricken king incapable of governing,[29] is an analogue of Biaurepaire, a city under siege that is bereft of most of its inhabitants, many of whom are imprisoned in the castle of a foreign enemy like Arthur's subjects in the *Charrete*, while the few defenders who remain suffer from starvation. Might Orkney also be under attack? If so, Gawain's messenger, again like Perceval before him, has managed to bypass the besiegers and enter the city unnoticed and unscathed.

In Arthurian geography, Orkney is a petty kingdom in northeastern Scotland that includes the islands of the same name. In the conventional history of Britain, it is technically not a part of Logres, which is more or less coextensive with the medieval kingdom of England south of Hadrian's Wall. Orkney is nonetheless subject to Logres because King Lot, initially ruler of Lothian, which lies south of the Firth of Forth, and later of Orkney as well, has sworn fealty to Arthur as Utherpendragon's legitimate successor[30]; Lot's son Gawain has done likewise. According to the protocol, Lot, as Arthur's vassal, should be serving his overlord as host at Orkney castle; they are brothers-in-law as well, for Utherpendragon gave Arthur's half-sister Anna to Lot in marriage when he wed her mother, Ygraine.[31] Yet King Lot is not mentioned in Chrétien's Orkney fragment—indeed, in the time frame of the Galloway Section, as in the Perceval Section, it is *matrilineal* succession that appears to dominate. Reminiscing with Gawain, Ygraine evokes her son-in-law Lot

"Hide your good deeds from your left hand"

with nostalgia (8093–94, B8135–36), but, in the *Conte del Graal*, he seems in fact simply to have vanished.[32] Not unlike Perceval earlier in the romance, Gawain himself, as his grandmother's successor—and sometime prisoner—at the Roche de Champguin, emerges as a, if not *the*, primary figure in the Orkney fragment even though he is not present physically: he is both the initiator of the episode and, in lieu of his absent father and an impotent Arthur, the moral and perhaps also the social and political authority of Orkney. Yet Lot remains alive somewhere, for Gawain is never referred to as king. More crucial, however, is the fact that any claim that Gawain might have to Arthur's kingdom is substantiated by his relationship to the king through his mother and grandmother Ygraine.

In an earlier event that imprints Perceval's image in the Orkney episode, the would-be knight arrives at Carlisle to find Arthur grieving because his able-bodied companions are absent; his woes are intensified by the threats and insults of a brash intruder whom the injured knights housed in the castle are too weak and too ill to confront. Orkney, with its infirm population and despondent king, is a counterpoise to Carlisle. The circumstances are relevant to the Orkney fragment in several ways, as we have seen, among them the fact that Arthur is again stricken by *tristitia* due in part to the absence of a knight whom he must consider the most worthy of his companions, and the kingdom appears to have suffered a blow that is far more severe than the Red Knight's earlier displays of hubris. There is as yet no Perceval—or, more to the point at present, no Gawain—to defend Arthur. Of particular interest is the fact that, as Gawain, the exemplary Arthurian knight, is notably absent at Carlisle, so Orkney is the only domain thus far represented in the romance where, after the defeat of King Ryon, he may have found a "meillor sejor" (836, B856) ([a place] where it is pleasanter to live) than with Arthur and his convalescing companions. The beggars in the street recall those days as a golden past brightened by Gawain's bestowals of charity—in Apollonian works of healing that mirror those of the *Christus medicus* in his encounter with Greoreas, no doubt, as well as acts of material largesse. Those days are no more. Gawain is constrained by Ygraine's custom to be absent, and a mad king holds court in what will be Gawain's own castle. Orcadian decay reflects in microcosm the waning of the Arthurian realm as a whole.

Conclusion

The *Conte del Graal* has produced the seeds to sow a "Mort Artu"[33] at the end of Chrétien's cycle of romances, and it promises to be a catastrophe as cataclysmic as Arthur's battle with Mordred in the traditional histories of Geoffrey of Monmouth and Wace that will subsequently be rewritten again in the *Didot Perceval* and the Lancelot-Grail Cycle. Donald Maddox and Joseph Duggan both have broken new ground in anticipating such a battle involving matters that concern knighthood and the rule of kings entailing the use of the Bleeding Lance.[34] The two kingdoms of significance that remain in the *Conte del Graal* are the realm of Arthur, which in the person of Gawain as perhaps his heir apparent could well be united with Champguin, and that of the Grail dynasty, which Perceval apparently stands to inherit in due time. Logres and its dependencies, paralyzed by a decline set in motion when Utherpendragon's kingdom fell to Arthur, will certainly strive for restoration under Arthur's enatic nephew[35] perhaps with the support of his five hundred new knights of all ages. Conditions in the even more mysterious Grail kingdom are less evident, but the Fisher King's domain may well require a sustained period of stability, perhaps to be secured by his heir, Perceval, before it can defend itself or attack those who threaten it. Meanwhile, on the sidelines, Escavalon, with its weak young king whose ambassador Guiganbresil is a blustering nonentity and whose "wise" advisor all too easily capitulates to expediency, suffers from delusions of grandeur. The successors to the pre-eminent kingdoms are destined to perform as models of knighthood, but of different orders. Gawain will remain what he is, the exemplar of the Arthurian era. Perceval, who was imprisoned in the Arthurian order but has been redeemed, will represent an ineffable knighthood of the Grail. When the cataclysm erupts, Gawain and Perceval will inevitably be pitted against each other.

In the interim, Gawain is trapped in the domain founded by his grandmother that lies in an Otherworld, a land where the living mingle with the dead. Galloway resembles no other locus in Chrétien's romances more closely than the land of Gorre in the *Charrete*, which is also in some ways reflected in Clamadeus's island kingdom, but in Galloway too Gawain seems incapable of matching Lancelot's feats of rescuing queens, liberating prisoners (as Perceval does when he defeats Clamadeus), or even returning to the Arthurian world of Logres. He has defeated the murderous guardian of the borderland and handed him over for customary imprisonment by the Ferryman—will he follow the Orgueilleus de la Roche as defender of the borderland, just as he has succeeded his grandmother as lord of Champguin, and will he be imprisoned in that role as well? In any case, he has won lordship of a powerful castle, a highly ambiguous reflection of the Grail Castle, which offers him honor, the status of a perfect knight,[36] and a compromised independence. Perceval too has won a castle and a lady whom he loves and has abandoned both of them. Will he have a chance to win them back? Come what may, he stands to inherit as well—or instead—the Grail Castle, the model reflected in Gawain's Roche de Champguin, and the mysterious, quasi-invisible kingdom that lies at the very heart of the *Conte del Graal*.

A critical difference between the predestined antagonists comes clear in light of Chrétien's Prologue. The key is St. Paul's use of the trope of human growth in body and in understanding found in I Corinthians 13, which it is tempting to consider alongside another Pauline image already alluded to, that of casting off the old man and putting on the new (Ephesians 4:22–24). The paradigm determines in charity the entire course of the *Conte del Graal* just as we have seen its development reflected darkly and clearly in a multiplicity of real and metaphorical mirrors. Perceval grows from boyhood to manhood, when he puts away childish things: he "casts off" his Welsh clothing and javelin and his childish ways of speaking, and he "puts on" new arms, courtly finery, and manly language. Eventually, however, he becomes entrapped in that "manhood," which is the Arthurian order idealized in a world of courtly sophistication. At the Hermitage, he is required in turn to cast off that man in order to acquire yet something else that is new: a liberation from guilt and *tristitia*, which implies a promise of higher knowledge in this life, a purposeful and charitable service in knighthood that mirrors his duties with respect to the *peccatum matris*, and still greater things to come.

Meanwhile, we learn from the beggars of Orkney that Perceval's erstwhile exemplar and potential future adversary has indeed exercised noble liberality and has shown mercy to the poor, yet without sustaining the benefits he has provided. In his worldly triumphs and his successes at reconciliation, he has acted charitably, but in a way that reflects the younger Perceval at Biaurepaire, which Chrétien condemns in his Pro-

Conclusion

logue. Gawain has allowed his left hand know what the right hand does, practicing his charity so that its beneficiaries can know about it and talk about it and spread his fame in beneficial "contes de Gauvain." He remains imprisoned in a debased and destructive chivalric code, and for this "old man" there is no escape. As the heir to the Grail kingdom, and in light of the Wise Vavassor's display of foreknowledge, Perceval, still wearing the armor of his first opponent in knighthood, seems destined to wield the Bleeding Lance against Gawain and ultimately to defeat him. As defender of the Grail kingdom against King Arthur's exemplary knight, Perceval may thus play a role in the collapse of the kingdom of Logres that, ironically, mirrors that of Mordred in the Geoffrey of Monmouth's *Historia* and Wace's *Brut*.[37]

Appendix A

The *Peccatum matris* as Original Sin: Psalm 108/109:14[1]

"In memoriam redeat iniquitas patrum eius in conspectu Domini, et *peccatum matris eius* non deleatur" (Psalm 108/09:14, my emphasis) (May the iniquity of his fathers be remembered in the sight of the Lord: and let not *the sin of his mother* be blotted out).[2] St. Augustine of Hippo, who interprets the psalmist's maligned enemy as Judas, calls attention to genealogical implications in the reference to the Second Commandment (Exodus 20:5–6, cf. Deuteronomy 5:8–10):

> No adorabis ea [sculptilia], neque coles: ego sum Dominus Deus tuus fortis, zelotes, visitans iniquitatem patrum in filios, in tertiam et quatram generationem eorum qui oderunt me: et faciens misericordiam in millia eis qui diligent me, et custodiunt praecepta mea.
>
> (Thou shalt not adore them [graven idols], nor serve them: I am the Lord thy God, mighty, jealous, visiting the iniquity of the fathers upon the children, unto the third and fourth generation of them that hate me: And shewing mercy unto thousands to them that love me, and keep my commandments.)

In this context, the hereditary *peccatum matris* and *iniquitas patrum* constitute Original Sin. Augustine further observes that

> Illud autem quod dictum est, *Reddam peccata patrum in filios*, additum est, *qui oderunt me* ..., hoc est, sicut me oderant parentes eorum: ut quemadmodum bonorum imitatio facit ut etiam propria peccata deleantur, sic malorum imitatio faciat ut non solum sua, sed etiam eorum quos imitati sunt, merita sortiantur. Si ergo Judas teneret illud ad quod vocatus est, nullo modo ad eum vel sua praeterita, vel parentum iniquitas pertineret: quia ergo non tenuit adoptionem in familia Dei, sed iniquitatem vetusti generis potius elegit.[3]

Appendix A

(God said, "I shall visit the iniquity of the fathers upon the children," and added, "who hate me," that is, as their forebears hated me. Just as emulation of those who are good causes one's own sins to be expunged, so emulation of those who are evil causes not only one's own sins but also those of the ones who are emulated to result in their just consequences. If therefore Judas had persevered in what he was called [by Christ] to do, neither his past deeds nor the iniquity of his parents would have affected him in any way, but he did not persist in his adoption into the family of God and chose instead the iniquity of the old way.)

Exculpation from Original Sin is achieved in conversion to God's law—the Old Law in terms of the Second Commandment, the New Law with respect to Judas—, but its effects are retained when, as in the case of unrepentant idol worshippers as well as Judas, God is disavowed and scorned.

Appendix B

The *Peccatum matris* as an Incentive to Charity: Foregrounding the Mother in the Vulgate Sirach[1]

The Book of Sirach, written in Jerusalem at the beginning of the second century B.C., is a book of the Hebrew apocrypha.[2] Also known as Ben Sira, the Wisdom of Yeshua or Jesus Ben Sira, and, in the Christian tradition, Ecclesiasticus (not to be confused with Ecclesiastes), it participates in the Jewish Wisdom Tradition. According to some biblical scholars, Sirach stands out among the later apocryphal works for its conservative position in reclaiming the pre-eminence of the Torah. It also manifests certain Essenic traits, and three small fragments of it are in fact found among the Dead Sea Scrolls. Much of the book takes the form of advice from a father to his children in general or to a son. What distinguishes Sirach from Proverbs, for example, is its single authorship, it thematic organization, and the sustained breadth and depth of its counsel on matters of religion, society, the family, commerce, and worldly sophistication. It also contains lengthy passages of remarkable poetic power such as the so-called Song of Wisdom (the whole of chapter 24) and the extensive "Let us now praise famous men" (AV) section in chapters 44–50.

Although Sirach was destined not to be accepted into the Hebrew canon, it was widely influential in its time. Several axioms, collectively known today as the Proverbs of Ben Sira, made their way anonymously into the Talmud, and references to Sirach have been identified in the New Testament. But over the centuries, Sirach as a book fell into oblivion

Appendix B

in Jewish culture and eventually ceased to be copied at all. The only known Hebrew manuscripts were copied in Egypt in the eleventh and early twelfth centuries. Large fragments of four of them were discovered at the turn of the last century in the *genizah*, a repository for discarded manuscripts containing the name of God, at the Ben Ezra Synagogue in Cairo. These fragments account for a little over one half of the text, but preserve nothing of the passage that most interests us. The Egyptian origin of these latest extant manuscripts is of interest, for modern scholars maintain that the Hebrew text of Sirach was virtually unknown in Europe in the Middle Ages. Even Salomon Rashi, the great rabbinic scholar of the Jewish school in Troyes who thrived at the turn of the twelfth century, probably knew nothing of the original text of Sirach apart from the proverbial statements anonymously incorporated into the Talmud.[3]

Although Sirach was gradually lost to Jewish tradition, it was preserved in the Christian Old Testament thanks to the Jewish compilers of the Septuagint Bible (LXX), who incorporated it, along with other late books, into their canon.[4] In fact, Yeshua Ben Sira's grandson (likewise named Yeshua), who had migrated to Alexandria, translated it into Greek around the year 130 B.C., at just about the time when the Septuagint project was nearing completion. It is this translation that appears in the Septuagint, which in turn was the basis of the later Latin translations.[5]

Compared with the Septuagint, Sirach 3:14–17 in the Vulgate (= 13–15 in LXX,[6] which AV follows) is unique in three important ways (the variants cannot of course be verified against the original Hebrew because the passage is not preserved in the existing fragments): (1) The Vulgate alone mentions a single sin in vs. 16 (cf. LXX and AV, vs. 14b), "pro peccato matris" (for the sin of thy mother), instead of sin in general, "ἀντὶ ἁμαρτιῶν" (= against sin, cf. NETS: against sins, AV: instead of sins), and (2) only in the Vulgate it is a question of a maternal sin. (3) Meanwhile, vs. 15 of the Vulgate (= LXX and AV, vv. 13–14a) anticipates the *father's* old age: "eleemosyna ... patris" (the relieving of the father), as do LXX and consequently AV (vs. 14a): "ἐλεημοσύνη γὰρ πατρὸς" (charity for a father [NETS]), cf. "the relieving of thy father" (AV); thus in vv. 16–17 the Vulgate creates—or uniquely preserves?—a pairing of father and mother in a passage that is devoted only to the father in LXX, vv.

The Peccatum matris *as an Incentive to Charity*

14–15, cf. AV: "For the relieving of thy father shall not be forgotten: and instead of sins it shall be added to build thee up. In the day of thine affliction it shall be remembered; thy sins also shall melt away, as the ice in the fair warm weather."

In fact, throughout the Sirach passage, filial piety is similarly demonstrated for the most part in parallel relationships with both parents, as in the Fourth Commandment: the father's honor and the mother's authority over their children (Vulgate, vs. 3); a son who honors his father atones for his sins, one who honors his mother stores up treasure (vv. 5–6), which is very close to the sense of vv. 14–17; a son who honors his father lives long, one who obeys God comforts his mother (vs. 7); one who fears God honors his parents and must serve them as though they were his masters (vs. 8) (Vulgate only); and so forth.[7] In the Vulgate text, the *peccatum matris* in vs. 16, which is mentioned alongside the reference to charity owed to the father, in fact brings the mother to the fore, for elsewhere in the passage the father is mentioned first when paired with the mother.

Of greater relevance to Chrétien de Troyes and the *Conte del Graal* is of course the text of the Vulgate, which is in all probability the only version of the Book of Sirach known to him.

Appendix C

The Custom of Logres in the *Charrete*[1]

Not without irony, the Amorous Maiden challenges Lancelot with a reference to the Custom of Logres, which Chrétien's narrator explains:

>"Sire, je m'an iroie
>O vos grant piece an ceste voie,
>Se vos mener m'an osïez
>Et se vos me conduisïez
>Par les us et par les costumes
>Qui furent ainz que nos ne fumes
>El rëaume de Logres mises."
>Les costumes et les franchises
>Estoient tex a cel termine
>Que dameisele ne meschine,
>Se chevaliers la trovast sole,
>Ne plus qu'il se tranchast la gole
>Ne feïst se tote enor non,
>S'estre volsist de boen renon,
>Et, s'il l'esforçast, a toz jorz
>An fust honiz an totes corz.
>Mes se ele conduit eüst,
>Uns autres, se tant li pleüst
>Qu'a celui bataille an feïst
>Et par armes la conqueïst,
>Sa volonté an poïst faire
>Sanz honte et sanz blasme retraire
>[1294–1316].

("My lord, I would ride a long way with you in this direction, if you dared to take me with you and if you treated me according to the customs that have existed in the kingdom of Logres since before we were born." The customs and rights were such at that time that, if a knight found a noble maiden or a girl alone, he should no more treat her dishonorably than he would slit his own throat, if he wished to keep his good name, and if he raped her, he would be shamed in every court. But if she was under escort, another [knight], if he wished to engage him [i.e., her escort] in battle and defeated him, could do with her as he pleased without incurring shame or blame.)

With respect to the *Conte del Graal*, Perceval, who is most certainly ignorant of the Custom, but aware that his mother has prohibited "le soreplus" (go[ing] any further [than kissing]) (530, B548), "innocently" violates its spirit in his clumsy attempts to seduce the Tent Maiden despite her objections when he finds her alone. Moreover, as the lady protests, she has an escort, albeit one who is absent. Assuming that the Custom of Logres is enforced throughout Galloway as well as in Logres, which appears to be the case according to the testimony of the Malevolent Maiden and others, Guiromelant won the Malevolent Maiden by killing her lover, as is permitted, and was protected from infamy when he attempted for force her to love him as he apparently loves her (8515–24, B8561–72; cf. 8884–98, B8932–46).

Gawain cites the first clause of the Custom, which Greoreas had violated when he punished him:

> an la terre le roi Artu
> Sont puceles asseürees.
> Li rois lor a trives donnees,
> Si les garde et si les conduit
> [7080–83, B7122–25].

(maidens are protected in King Arthur's land. The king has given them safe conduct and watches over and protects them.)

Greoreas, certain that he is about to die and aware of his own transgression against the Custom, begs Gawain to take his lady under his protection in order to assure her safety as best he can.

From the case of the Malevolent Maiden and the base conduct of the Orgueilleus de la Lande and perhaps Guiromelant also, it is clear that the Custom of Logres can be used to justify both the mistreatment of women and the entrapment of solicitous knights, as when Perceval meets the Tent Maiden for the second time and, presumably, in the case of the Weeping Maiden's lover as well.

Chapter Notes

Preface

1. The edition of reference is Chrétien de Troyes, *The Story of the Grail (Li Contes del Graal), or Perceval*, ed. Rupert T. Pickens, trans. William W. Kibler (New York and London: Garland, 1990), base manuscript: *A*, with regular consultation of *Le Roman de Perceval ou le Conte du Graal*, ed. Keith Busby (Tübingen: Max Niemeyer, 1993), base manuscript: *T*. For manuscripts of the *Conte del Graal* cited below, see the Bibliography. Other editions cited include Chrétien de Troyes, *Le Conte del Graal ou le Roman de Perceval*, ed. and trans. Charles Méla, Lettres Gothiques (Paris: Livre de Poche, 1990), base manuscript: *B*; Alfons Hilka, ed., *Der Percevalroman von Christian von Troyes*, Christian von Troyes' Sämtliche Werke 5, gen. ed. Wendelin Foerster (Halle: Niemeyer, 1932; rpt. Amsterdam: Rodopi, 1966), base manuscript: *A*; and Chrétien de Troyes, *Le Roman de Perceval ou le Conte del Graal*, ed. William Roach, Textes Littéraires Français 71 (Geneva: Droz and Paris: Minard, 1959), base manuscript: *T*. References to line numbers in Busby's edition that differ from Pickens, ed., are preceded by B. Busby's numbering conforms with that of Hilka and Roach; differences are due for the most part to apparent interpolations accepted by Hilka (see Pickens, ed., pp. 502–05) and rejected by both Roach and Busby. Translations in parentheses throughout are Kibler's; deviations, which are intended to highlight shades of meaning and syntactic elements pertinent to particular arguments, appear in square brackets. Translations from other works by Chrétien are my own.

2. See the editions by Anne Berthelot in Chrétien de Troyes, *Œuvres complètes*, gen. ed. Daniel Poirion, Bibliothèque de la Pléiade (Paris: Gallimard, 1994), pp. 915–52, 1391–1410 (*Philomena*) and 953–1036, 1410–51 (*Guillaume d'Angleterre*). Chrétien refers to earlier works in the opening of *Cligés*, ed. Charles Méla, Lettres Gothiques (Paris: Livre de Poche, 1994), 1–7: (1) *Erec et Enide*, ed. Jean-Marie Fritz, Lettres Gothiques (Paris: Livre de Poche, 1992); (2) a tale involving King Mark and Isolda the Blonde (lost); and three French translations of Ovidian texts: (3) *Ars amatoria (Art of Love)* (lost), (4) "The Shoulder Bite" (story of Pelops, *Metamorphoses* 6: 400–14) (lost), and (5) the "Metamorphosis of the Hoopoe, the Swallow, and the Nightingale" (= *Philomena*?), cf. *Metamorphoses*, ed. and trans. Frank Justus Miller, Loeb Classics Library, 2 vols. (1921–1922; rpt. London: W. Heinemann and Cambridge, MA: Harvard University Press, 1960), 6: 430–673).

3. On the order of composition, see Ch. 4., n. 30.

4. In addition to the edition cited in n. 1 above: *The Welsh Knight: Paradoxicality in Chrétien's Conte del Graal*, French Forum Monographs 6 (Lexington, KY: French Forum, 1977); "*Le Conte del Graal (Perceval)*," in *The Romances of Chrétien de Troyes: A Symposium*, ed. Douglas Kelly, Edward C. Armstrong Monographs on Medieval Literature 3 (Lexington, KY: French Forum, 1985), pp. 232–86, 335–39; and "*Le Conte du Graal*: Chrétien's Unfinished Last Romance," in *A Companion of Chrétien de Troyes*," ed. Norris J. Lacy and Joan Grimbert (Cambridge: Boydell and Brewer, 2005), pp. 169–87.

5. Joan Tasker Grimbert, *"Yvain" dans le miroir* (Amsterdam and Philadelphia: John Benjamins, 1988).

6. In Donand Maddox, *Fictions of Identity in Medieval France* (Cambridge: Cambridge University Press, 2000), passim.

Notes—Introduction

7. Norris J. Lacy, *The Craft of Chrétien de Troyes: An Essay on Narrative Art* (Leiden: Brill, 1980), pp. 100–12.

8. Antoinette Saly, "Beaurepaire et Escavalon," in *Mélanges d'études romanes du Moyen-Âge et de la Renaissance offerts à Jean Rychner, Travaux de Linguistique et de Littérature*, 16 (1978): 469–81, and "La Récurrence des motifs en symétrie inverse dans la structure du *Perceval* de Chrétien de Troyes," *Travaux de Linguistique et de Littérature*, 21 (1983): 21–41.

9. Lucien Dällenbach, *Le Récit spéculaire: Essai sur la mise en abyme* (Paris: Seuil, 1977); see also Maddox, *Fictions of Identity*, pp. 14–20.

10. For example, Frederick Goldin, *The Mirror of Narcissus in the Courtly Lyric* (Ithaca, NY: Cornell University Press, 1967); Jeanne A. Nightingale, "Erec in the Mirror: The Feminization of the Self and the Reinvention of the Chivalric Hero in Chrétien's First Romance," in *Arthurian Romance and Gender/Masculin-Féminin dans le roman arthurien médiéval/Geschlichterrollen im mittelalterlichen Artusroman*, ed. Wolfgang Wolfzettel (Amsterdam and Atlanta: Rodopi, 1995), pp. 130–46; Henri Rey-Flaud, *Le Chevalier, l'Autre et la Mort: Les aventures de Gauvain dans* Le Conte du Graal (Paris: Payot & Rivages, 1998), esp. ch. 6 ("Narcisse meurtrier de son image," pp. 128–54) and ch. 7 ("Comme en des miroirs confrontés," pp. 155–78), where doubles are explored, cf. Barbara N. Sargent[-Baur], "L'Autre chez Chrétien de Troyes," *Cahiers de Civilisation Médiévale* 10 (1967): 199–205; Claire Nouvet, "An Allegorical Mirror: The Pool of Narcissus in Guillaume de Lorris' *Romance of the Rose*," *Romanic Review*, 91 (2002): 353–74, and Frank Brandsma, "Mirror Characters," in *Courtly Arts and the Art of Courtliness*, ed. Keith Busby and Christopher Kleinhenz (Cambridge: D.S. Brewer, 2006), pp. 275–82. Essays in *Miroirs et jeux de miroirs dans la littérature médiévale*, ed. Fabienne Pomel (Rennes: Presses Universitaires de Rennes, 2003) are devoted to texts from the thirteenth through the fifteenth centuries. See also Mark Pendergrast, *Mirror/Mirror: A History of the Human Love Affair with Reflection* (New York: Basic Books, 2003).

11. "Videmus nunc per speculum in ænigmate: tunc autem facie ad faciem." Unless indicated otherwise, the Vulgate text used is *Biblia sacra iuxta Vulgatam clementinam* (Madrid: Biblioteca de Autores Cristianos, 1994); translations are from the Douay-Rheims Version, *The Holy Bible* (Baltimore: John Murphy, 1899).

Introduction

1. Cf. "Qui petit seme petit queut" (no. 2074), in Joseph Morawski, ed., *Proverbes français antérieurs au XVe siècle*, Classiques Français du Moyen Age 47 (Paris: Champion, 1925); Elisabeth Schulze-Busacker, *Proverbes et expressions proverbiales dans la littérature narrative du moyen âge français* (Paris: Champion, 1985), p. 294. As Danièle James-Raoul points out in *Chrétien de Troyes, la greffe d'un style* (Paris: Champion, 2007), pp. 183–86, the biblical references (II Corinthians 9:6, the Parable of the Sower, Matthew 6:3–4, I John 4:16) underscore the unique status of this prologue among Chrétien's in its appeal to God as textual guarantor; she omits Chrétien's translation of I Corinthians 13:4. Matilda Tomaryn Bruckner, *Chrétien Continued: A Study of the* Conte du Graal *and Its Verse Continuations* (Oxford: Oxford University Press, 2009), pp. 72–85, lays the foundation for her groundbreaking study with an insightful analysis of the Prologue; also highly pertinent is Bruckner, "Weaving a Tapestry from Biblical Exegesis to Romance Textuality: Caught in the Web of Chrétien's *Conte du Graal*," forthcoming.

2. Mark 4:1–20, Matthew 13:1–23, Luke 8:1–15; here, "Et aliud [semen] cecidit in terram bonam: et dabat fructum ascendentem et crescentem" (Mark 4:8, cf. Matthew 13:8, Luke 8:8) (And some [seed] fell upon good ground; and brought forth fruit that grew up, and increased).

3. Discussed by Jeff Rider, " 'Wild Oats': The Parable of the Sower in the Prologue of Chrétien de Troyes' *Conte del Graal*," in *Philologies Old and New: Essays in Honor of Peter Florian Dembowski*, ed. Joan Tasker Grimbert and Carol J. Chase, ECAMML 12 (Princeton, NJ: Edward C. Armstrong Monographs, 2001), pp. 251–66. Although he does not mention charity, Rider offers many significantly pertinent views on sowing and harvesting in the Prologue in terms of education and sexuality throughout the *Conte del Graal*.

4. Nathan Edelman, "A Scriptural Key to Villon's *Testament*," *Modern Language Notes* 72 (1957): 345–51, rpt. in Edelman, *The Eye of the Beholder: Essays in French Literature*, ed. Jules Brody (Baltimore and London:

Notes—Introduction

Johns Hopkins University Press, 1974), pp. 31-37. In the passage in question, Villon takes as his "prayer" for his archenemy, Bishop Thibaud d'Aussigny, "Le ver[se]let escript septiesme / Du pseaulme *Deus laudem*" (*Testament*, 47-48) (verse 7 from the Psalm *Deus laudem*), i.e., Psalm 108 (Vulgate)/109 (Authorized King James Version, hereafter AV):8: "Fiant dies eius pauci et episcopatum eius accipiat alter" (May his days be few: and his bishopric let another take); François Villon, *Poésies complètes*, ed. Claude Thiry, Lettres Gothiques (Paris: Livre de Poche, 1991).

5. Cf. "proficiscar in Hierusalem ministare sanctis" (I shall go to Jerusalem to minister unto the saints) (Romans 15:25).

6. On Philip, see John W. Baldwin, "Chrétien in History," in *A Companion to Chrétien de Troyes*, ed. Norris J. Lacy and Joan Tasker Grimbert, pp. 3-13; June Hall McCash, "Chrétien's Patrons," in *Companion to Chrétien de Troyes*, pp. 15-25; and Joseph J. Duggan, *The Romances of Chrétien de Troyes* (New Haven/London: Yale University Press, 2001), pp. 19-21

7. Cf. more restricted readings by Peter Haidu, *Aesthetic Distance in Chrétien de Troyes: Irony and Comedy in "Cligès" and "Perceval"* (Geneva: Droz, 1968), pp. 115-17; D.D.R. Owen, *The Evolution of the Grail Legend* (Edinburgh and London: Oliver and Boyd, 1968), pp. 130-31; and Tony Hunt, "The Prologue to Li Contes del Graal," *Romania* 92 (1971): 359-79. For an overview of interpretations of the Prologue, and for a more expansive reading, see Barbara N. Sargent-Baur, *La Destre et la senestre: Etude sur le "Conte del Graal" de Chrétien de Troyes* (Amsterdam/Atlanta: Rodopi, 2000), pp. 1-23; also Keith Busby, *Chrétien de Troyes, Perceval (Le Conte du Graal)* (London: Grant and Cutler, 1993), pp. 12-15.

8. Explicitly in *Erec et Enide*, 2259-66, 6665-77; implicitly in *Cligés*, where the Greek emperor Alexandre instructs his son, also named Alexandre, on the virtue of liberality (192-217). On Alexander the Great in Chrétien's last romance, see Hunt, "Prologue," pp. 366-77, and Sargent-Baur, "Alexander and the *Conte du Graal*," in *Arthurian Literature* 14, ed. James P. Carley and Felicity Riddy (Cambridge: Brewer, 1996), pp. 1-18.

9. Chrétien's judgment is consonant with that of writers of Alexander romances who often borrow the epic topos of the noble Saracen to describe the pagan emperor as unenlightened by Christianity and therefore flawed despite his many virtues: for example, "Se il fust crestïens, ainc tels rois ne fu nes, / Si cortois ne si larges ..." (If he had been a Christian, never would such a king been have born, one so valiant or generous); *The Medieval French Roman d'Alexandre*, vol. 2: *Version of Alexandre de Paris*, ed. E.C. Armstrong, D.L. Buffam, Bateman Edwards, and L.F.H. Lowes (Princeton: Princeton University Press, 1938; rpt. New York: Kraus, 1965), Branch 4, 1556-57, my translation. See esp. Michel Zink, "The Prologue to the *Historia de Preliis*: A Pagan Model of Spiritual Struggle," in *The Medieval French Alexander*, ed. Donald Maddox and Sara Sturm-Maddox (Albany: State University of New York Press, 2002), pp. 21-27, who relates the *Historia* specifically to the *Perceval* prologue.

10. "L'evangile, por coi dit ele: / 'Tes biens a ta senestre cele?' / La senestre, selonc l'estoire, / Senefie la vainne gloire / Qui vie[n]t de fause ypocrisie. / Et la destre, que senefie? / Charité qui de sa bone oevre / Pas ne se vante, ençois la coevre" (Why does the Gospel state: "Hide your good deeds from your left hand?" The left hand, according to tradition, stands for vainglory, which comes from false hypocrisy. And what does the right hand stand for? Charity, which does not boast of its good deed, but hides it) (37-44).

11. In 44-45 ("ençois la coevre, / Que nus ne le set que cil non") Chrétien returns to Matthew 6:4, "ut sit eleemosyna tua in abscondito, et Pater tuus, qui videt in abscondito, reddet tui" (That thy alms be made in secret, and thy Father who seeth in secret will repay thee).

12. "Deus charitas est: et qui manet in charitate, in Deo manet, et Deus in eo" (God is charity: and he that abideth in charity, abideth in God, and God in him). The word *charité* occurs six times in the Prologue and twice in the Galloway Section.

13. "Sainz Pos lo dit et je le lui" (49) (St. Paul states and I read it there). See Bruckner, "Weaving a Tapestry."

14. For example, Sargent-Baur, *La Destre*, pp. 10-11, and Evelyn Birge Vitz, *Orality and Performance in Early French Romance* (Cambridge: D.S. Brewer, 1999), pp. 126-26; but see Zink, "Prologue," p. 27. In James-Raoul's rhetorical analysis, the misattribution is inconsequential (*Chrétien de Troyes*, p. 184).

15. Subsequent quotes from I Corinthians 13 are discussed below, pp. 58-61.

16. See Henri de Lubac, *Exégèse médiévale: Les quatre sens de l'Écriture* (Paris: Auber, 1959), vol. 1.2: 134-43; Joseph G. Prior, *The Historical Critical Method in*

Notes—Chapter 1

Catholic Exegesis (Rome: Editrice Pontifica Università Gregoriana, 2001), pp. 34–56; and Karen Armstrong, *The Bible: A Biography* (New York: Grove/Atlantic, 2007), pp. 102–54. See Jeff Rider, "Perpetual Enigma of Chrétien's Grail Episode," *Arthuriana* 8.1 (1998): 6–21. On *aenigma* as riddle, see Eleanor Cook, *Enigmas and Riddles in Literature* (Cambridge/New York: Cambridge University Press, 2009, ch. 2 ("Enigma as Trope: History, Function, Fortunes"), esp. pp. 29–47.

17. See Sabine Melchior-Bonnet, *Histoire du miroir* (Paris: Hachette, 1994), trans. Katherine H. Jewett, *The Mirror: A History* (New York: Routledge, 2001), and "Présentation: Réflexions sur le miroir," in *Miroirs et jeux de miroirs*, ed. Fabienne Pomel, pp. 17–26; also R.W. Douglas and Susan Frank, *A History of Glassmaking* (Henley-on-Thames: Foulis, 1972).

18. *Isidori Hispanensis episcopi Etymologiarum sive originum Libri XX*, ed. W.M. Lindsay, 2 vols. (1911; rpt. Oxford: Clarendon Press, 1957), 2: XVI.4.

19. See above, pp. 5–7; also Pickens, "*Le Conte du Graal*," in *A Companion to Chrétien de Troyes*, ed. Lacy and Grimbert, pp. 175–76.

20. "De marbre furent les meisieres, / Au chef desus avoit verrieres / Si *clere[s], qui garde i preïst,* / Que par mi le voirre veïst / Toz ces qui el pales antrassent / Et par mi la porte passasent. / Li voirres fu painz a colors, / Des plus riches et des mellors / Qu'an sache deviser ne fere ..." (7677–85, B7719–27, my emphasis) (the walls were marble, with glass windows above so *clear that if you were attentive* you could see through the glass everyone entering the hall and passing through the door. The glass was stained with the most costly and finest colors one could conceive of or create). On these windows, see Michèle Vauthier, "Le Paradoxe des fenêtres colorées dans *Le Conte du Graal*: une interprétation possible à la lecture des couleurs chez Chrétien de Troyes," in *Les Couleurs au moyen âge*, Senefiance 24 (Aix-en-Provence: Publications du CUER-MA, 1988): 423–48.

Chapter 1

1. "Et quant il les vit an apert, / Que del bois furent descovert, / Si vit les haubers fremïanz / Et les hiaumes clers et luisanz / Et les lances et les escuz / Que onques mes n'avoit veüz, / Et vit le vert et le vermeil / Reluire contre le soleil / Et l'or et l'azur et l'argent, / Se li fu mout et bel et gent" (127–36) (But when he caught sight of them coming out of the woods, he saw the glittering hauberks and the bright, shining helmets, the lances and the shields, which he had never seen before, and he beheld the green and vermilion glistening in the sunshine, and the gold, the blue, and silver; he found it most fair and noble). Jeff Rider mentions light and shining colors throughout "The Perpetual Enigma of Chrétien's Grail Episode."

2. "Ci voi ge Damedeu, ce cuit, / Car un si bel an i esgart / Que li autre, se Dex me gart, / N'ont mie de biauté le disme" (Yet there I see God Almighty in person, I think, for one of them, so help me God, is more than ten times more beautiful than any of the others) (144–47).

3. "Et li vaslez dist as boviers: / 'Veïstes vos cinc chevaliers / Et trois puceles ci passer? / —Il ne finerent hui d'aler / Par ces forez,' font li bovier. / Et li vallez au chevalier / Qui tant avoit a lui parlé / Dist: 'Sire, par ci sont alé / Li chevalier et les puceles'" (323–31) (And the boy said to the ox-drivers, "Have you seen five knights and three maidens pass this way?" "This very day they went through these woods." And the boy said to the knight who had spoken to him at such length, "My lord, the knights and maidens passed this way").

4. In the *Charrete*, Arthur's barons and "Mainte bele dame cortoise / Bien parlant an lengue françoise" (39–40) (many a beautiful, courtly lady speaking properly in the French language) are present at court when Meleagant kidnaps the queen; Chrétien de Troyes, *Le Chevalier de la Charrete*, ed. Charles Méla, Lettres Gothiques (Paris: Livre de Poche, 1992).

5. In fact, in the earliest medieval depiction of harrowing, the Bayeux Tapestry portrays a sower casting seed over a plowed field as it is being harrowed; *La Tapisserie de Bayeux-The Bayeux Tapestry-Wandteppich von Bayeux* (Bayeux: Édition Ville de Bayeux, n.d.), scene 10. The size and wealth of the manor of Perceval's mother are indicated by the fact that she owns six harrows drawn by twelve oxen (80–84).

6. Rider, "Wild Oats," 255–56, mentions the harrowers in terms of the springtime opening (69–84) and conventional use of fields and field labor as sources of sexual metaphors, but not with respect to Perceval's engagement with them on behalf of Arthur's knights.

Notes—Chapter 1

7. Later, Gornemant de Gohort explicitly associates Perceval with Chrétien's name (1647-50, B1667-70); see below, p. 55 and Ch. 2, n. 3.

8. "Galois sont tuit par nature / Plus fol que bestes an pasture: / Cist [Perceval] est ausi come une beste" (243-45) (all Welshmen are by nature stupider than beasts in the field: this one is just like a beast). See Pickens, "Rencontres culturelles: monde francophone et matière de Bretagne," in *A French Forum: Mélanges de littérature française offerts à Raymond C. et Virginia A. La Charité*, ed. Gérard Defaux and Jerry C. Nash (Paris: Klincksieck, 2000), pp. 21-30.

9. On monsters as portentous creatures, see Isidore of Seville, *Etymologiarum sive originum Libri XX*, vol. 1: IX.3, who quotes Varro and St. Augustine of Hippo.

10. Laudatory accounts reflecting certain "contes de Gauvain" are limited to the little girl's defense of him at Tintagel and a beggar's lament over his absence from Orkney (9154-64, B9204-14).

11. Gawain defends himself against Greoreas's charge (7076-89, B7118-31); see ch. 3, pp. 97-98), while Guiromelant has lied on other matters: according to Clarissant, Gawain's sister, Guiromelant falsely claimed that she would love him more than her brother (8961-92, B9009-40). On the Malevolent Maiden's evil connivance with Greoreas's nephew and the Orgueilleus de la Roche a l'Estroite Voie in context with the Custom of Logres, see Donald Maddox, *Arthurian Romances of Chrétien de Troyes: Once and Future Fictions* (Cambridge: Cambridge University Press, 1991), pp. 104-08; ch. 4, "*Rexque futurus*: the Anterior Order in *Le Conte du Graal*," pp. 82-118, is reprinted in Arthur Groos and Norris J. Lacy, eds., *Perceval/Parzifal: A Casebook* (New York and London: Routeledge, 2002), pp. 53-96.

12. Maddox, *Fictions of Identity*, pp. 1-19 and ch. 2, esp. pp. 87-90

13. See below, pp. 177-79.

14. Ivor Arnold, ed., *Le Roman de Brut de Wace*, 2 vols. Paris (Société des Anciens Textes Français, 1938-40), 11561-609. Translations are my own. See also Judith Weiss, ed. and trans., *Wace's Roman de Brut: A History of the British* (1999; rev. Exeter: University of Exeter Press, 2002), pp. 290-93; *The Historia regum Britannie of Geoffrey of Monmouth*, ed. Neil Wright, vol. 1 (Cambridge: D.S. Brewer, 1984); Geoffrey of Monmouth, *History of the Kings of Britain*, trans. Sebastian Evans, rev. Charles W. Dunn (New York: Dutton, 1958). See Pickens, "Courtesy and *Vasselage* in Chrétien de Troyes's *Conte del Graal*," in *Echoes of the Epic: Studies in Honor of Gerard J. Brault* (Birmingham, AL: Summa, 1998), 189-221, esp. 209-13, and "Arthurian Time and Space: Chrétien's *Conte del Graal* and Wace's *Brut*." *Medium Ævum* 75 (2006): 219-46.

15. No king involved in the conquest of islands is named Ryon or anything like it; however, in the Vulgate *Merlin*, ed. H. Oskar Sommer, *The Vulgate Version of the Arthurian Romances*, 8 vols. (Washington, D.C.: The Carnegie Institute, 1908-1916, 2: 407-19, a King Rion of Denmark is the last and fiercest of the Saxon invaders of Britain to overwhelm the young Arthur's kingdom of Logres after the murder of his father, Utherpendragon. In Geoffrey of Monmouth, ed. Wright, ch. 165, and Wace's *Brut*, ed. Arnold, 11517-11608, Arthur fights a giant at Mont St. Michel and remembers Rion; in the Vulgate *Merlin* (2: 430), he kills the giant with Rion's sword. See Pickens, "Arthur's Channel Crossing: Courtesy and the Demonic in Geoffrey of Monmouth and Wace's *Brut*," *Arthuriana* 7 (1997): 3-19. Perceval's mother is the first to mention "islands of the sea" when she boasts of Perceval's heritage: "N'ot chevalier de si haut pris, / Tant redoté ne tant cremu, / Biax filz, con vostre pere fu / An totes les isles de mer" (398-401, B410-13) (There was no worthier knight, no knight more feared and respected, fair son, than your father in all the isles of the sea), and "Es isles de mer n'ot linage / Meillor del mien an mon aage" (407-08, B419-20) (In the isles of the sea there was no finer lineage than mine in my day). Her expression, "An totes les isles de mer" and "Es isles de mer," which is taken up by Gawain (4057, B4091), is used in superlative constructions (see Pickens, ed., p. 453n) and appears not to indicate a location apart from Great Britain, nor does it necessarily refer to the realm associated with Ryon and Clamadeus; but see Brigitte Cazelles, *The Unholy Grail: A Social Reading of Chrétien de Troyes's "Conte du Graal"* (Stanford, CA: Stanford University Press, 1996), pp. 49-53.

16. See also below, pp. 134-36, also 181-82.

17. We learn still later from Perceval's Hermit Uncle (6375-97, B6409-31) that the Fisher King is the son of an old king who has lain ill for twelve years and has been sustained only by a consecrated host brought to him daily in the Grail. This Grail King is the brother of the Hermit and of Perceval's

Notes—Chapter 1

mother. Thus Perceval too descends from Grail royalty.

18. On Perceval's mother, see especially Debora B. Schwartz, "A la guise de Gales l'atorna': Maternal Influence in Chrétien's *Conte del Graal*," *Essays in Medieval Studies* 12 (1996): 94–118.

19. See below, pp. 78–80. As Bruckner, *Chrétien Continued*, p. 134, suggests, Perceval's departure in search of his mother and his promise to bring her back to Biaurepaire suggest his desire to reconcile sexual love for Blanchefleur with his mother's injunction against "le soreplus"—i.e., seeking her "approval" to go for the "soreplus" in marriage.

20. Barbara N. Sargent[-Baur], "Medieval *ris*, *risus*: A Laughing Matter?," *Medium Ævum* 43 (1974): 116–32.

21. Three manuscripts of the *Conte del Graal*, HPT (T's twin V is in lacuna) bear, following 3892 (B3926), different interpolated accounts of the sword's breaking during Perceval's battle with the Orgueilleus de la Lande: see Busby, ed., Appendices 1–3, pp. 395–412, and also Bruckner, *Chrétien Continued*, pp. 207–09.

22. Within sight of the tents (4137, B4171). On the one hand, the tents align the episode with Chrétien's description of the Tent Maiden, whose beauty has been restored by this time; on the other hand, like the pavilion of the Orgueilleus de la Lande and his lady, Arthur's tents are a locus of courtly civilization in the wilderness where Gawain will provide fine clothing to replace Perceval's armor before being received by King Arthur (4500–06, B4534–40; 4534–40, B4568–74).

23. See the seminal article by Grace Armstrong, "The Scene of the Blood Drops on the Snow: A Crucial Narrative Moment in the *Conte del Graal*, *Kentucky Romance Quarterly*, 19 (1972): 127–47; also Michelle A. Freeman, *The Poetics of* Translation studii *and* Conjointure *in Chrétien de Troyes's* Cligés (Lexington, KY: French Forum 1979), esp. pp. 74–88, Henri Rey-Flaud, "Le Sang sur la neige: analyse d'une image-écran de Chrétien de Troyes," *Littérature* 37 (1980): 15–24, and Busby, *Perceval (Le Conte du Graal)* (London: Grant & Cutler, 1993), pp. 42–46.

24. On Blanchefleur, see Alice M. Colby[-Hall], *The Portrait in Twelfth-Century French Literature: An Example of the Stylistic Originality of Chrétien de Troyes*, Histoire des Idées et Critique Littéraire 61 (Geneva: Droz, 1965), esp. pp. 164–69.

25. Agreement of the adjective *blanche* in the singular is with the closer of the two nouns.

26. Not naming it, but suggesting it by the verb *(se) mirer* (6636, B6676; 6754, B6796; 6789, B6839) (to look at oneself in a mirror). As for Oiseuse, see Guillaume de Lorris and Jean de Meun, *Le Roman de la Rose*, ed. Armand Strubel, Lettres Gothiques (Paris: Librairie Générale Française, 1992), vs. 557.

27. On the Malevolent Maiden's characterization, see Frédérique Le Nan, "La *Male Pucele* aux bornes de Galvoie," in *"Le Conte du Graal: Chrétien de Troyes*," ed. Danielle Quéruel (Paris: Ellipses, 1998), pp. 74–88. For Le Nan, however, the Malevolent Maiden's mirror is more like the perilous mirror of Narcissus than that of Oiseuse (pp. 77, 87–88); however, it does not threaten the one who gazes into it but those who fall into her trap.

28. See Colby[-Hall], *The Portrait*, pp. 173–77, and Corinne Pierrevieille, "Figures féminines dans *Le Conte du Graal*," in *Le Conte du Graal: Chrétien de Troyes*, ed. Quéruel, pp. 89–101, esp. 91–92 and n. 4.

29. In "Arthurian Time and Space" I suggest that the condition of the Tent Maiden's skin, which has been subjected to extreme heat and cold (cf. 3695, B3729, below), indicates at least a year's exposure to the elements. My thanks to Monica E. Wright of the University of Louisiana at Lafayette for confirming that the quality of the dress she is likely to be wearing as a wealthy knight's lady is such that it would also have taken a much longer time to reach the state of disintegration described by Chrétien than seems to have lapsed in the plot since Perceval left her in her tent.

30. See Maddox, *Arthurian Romances of Chrétien de Troyes*, pp. 113–14, and below, MS. pp. 182–84, 189–93.

31. On arms for hunting and fighting, see Bruckner, *Chrétien Continued*, pp. 148–65, esp. 153–57.

32. An example of destructive speech, "Vilain gap" (wicked [uncouth] gossip) and "parole estote" (prideful words) (22), which Count Phillip, in charity, does not tolerate and for which Arthur rebukes Kay: "Vilenie est d'autrui gaber / Et de promettre sans doner" (997–98, B1017–18) (It is a wicked thing to mock another and to promise without giving). See Micheline de Combarieu du Grès, "Les Enjeux de la langue dans *Le Conte du Graal*," in *Le Conte du Graal: Chrétien de Troyes*, ed. Quéruel, 43–61, esp. 48–50.

33. Above, pp. 24–25.

Notes—Chapter 1

34. *Guigemar*, 76–102, in *Lais de Marie de France*, ed. Karl Warnke, trans. Laurence Harf-Lancner, Lettres Gothiques (Paris: Livre de Poche, 1990).

35. Perceval in fact encounters a relatively new technology in the knight's lance. Gerard J. Brault, *The Song of Roland: An Analytical Edition*, 2 vols. (University Park and London: Pennsylvania State University Press, 1978), 1: 355, n. 192, comments that the terms *espiet* (spear, *also* javelin) and *lance* (= *hanste*) are interchangeable in the Oxford *Roland* (ca. 1130), but adds that lances are not thrown. However, the Bayeux Tapestry (ca. 1075) shows knights holding lances both underhanded (esp. scene 19), ready to thrust, and overhanded, some apparently preparing to hurl them (scenes 18 and esp. 51, where lance-length weapons are sailing through the air, and scenes 55–56; in scene 52, knights are thrusting overhanded like foot soldiers generally, who most often thrust and hurl overhanded (scenes 19, 51). Scene numbers are standard in images of the Tapestry published by the Ville de Bayeux, e.g., *La Tapisserie de Bayeux-The Bayeux Tapestry-Wandteppich von Bayeux*, but in David M. Wilson, *The Bayeux Tapestry* (New York: Thames & Hudson, 1985), p. 21 = scene 18, pp. 22–23 = scene 19, pp. 59–60 = scene 51, pp. 62–63 = scene 52, pp. 67–69 = scenes 55–56. Michael Prestwich, *Armies and Warfare in the Middle Ages: The English Experience* (New Haven and London: Yale University Press: 1999), pp. 26–27, describes ash lances at the time of the Norman Conquest as light weapons to be thrown or thrust; only later did they develop into longer, heavier lances that were carried upright and lowered to strike. According to Kelly DeVries and Robert D. Smith, *Medieval Weapons: An Illustrated History of Their Impact* (Santa Barbara: ABC-CLIO, 2007), pp. 129–30, who describe weapons in the Bayeux Tapestry, the conversion began in roughly the mid-twelfth century. See esp. Michel Zink, "Renouart et Perceval: le tinel et le javelot," in *Literatur, Geschichte und Verstehen: Festschrift für Ulrich Mölk zum 60. Geburtstag*, ed. Hinrich Hugge and Udo Schöning with Friedrich Wolfzettel (Heidelberg: Winter, 1997), pp. 277–86.

36. The Red Knight raises his lance with both hands and strikes Perceval with the shaft (1083–88, B1103–08) in a show of contempt indicating that he does not consider his challenger worthy of being attacked as though he were a knight.

37. Ernst Robert Curtius, *European Literature and the Latin Middle Ages*, trans. Willard Trask (1953; rev. Princeton: Princeton University Press, 1953), pp. 512–13. See Lionel J. Friedman, "Gradus amoris," *Romance Philology* 19 (1965): 167–77; Douglas Kelly, "The Logic of the Imagination in Chrétien de Troyes," in *The Sower and His Seed: Essays on Chrétien de Troyes*, ed. Rupert T. Pickens (Lexington, KY: French Forum, 1983), 9–30; and Don A. Monson, *Andreas Capellanus, Scholasticism, and the Courtly Tradition* (Washington: Catholic University of America Press, 2005), pp. 303–05 and *passim*.

38. Matthieu de Vendôme, *Ars versificatoria*, 4.30, in *Arts poétiques du XIIe et du XIIIe siècles*, ed. Edmond Faral (Paris: Champion, 1962), p. 183, mentions six steps: *intuitus* (looking), *concupiscentia* (desire), *accessus* (approach), *colloquium* (conversation), *blandimentum* (caressing), and *congressio*. Andreas Capellanus (Book 1, ch. 6, First Dialogue) reduces the number to four, omitting looking because it is a given (Monson, *Andreas Capellanus*, p. 304) and paraphrasing the others: *spei datio* (giving hope: *alloquium*), *osculi exhibitio* (granting a kiss: *basia*), *amplexus fructio* (enjoying an embrace: *contactus*), *totius personae concessio* (surrendering the whole person: *factum*); see P.G. Walsh, ed. and trans., *Andreas Capellanus on Love* (1982; rpt. London: Duckworth, 1993), and André le Chapelain, *Traité de l'amour courtois*, trans. Claude Buridant (Paris: Klincksieck, 1974), n. 19, pp. 214–16.

39. As he naïvely tells the Tent Maiden, "mout meillor beisier vos fet / Que chanbriere que il et / An tote la meison ma mere, / Que n'avez pas la boiche amere" (your kiss is much better than that of any chambermaid in all my mother's household, because your mouth is not bitter) (707–10, B725–28).

40. Later the Orgueilleus de la Lande uses the same expression in relationship to kissing as he degrades the Tent Maiden (3830, B3863).

41. See Lori Walters, "The Image of Blanchefleur in Montpellier, BI, Sect. Méd. H 249," in *Les Manuscrits de/The Manuscripts of Chrétien de Troyes*, ed. Keith Busby, Terry Nixon, Alison Stones, and Lori Walters, 2 vols. (Amsterdam and Atlanta: Rodopi, 1993), 1: 437–52, a comprehensive codicological study of the manuscript in question with an extensive analysis of Blanchefleur's character and her relationship with Perceval.

42. "Et se je onques fis devise / An biauté

Notes—Chapter 1

que Dex eüst mise / An cors de fame ne an face, / Or me replest que une an face / Ou ge ne mantirai de mot" (And if ever before I have described the beauty God formed in a woman's face or body, I would like to [make one now] that would never vary from the truth) (1885-89, B1905-09). See Colby[-Hall], *Portrait*, pp. 164-69, and Duggan, *Romances of Chrétien de Troyes*, pp. 300-03.

43. Summarized by Ruth Harwood Cline, trans., *Perceval or the Story of the Grail* (Athens: University of Georgia Press, 1985), p. 59n. See also Lacy, *Craft of Chrétien*, pp. 62-66.

44. Perceval acquires other rhetorical powers at Biaurepaire (ch. 2, pp. 79-80).

45. On speech as sustenance, see *Cligés*, 4314-27, where Fenice is nourished by her lover's ambiguous parting words—he asks her leave "Come a cele qui je sui touz" (as the one [*his empress? his lover?*] to whom he belongs totally) (4269)—and her interpretation of them.

46. P.G. Walsh, *Andreas Capellanus*, p. 20, borrows the term from "the sublime language of the sociologists."

47. The pattern of simultaneity and chronological advancement here is a reflection of a similar construction in Anguigneron's and Clamadeus's parallel voyages from Biaurepaire to Arthur's court in Disnadaron, for example, as well as in the interlace of the Tent Maiden's story and, on a larger scale, in the intertwining trajectories of the Perceval and Gawain adventures.

48. *Joie* and *mervoille* (4677) are near-synonyms. At first Chrétien's narrator appears to follow the Old French rule concerning compounds, i.e., that subsequent adjectives and verbs agree in number and gender with the closer member, but by 4682 it is clear that he singles out *joie*, which is more highly charged erotically.

49. Compare *Erec et Enide*: after the couple's wedding, "Mout fu granz la *joie* ou palés, / Mais tot *le soreplus* vos les, / S'orroiz la *joie* et le delit / Qui fu en la chambre et ou lit" (2065-69, my emphasis) (Great was the *joy* in the palace, but I spare you *the rest*, and you will hear about the *joy* and delight there were in the bedchamber and in the bed). In the latter scene, Chrétien uses the erotic terms in reference to joyful celebration and to his own composition; a merging of celebratory and erotic joy also occurs in *Cligés*: concerning Soredamors and Alexandre's wedding, "De lor [i.e., des espousailles] richesce et des vitailles / Et de la *joie* et dou deduit, / Nus nel savroit dire, ce cuit, / Tant qu'as noces plus n'en eüst / ... / Trois *joies*, trois ennors i ot. / L'une fu dou chastel qu'il prist, / L'autre de ce que li promist / Li rois Artus qu'il li donroit / ... / Le meillor roiaume de Gales. / ... / La graindre [joie] fu la tierce, / De ce que sa fame fu fierce / De l'eschequier dont il fut rois" (2312-31) (about the wedding's richness and abundant foods, the joy and the delight, no one could tell before there are no more weddings.... There were three joys and honors for Alexandre: one was the castle he had won, the second that King Arthur promised him the best kingdom in Wales; the greatest joy was the third, that his wife was the queen of the chessboard where he was king).

50. "... dui valet ont aportee / Une table lee d'ivoire / ... dui autre vaslet vindrent / Qui aporterent deus eschaces / ... furent eles d'ebeneus" (3226-27, 3232-33, 3237; B3260-61, 3266-67, 3271) (two squires carried in a broad ivory table ... two other squires came bearing two trestles ... they were of ebony). Duggan, *The Romances of Chrétien de Troyes*, apropos of the Roche de Champguin as an otherworldly kingdom of the living and the dead, draws attention to the gates of Hell in the *Roman d'Eneas*. In the *Æneid*, which the *Eneas* translates, the gates are of horn, from which true dreams issue, and ivory, source of false dreams; Vergil's *Aeneid, Books I-VI*, ed. Clyde Pharr (Boston: D.C. Heath, 1930), VI: 892-96. There can be no doubt that Chrétien knew the *Eneas*: see, for example, Karl D. Uitti, with Michelle A. Freeman, "Christine de Pisan and Chrétien de Troyes: Poetic Fidelity to the City of Ladies," in *The Legacy of Chrétien de Troyes*, ed. Norris J. Lacy, Douglas Kelly, and Keith Busby 2 vols. (Amsterdam: Rodopi, 1987-1988), 2: 229-53, esp. 229-36, and esp. *Chrétien de Troyes Revisited* (New York: Twayne, 1995), pp. 104-18. Here the *Eneas* reads: "Dous grant portes a en enfer, / n'a en nule ne fust ne fer: / l'une porte est eborine [*through which false dreams pass, cf.* 3002] / et l'autre anprés si est cornine [*true dreams, cf.* 3004]" (2997-3000) (There are two gates in Hell, and in neither one is there wood or iron: one gate is of ivory [*false dreams*] and the other is of horn [*true dreams*]; *Eneas: Roman du XIIe siècle*, ed. J.-J. Salverda de Grave (Paris: Champion, 1968), my translation. If Chrétien had this passage in mind, which is plausible, he must have misread *eborine* (of ivory) as "of ebony," cf. *eborin* (of ivory) vs. *ebeine*, *ebenus* (ebony) in Alan Hindley, Frederick W. Langley, and Brian J. Levy, eds., *Old French-*

English Dictionary (Cambridge: Cambridge University Press, 2000); Chrétien's reading of the *Eneas* may also influence the description of the high table at the Grail Castle.

51. Haidu, *Aesthetic Distance*, pp. 247–49, is the first to remark on importance of the peg-leg.

52. See below, p. 85, and Ch. 3, n. 3.

53. "Vos oïssiez ja tex noveles / Qui vos enuiassent mout fort, / Se fust ce que ge vos port / Conpaignie et si vos condui" (7630–33, B7672–75) (You would already have heard some news that would have been most distressing were I not accompanying you and serving as your escort). By its name, the guardian's prosthesis (*eschace*, 7610, B7652) also recalls the ebony trestles that support the high table at the Grail Castle (see above, Ch. 1, n. 50).

54. Algirdas-Julien Greimas, *Grand Dictionnaire ancien français* (Paris: Larousse, 2007), s.v. *fraisne*: "*fraisnin* adj. (1080 [sic], *Rol[and]*)." De frêne, épithète fréquent de lance" (*fraisnin* adj. ... Made of ash wood, frequent descriptor of *lance*). Cf. Ovid, *Metamorphoses*, 10: 93: "coryli fragiles et fraxinus utilis hastis" (breakable hazels and the ash good for making spears).

55. That is, his *niece* (1881, B1901). Busby is right to define *niece* in the *Conte del Graal* as granddaughter (Busby, ed., p. 569, s.v. *niece*) and not "niece," as, for example, in Greimas, *Grand Dictionnaire*, s.v. *nieçain*. Blanchefleur implies a distinction in relationship between Gornemant and "un[s] miens oncles" (1891, B1911) ([an] uncle [of mine]), a prior, who has provided her with meager food supplies. In the Galloway Section, Clarissant (8227, B8269), the Old Queen's *niece* (8249, B8275), is clearly her granddaughter. See below, Ch. 2, n. 5.

56. "Ce[l] jor meïsmes uns granz vanz / Ot par mer chaciee une barge / Qui de froumant portoit grant charge / Et d'altre vitaille estoit plainne: / Si con Deu plot, antiere et sainne / Est devant le chastel venue" (2490–95, B2524–29) (That very day a powerful storm had driven across the waters a ship heavily laden with wheat and filled with other provisions; it was God's will that it came whole and undamaged to the foot of the castle). In a superb example of paralepsis, Haidu, *Aesthetic Distance*, p. 165, appears to underrate the significance of the event: "The Clamadeus sequence is also enlivened by the pleasant scene in which a merchant ship arrives with victuals ...," etc. Chrétien's narrator regards the ship's arrival as an act of divine intervention, but his view is undercut by the fact that the merchants sell their food to the starving populace. As for churches in the conventional Gawain adventures, church bells are rung in Escavalon to alert the populace that their enemy Gawain is in town (5908, B5942), while in Tintagel Gawain goes to early morning Mass with his host's family the day he fights Meliant de Lis (5446–53, B5480–87).

57. Yet there also appears to be a larger gate (5136, B5170) through which, at certain times, a crowd of armed knights (5132–47, B5166–81) and at least one horse (5483–97, B5517–31) may pass more easily than they might through a narrow postern.

58. For details, see Pickens, "*Le Conte du Graal*: Chrétien's Unfinished Last Romance," pp. 171–76. On hospitality as a structuring device, see Matilda T. Bruckner, *Narrative Invention in Twelfth-Century French Romance: The Convention of Hospitality (1160–1200)* (Lexington, KY: French Forum, 1980).

Chapter 2

1. The term *charité* occurs nine times in Chrétien's works: once in *Yvain*: Chrétien de Troyes, *Le Chevalier au lion ou le Roman d'Yvain*, ed. and trans. David Hult, Lettres Gothiques (Paris: Livre de Poche, 1994), 2839, apropos of the Charitable Hermit who feeds the insane wildman Yvain, and eight in the *Conte del Graal*: 43, 46, 47, 48, 52, and 59 (Prologue); 6599 (B6639) and 9161 (B9211). See Marie-Louise Ollier, *Lexique et concordance de Chrétien de Troyes d'après la copie de Guiot* (Montréal: Institut d'Études Médiévales, Université de Montréal, and Paris: Vrin, 1986). On the Charitable Hermit and Perceval's Hermit Uncle, see Debora B. Schwartz, "*Par bel mentir*: Chrétien's Hermits and Clerkly Responsibility," in *Translatio Studii: Essays in Honor of Karl D. Uitti for His Sixty-Fifth Birthday*, eds. Renate Blumenfeld-Kosinski, Kevin Brownlee, Mary B. Speer, and Lori J. Walters (Birmingham, AL: Summa, 2000), pp. 287–309.

2. "Diliges proximum tuum, sicut teipsum" (Thou shalt love thy neighbour as thyself) (Matthew 22:39); "dimitte nobis debita nostra sicut et nos dimisimus debitoribus nostris" (And forgive us our debts, as we also forgive our debtors) (Matthew 6:12).

3. The recurrence of Chrétien's name in 1650 (B1670) is noteworthy. The allusion is amusing, to be sure, but it also recalls other ways in which Perceval reflects the poet

Notes—Chapter 2

(above, pp. 17–20). Cf. Chrétien's play on his name in the *Erec et Enide* prologue: "Des or comencerai l'estoire / Que toz jors iert en memoir / Tant con durra crestïenté. / De ce s'est Chrestïens ventez" (ed. Fritz, 23–26) (Now I'll begin the story, which will be remembered forever, as long as Christendom shall endure. Chrétien has boasted of this).

4. The passage 1637–42 (B1657–62) is obscure in the manuscript tradition (Pickens, ed., pp. 455–56n), but despite "pucele ou fame" (maiden or woman) in 1637, the feminine participle in 1639, and feminine pronouns in 1640–41, Busby's reading is superior: "home ne fame" (man or woman) (B1657). See B1657–61 and variants, Busby, ed., pp. 69 and 448nn.

5. See above, Ch. 1, n. 55. She is his *niece* (1881) (granddaughter). Gornemant is an extraordinarily rich, powerful and courtly nobleman, she says, but she has not had contact with him for a long time (1864–89, B1884–1909). Like Perceval at first, Blanchefleur lacks the protection of a father or any other male adult.

6. As Perceval's Hermit Uncle tells him, another *parole* (6372; B6406: *proiere*) of his mother, i.e., her prayers on his behalf, has saved him from utter destruction.

7. Although Saly, "La Récurrence des motifs en symétrie inverse," rightly regards the Hermitage episode as pivotal, she does not analyze it in relation to the Waste Forest but instead pairs it with the Grail Castle (p. 29), a *rapprochement* that is also rich in signification.

8. She is "la veve dame / De la Gaste Forest soutainne" (the widowed lady of the [isolated] Waste Forest) (74–75). She tells Perceval, "Vostre peres cest manoir ot / Ici an ceste forest gaste" (Your father had this manor in this [waste] forest) (432–33).

9. As are in truth lands around Biaurepaire, certain parts of Galloway, Orkney, etc. Cf. *gaste*: "abandoned, wild, deserted; laid waste, in poor condition, ravaged, devastated, ruined, arid, uncultivated; violated (of a woman); terre g., wasteland" (Hindley, Langley, and Levy, *Old French-English Dictionary*).

10. The day Perceval meets the five knights on his mother's estate, six harrows drawn by two oxen each are at work in her oat field (80–84).

11. Hindley, Langley, and Levy, *Old French-English Dictionary*: *desert*[1] (noun): "desert; wilderness; wasteland; destruction, ruin."

12. Unlike what is implied by *forest gaste* or *gaste forest*, a medieval *forest* unqualified (in post-Merovingian France, or post-Conquest England) should not necessarily be construed as a forest wildwood in the usual American sense, but as managed hunting preserve with wooded areas, coppices, and open spaces such as fields and meadows. See Oliver Rackham, *Ancient Woodland: Its History, Vegetation and Uses in England* (London: Edward Arnold, 1980), pp. 1–6, 106–54, esp. 131–44, etc., and *Woodlands* (London: Harper Collins, 2006), pp. 25–27, 116–33; also Logan E. Whalen and Rupert T. Pickens, "Gardens and Anti-Gardens in Marie de France's *Lais*," *Romance Philology* 66 (2012): 185–210.

13. That is, if they are like the Charitable Hermit in *Yvain*. Their quality of life is in fact considerably higher than his before Yvain begins bringing him venison. Like him, they eat bread and drink clear water, but his moldy barley bread, kneaded with straw, is tough and bitter-tasting, while even on Good Friday, when the anchorites eat only bread and wild herbs, the bread they share is made of barley and oats; they also have grain and straw enough to feed Perceval's horse (6463–68, B6501–06). The Charitable Hermit's lot improves markedly after he befriends Yvain. Then he has venison to eat and sells the hides to buy bread superior to that to which he has been accustomed (2831–95). The anchorites' means of acquiring good bread may well mirror that of Yvain's benefactor; see Peter Haidu, "The Hermit's Pottage: Deconstruction and History in *Yvain*," *The Sower and His Seed: Essays on Chrétien de Troyes*, ed. Pickens, pp. 127–45, rpt. *Romanic Review* 74 (1983): 1–15.

14. As above: "Volantiers alez au mostier / Proier Celui qui tot a fait / Que de vostre ame merci ait / Et qu'an cest siegle terrïen / Vos gart come son crestïen" (go gladly to church and pray Him who made all to have mercy on your soul and keep you [His] true Christian in this earthly life).

15. Chrétien does not account for any previous attendance at church except implicitly, perhaps, at Blanchefleur's city of Biaurepaire, where Perceval displays knowledge of the convent and monastery (below, pp. 79–80). Having mistaken the Tent Maiden's pavilion for a church, Perceval stumbles upon the Grail Castle when, in terms of his mother's determination of subsequent events, he might have visited a real church.

16. As a knight customarily "de-*fies*,"

170

Notes—Chapter 2

breaks faith with, an enemy before attacking him. Similarly, Blanchefleur's enemy *Clamadeu(s) des Isles* may be one who accuses or makes perhaps unwarranted demands of God (Old French *clamer* in some senses of modern *réclamer*).

17. See below, pp. 64–66 and esp. Ch. 2, n. 33.

18. Matthew 22:37-39: "Ait illi Iesus: Diliges Dominum Deum tuum ex toto corde tuo, et in tota anima tua, et in tota mente tua. Hoc est maximum, et primum mandatum. Secundum autem simile est huic: Diliges proximum tuum, sicut teipsum. In his duobus mandatis universa lex pendet et prophetae" (Jesus said to him [a Pharisee]: Thou shalt love the Lord thy God with thy whole heart, and with thy whole soul, and with thy whole mind [= Deuteronomy 6:5]. This is the greatest and the first commandment. And the second is like unto this: Thou shalt love thy neighbour as thyself [= Leviticus 19:18]. On these two commandments dependeth the whole law and the prophets). On spiritual *caritas* in the twelfth century, see Michael S. Sherwin, O.P., "Aquinas, Augustine, and the Medieval Scholastic Crisis Concerning Charity," in *Aquinas the Augustinian*, ed. Michael Dauphinais, Barry David, and Matthew Levering (Washington, D.C.: Catholic University of America Press, 2007), pp. 182–204, who draws on Robert Wielockx, "La Discussion scolastique sur l'amour d'Anselme de Laon à Pierre Lombard d'après les imprimés et les inédits" (diss. Université Catholique de Louvain, 1981), cf. Wielockx, "La Sentence '*De caritate*' et la discussion scolastique sur l'amour," *Ephemerides Theologicae Lovaniensis* 58 (1982): 50–86, 334–56; 59 (1983): 26–45. The anonymous *De caritate*, which is associated with the cathedral school of Laon, advances a pseudo-Augustinian doctrine: " 'We should love ourselves for God's sake ... [i.e.,] we should love God and serve him,' ... [and] 'just as we love ourselves that God may be served, likewise should we love our neighbor that God may be served' " (Sherwin's translation, p. 186, of *De caritate*, §§8–9, 18–19). This view was attacked by Hugh of St. Victor (*De sacramentis*, PL 176: 534) and is opposed to a *caritas* springing from the desire to love and take joy in the beloved (also Augustinian) that is expressed in much courtly literature (Sherwin, pp. 181–83) and in Victorine and Cistercian traditions. According to Sherwin, both sides failed to understand the true essence of Augustinian charity (pp. 194–95) before the elegant solution offered in the next century by Aquinas (pp. 195–204). See also Ann Astell, *The Song of Songs in the Middle Ages* (Ithaca and London: Cornell University Press, 1990), pp. 1–104, and Kathleen Andersen-Wyman, *Andreas Capellanus on Love? Desire, Seduction, and Subversion in a Twelfth-Century Latin Text* (New York: Palgrave Macmillan, 2007), pp. 116–57.

19. The term occurs of John of Salisbury's *Policraticus*, book 6, ch. 5, in *Johannis Saresberriensis Opera Omnia*, ed. J.A. Giles, vol. 4 (Oxford: J.H. Parker, 1848), p. 15.

20. "...secundum primum modum lex nova non est alia a lege veteri, quia utriusque est unus finis, scilicet ut homines subdantur Deo ... Alio modo lex nova est alia a lege veteri, quia lex vetus est quasi paedagogus puerorum, ut Apostolus dicit, ad Gal. [3:24]; lex autem nova est lex perfectionis, quia est lex caritatis, de qua Apostolus dicit, ad Coloss. [3:14], quod est *vinculum perfectionis*." (... in the first sense, the New Law does not differ from the Old Law, because both have the same end, which is that man should be subject to God.... In the second sense, the New Law does differ from the Old. For the Old Law is a tutor for the young, as Paul says [Galatians 3:24], but the New Law is a law of perfection, since it is the law of charity, which Paul calls the *bond of perfection* [Colossians 3:14]); Thomas Aquinas, *Summa Theologica: Latin Text and English Translation*, vol. 30, ed. and trans. Cornelius Ernst, O.P., (Cambridge, Blackfriars, 1972), *Prima Secundae*, Quaestio 107, pp. 22–23. Cf. "... quia invicem onera vestra portatis, impletis legem sacratissimam caritatis. Ipsa est enim lex Christi; lex caritatis est lex Christi" (because you bear one another's burdens, you have fulfilled the most holy Law of Charity, that is, the very law of Christ: the Law of Charity is the law of Christ), Sermon 5 of "De verbis Apostolis ad Galatas," attributed to St. Augustine of Hippo, *Sancti Aurelii Augustini, Hipponensis episcopi, Operum supplementum quarta*, ed. D.A.B. Caillau (Paris: Parent-Desbarres, 1839), p. 83, commenting on Galatians 6:2, "Alter alterius onera portate, et sic adimplebitis legem Christi" (Bear ye one another's burdens: and so you shall fulfill the law of Christ). Cf. Matthew 22:37–39, above, Ch. 2, n. 13.

21. See, for example, Marie Anne D'Arcy, "*Li Anemis meismes*: Satan and Synagogue in *La Queste del Saint Graal*," *Medium Ævum* 66 (1997): 207–35, which establishes a 12th-century context of anti-Semitism; Peter Viereck, "Metapolitics Revisited," *Humanitas* 16 (2003): 48–75; Paul Lawrence Rose, *Wag-*

Notes—Chapter 2

ner: *Race and Revolution* (New Haven and London: Yale University Press, 1992), esp. pp. 158–69, cf. Nazi regalia in Hans Jürgen Syderberg's filmization of Wagner's *Parsifal* (1982), see Ulrich Müller, "Blank, Syberberg, and the German Arthurian Tradition," in *Cinema Arthuriana: Twenty Essays*, ed. Kevin J. Harty, (rev. Jefferson, NC: McFarland, 2002), pp. 177–84, esp. 181, 183 n. 5. A contributor to neo-Nazi websites is self-identified as Parsifal.

22. On the basis of the variant "preudome" (noble man) in reference to the Hermit for "boen home/saint home " (good man/holy man) (6269, B6303; 6283, B 6317) found in several manuscripts, Sargent-Baur, *La Destre*, pp. 150–51, makes the point that Perceval's quest for the Hermit conforms with his mother's counsel to seek out *prodomes* (gentlemen [noble men], 545, B563). *Boen home* is in fact a near synonym of *preudome*, see discussion of "le bon roi Artu" (good King Arthur) below, p. 138.

23. He hears confession and assigns penance as a precondition for absolution, which he is apparently authorized to grant. The text does not specify whether it is he or the second priest who celebrates the Easter Mass.

24. Significantly, at Biaurepaire Perceval fights Anguigneron under the sign of the True Cross, which, like much else, he later forgets (6189, B6223): he is sent out from the castle with the prayer "... icele voire croiz / Ou Dex sofri pener son fil / Vos gart hui de mortel peril / Et d'anconbrier et de prison, / Et vos remaint a garison / An leu ou vos soiez a eise / Qui vos delit et qui vos pleise" (may the true Cross on which God let His own Son suffer protect you today from death, difficulty or capture, and bring you back safely to where you will find comfort, happiness, and pleasure) (2134–40, B2168–74).The blessing is consonant with his mother's efficacious prayer (below, MS. pp. 80–85).

25. See Bonnie Buettner, "The Good Friday Scene in Chrétien de Troyes' *Perceval*," *Traditio* 36 (1980): 415–26. Eric Rohmer's film *Perceval le Gallois* concludes with a much-criticized "Passion Play," which is in fact a sung performance of the Passion Gospel chanted in the style of Notre-Dame de Paris at the end of the twelfth century, which Perceval may well have heard read or changed on Good Friday; see Jeff Rider, *et al.*, "The Arthurian Legend in French Cinema: Robert Bresson's *Lancelot du Lac* and Erich Rohmer's *Perceval le Gallois*," in *Cinema Arthuriana: Twenty Essays*, ed. Kevin J. Harty, pp. 149–62, esp. 156–58.

26. The significance of names and surnames is alluded to by Perceval's mother in her advice to seek out noble men: "N'aiez longuement conpaignon / Que vos ne demandez son non; / Le non sachiez par la parsome, / Car par le non conuist an l'ome" (never keep company with anyone for very long ... without asking his name; learn his name well, for by the name one knows the man) (541–44, B561–64), cf. Morawski, 1100: "Le nom ensuit l'ame" (the name follows from the soul). Six manuscripts (*BEHQTV*) read "sornon" (surname) in either 543 or 544 (B561–62) (see Busby, ed., variants). On names and surnames, see esp. Sargent-Baur, *La Destre*, pp. 119–38. The theme of naming is also reflected in the powerful prayer with the Holy Names of God which the Hermit teaches Perceval (6445–55, B6481–91).

27. Except according to an interpolation in *AL*, f. 339 (B342), where the knights' captain asks the boy's name and he responds with terms of affection or respect which his mother and her serfs have used to address him: "Biax Filz" (Fair Son), "Biau[s] Frere" (Fair Brother), and "Biau[s] Sire" (Fair Lord); see Pickens, ed., Appendix I, pp. 502–03; Busby, ed., pp. 427–28, n. to 343–60.

28. For example, Duggan, *The Romances*, pp. 80–81, and Ben Ramm, *A Discourse for the Holy Grail in Old French Romance*, Gallica 2 (Cambridge: D.S. Brewer, 2007), pp. 115–19. On the nature of Perceval's sin, see David G. Hoggan, "Le Péché de Perceval: pour l'authenticité de l'épisode de l'ermite dans le *Conte du Graal* de Chrétien de Troyes," *Romania* 93 (1972): 50–76; Amelia A. Rutledge, "Perceval's Sin: Critical Perspectives," *Œuvres et Critiques* 5.2 (1981): 53–60; Fanni Bogdanow, "The Mystical Theology of Bernard de Clairvaux and the Meaning of Chrétien de Troyes' *Conte du Graal*," in *Chrétien de Troyes and the Troubadours: Essays in Memory of the Late Leslie Topsfield*, ed. Peter S. Noble and Linda Paterson (Cambridge: St. Catherine's College, 1984), pp. 249–82; Claude Lachet, "La Confession de Perceval chez l'ermite: étude littéraire des vers 6136 à 6217 [= 6314–99, B6348–6475]," in *Le Conte du Graal: Chrétien de Troyes*, ed. Quéruel, pp. 62–72; Sargent-Baur, *La Destre*, pp. 139–64, 189–207; Uitti, with Freeman, *Chrétien de Troyes*, pp. 120–25; and Bruckner, *Chrétien Continued*, pp. 119–32. Bruckner succinctly restates the core paradox of the *felix culpa* (cf. Pickens, *Welsh*

Knight, pp. 108–33): "Perceval cannot arrive at the [Fisher King's] castle to ask the questions without causing his mother's death and thus incurring the very sin that prevents him, according to his maternal relatives, from asking the healing questions" (p. 125). Kibler's translation of 3560-61 (B3594-95) is unambiguous: misfortune "befell you because you sinned against your mother, who has died of grief on your account." In another light, Joseph Campbell, *The Masks of God: Creative Mythology* (New York: Viking, 1970), who has nothing but contempt for Chrétien's romance (pp. 226-30), discusses the *felix culpa* in Wolfram von Eschenbach's *Parzifal* (pp. 257-62, and *passim*). In fact, if the Paschal Vigil, the third of the Triduum observances, is celebrated at the Hermitage, Perceval would hear the *felix culpa* extolled in the *Exsultet*, where the paradox is expressed in terms of Adam's sin as a necessary prerequisite to redemption in Christ: "O felix culpa quae talem ac tantum meruit habere Redemptorem" (O happy fault that earned [for us] such a great and remarkable Redeemer).

29. Seven (*BFLMQRS*) of 15 manuscripts, two of which (*TV*) are "twins"; three of the seven (*BLR*) are close to Guiot's copy (*A*) (see Pickens, ed., pp. xxx-xxxii, and variants in Busby, ed., 3595).

30. Ewa Slojka, "Escape from Paradox: Perceval's Upbringing in the *Conte du Graal*," *Arthuriana* 18.4 (2008): 66-86.

31. M. Victoria Guerin, *The Fall of Kings and Princes: Structure and Destruction in Arthurian Tragedy* (Stanford: Stanford University Press, 1995), esp. pp. 140-95; cf. Duggan, *The Romances of Chrétien de Troyes*, pp. 78-79, 91, 259-60; David C. Fowler, *Prowess and Chivalry in the* Perceval *of Chrétien de Troyes* (Seattle: University of Washington Press, 1959), *passim*, and Daniel Poirion, "L'Ombre mythique de Perceval dans le *Conte du Graal*," *Cahiers de Civilisation Médiévale* 16 (1973): 191-98.

32. See Duggan, *The Romances of Chrétien de Troyes*, pp. 80-81, but absolute homophony depends on whether or not in Chrétien's language the /s/ before the voiceless affricate /tʃ/ represented by *ch* in *peschiere* was still articulated as /χ/ or had already fully disappeared.

33. I am most grateful to two eminent colleagues, both very good friends, who suggested, in discussion of my paper "*Perceval* and the Book of Sirach" (Kalamazoo, Michigan, May 11, 2013), that Perceval's mother is subject to the sin of *tristitia* (sorrow), a manifestation of an incapacitating passion or emotion close to a despair born of grief that is comparable with *acedia* (boredom, ennui), which is a gateway to the capital sin of *pigritia* (sloth). *Tristitia* is the emotion most frequently discussed by St. Thomas Aquinas (see reference to Robert Miner below). The sorrow that Perceval's mother feels is, however, of another order altogether. To be sure, she deeply grieves the certain loss of her youngest and last remaining son, who is soon to leave her. This is the last blow left for her to bear after the heartrending deaths of her husband and elder sons and her loss of fortune and status, but she does not hide from the light or will herself to die. Nor does she show signs of the kinds of indolence and despair stemming from *tristitia* or *acedia* that are suffered, according to Aquinas, by cloistered religious who are so distressed that they are incapable of contributing to the well-being of their community. Instead, she spends the last three days of her life fashioning a sturdy shirt, a pair of Welsh pants, and a buckskin cloak for her son to wear in his new life of adventure (478-86, B498-506). More to the point, she was in such a state of grace when she died, according to the Hermit, that her prayer to God to watch over and guide her son has had the power to sustain him through thick and thin for over five years (6369-74, B6411-16). If I cannot agree that Perceval's mother is afflicted with *tristitia*, the condition does indeed shed light on the kinds depression suffered by Perceval when he arrives at the Hermitage and Gawain when he is confined to the Roche de Champguin (see above, pp. 59-60), by the Malevolent Maiden when she seeks to commit "suicide by knight" (below, pp. 118-20), and by Arthur at Orkney (below, pp. 128-29, 148). The fatal grief suffered by Perceval's father because of the death of two sons, when he had a third who was alive (389-470, B407-88), represents perhaps the most extreme instance of *tristitia* in the romance. See St. Thomas Aquinas, *Summa Theologiae: Latin Text and English Translation*, vol. 35, ed. and trans. Thomas R. Heath, O.P. (Cambridge, Blackfriars, 1972), *Secunda Secundae*, Quaestio 35, pp. 20-35; also Robert Miner, *Thomas Aquinas on the Passions* (Cambridge, New York, et al.: Cambridge University Press, 2009), esp. pp. 188-212, and Ian Irvine, "*Acedia*, *Tristitia* and Sloth: Early Christian Forerunners to Chronic Ennui," *Humanitas* 12 (1999): 89-103, esp. 93-102.

Notes—Chapter 2

34. Half of the manuscripts including, Busby's base (*T*), read *parole* (*ABCHRTV*).

35. The very text discussed in Edelman, "A Scriptural Key," see above, p. 12, and Introduction, n. 4.

36. Cf. also Psalm 50:7/51:5: "ecce enim in iniquitatibus conceptus sum et in peccatis concepit me mater mea" (For behold I was conceived in inquities; and in sin did my mother conceive me).

37. *Enarratio in Psalmum CVIII*, Migne, *PL* 37: 1437. For details, see Appendix A.

38. In reference to Villon's *Testament*, for example, or in the curse of Ethelred the Unready attributed to St. Dunston inscribed on his tomb in Old St. Paul's Cathedral in London (destroyed in the Great Fire of 1666): "Quoniam aspirasti ad regnum per mortem fratris tui, in cujus sanguine conspiraverunt Angli cum ignominiosa matre tua, ... nec expiabitur nisi longa v[i]ndicta peccatum tuum, & *peccata matris tue*, & peccatum virorum qui interfuere consilio illius nequam" (Because you sought to acquire the kingdom through the death of your brother, in whose murder Anglians plotted with your reprehensible mother, ... may your sin, *the sins of your mother*, and the sin of the men who took part in her evil scheme not be forgiven except after a long punishment); John Weever, *Antient [sic] Funeral Monuments of Great-Britain, Ireland, and Islands Ajdacent* ... (London: W. Tooke, 1767), p. 148, my emphasis. More charitably, when St. Augustine hears of his mother's death, he entreats God concerning her sins: "Nunc pro peccatis matris meae deprecor te" (I now entreat you for my mother's sins); *The Confessions of Augustine*, ed. John Gibb and William Montgomery (Cambridge: Cambridge University Press, 1908), IX, 13, my translation.

39. Rabanus Maurus, *Commentarium in Ecclesiasticum* (840), Migne, *PL* 109: 763–1126, here 777. Translations are my own. On the Book of Sirach and esp. the passage Sirach 3:14-17, see Appendix B.

40. Cf. "... agat poenitentiam ori peccati, et offerat de gregibus agnam sive capram" (Leviticus 5:5-6) (Let him do penance for his sin, and offer of the flocks an ewe lamb, or a she goat).

41. *The Holy Bible* [Douay-Rheims] (3 vols. 1811–1814; rpt. in 1 vol. New York: Thomas Kelly, 1873), at Ecclesiasticus 3:16.

42. On the Vulgate's unique text by comparison with the Septuagint, see Appendix B.

43. See below, pp. 76–79.

44. Perceval's reticence in noble company surfaces in comedy when he arrives at Biaurepaire and sits in silence beside Blanchefleur along with a group of six knights who expect him to initiate conversation: they "virent celui qui se sist / Delez lor dame et mot ne dist" (looked at the knight who sat beside their lady and said nothing) (1835–36, B1855–56), and they whisper to one another that he must be mute, which is too bad for a knight whose beauty matches hers (1840–54, B1874–88). Without judgment, which he leaves to the knights, Chrétien's narrator explains, meanwhile, that "Por ce de parler se tenoit / Que del chasti li sovenoit / Que li prodom li avoit fet" (He refrained from speaking because he recalled the lesson the gentleman had given him) (1837–39, B1871–73).

45. Morawski 125: "A sage home afiert pou de parole" (Discretion in speech is becoming to a wise man), 1236: "Mieuz se vaut tere que folie dire" (It is better to keep silent than to speak folly) (cf. 1254), 2276: "Sovant est blamez qui trop est emparlez" (One who is too talkative is often blamed), 2428: "Trop parler nuist" (Talking too much does harm); cf. Schultze-Busacker 2276 (below), 2278 (quotes Gornemant), 2428, cf. 1236 and 1254.

46. In discussion of social aspects of verbal communication in general, see Danièle James-Raoul, *La Parole empêchée dans la littérature arthurienne* (Paris: Champion, 1997), pp. 110–11, who cites Sirach 27:5-8: "Sicut in percussura cribri remanebit pulvis, sic aporia hominis in cogitatu illius. Vasa figuli probat fornax, et homines iustos tentatio tribulationis. Sicut rusticatio de ligno ostendit fructum illius, sic verbum ex cogitatu cordis hominis. Ante sermonem non laudes virum; haec enim tentatio est hominum" (As when one sifteth with a sieve, the dust will remain: so will the perplexity of a man in his thoughts. The furnace trieth the potter's vessels, and the trial of affliction just men. The dressing of a tree sheweth the fruit thereof, so a word out of the thought of the heart of man. Praise not a man before he speaketh, for this is the trial of men). Concerning the *Conte del Graal* specifically, however, she discusses Perceval's silent distraction in the Blood Drops episode (esp. 4211–19, B4245–53), pp. 122–23, and his silence generally, in reference to Ecclesiastes 3:7, pp. 119–21.

47. Rabanus Maurus comments on vs. 7: "Mos est semper prudentium, ut moderent sermones suos, et aptum tempus observent: stultorum vero ut nec locum, nec tempus,

nec modum custodiant ..." (*PL* 109: 895) (It is always the way of the prudent to moderate their speech and to observe an appropriate time for it; it is most often the way of fools to take no notice of place or time or manner). The verse and commentary are reflected particularly in the Hideous Damsel's assessment of Perceval's behavior at the Grail Castle: "Ce est tu li maleüreus / Qui veïs qu'il fu tans et leus / De parler et si te taüs!" (And you are that wretched man, for you saw that it was the time and place to speak and you kept your silence) (4631-34, B4665-68).

48. Morawski and Schulze-Busacker 2276, cf. Morawski 1562: "On se puet bien trop teire" (One can refrain too much from speaking).

49. Which Rabanus Maurus (*PL* 109: 895) relates to Sirach 20:6.

50. The sequence in Sirach 20 concludes with a double warning (vs. 8): "Qui multis utitur verbis laedet animam suam" (He that useth many words shall hurt his own soul), which in fact recalls Proverbs 10:19, quoted by Gornemant de Gohort, and the social consequences of arrogant verbosity: "qui potestatem sibi sumit iniuste, odietur" (he that taketh authority to himself unjustly shall be hated).

51. Kathryn Gravdal perfectly captures the tenor in the latter episode when she comments that "rarely has sexual assault looked so endearing," in *Ravishing Maidens: Writing Rape in Medieval French Literature and Law* (Philadelphia: University of Pennsylvania Press, 1991), p. 51, cited by James R. Simpson, *Troubling Arthurian Histories: Court, Culture, Performance and Scandal in Chrétien de Troyes's* Erec et Enide, Medieval and Early Modern Studies 5 (Oxford: Peter Lang, 2007), pp. 231-32. See also Bruckner, *Chrétien Continued*, pp. 91-100.

52. The standard being the depth of the Hermit's analysis.

53. Cf. also "ceste forest gaste" (433, B451) (this wild forest). Later Gawain rides through "forez gastes et sostainnes" (7183, B7225) (lonely and uninhabited forests) in Galloway.

54. As in the Parable of Lazarus and the Rich Man: "Factum est ut moriretur mendicus, et portaretur ab angelis in sinum Abrahae. Mortuus est autem et dives, et sepultus est in inferno. Elevans autem oculos suos cum esset in tormentis, vidit Abraham a longe, et Lazarum in sinu eius" (Luke 16: 22-23) (And it came to pass, that the beggar died, and was carried by the angels into Abraham's bosom. And the rich man also died: and he was buried in hell. And lifting up his eyes when he was in torments, he saw Abraham afar off, and Lazarus in his bosom).

55. In the First Continuation and in Wolfram von Eschenbach's *Parzifal*, however, it also provides food for the banqueters. In Chrétien, the procession is apparently modeled on the presentation of courses at elegant medieval banquets. On Old French *graal*, see Joseph Goering's commentary on Héliant de Froidmont's well-known description of grails used to serve meat dishes at noble banquets in *The Virgin and the Grail* (New Haven and London: Yale University Press, 2005), pp. 59-70; Richard O'Gorman, "Grail," in *The New Arthurian Encyclopedia*, ed. Norris J. Lacy (New York and London: Garland, 1996), pp. 212-13; Pickens, "Grail," in *Medieval France: An Encyclopedia*, ed. William W. Kibler and Grover A. Zinn (New York and London: Garland, 1995), pp. 409-10; and Alfred Foulet, "Chrétien's Indebtedness to the *Alexandre décasyllabique*," in *The Romances of Chrétien de Troyes: A Symposium*, ed. Douglas Kelly, pp. 305-09. However, Jean-René Valette, *La Pensée du Graal: Fiction littéraire et théologique (XIIe-XIIIe siècle)* (Paris: Champion, 2008), pp. 146-47, following Daniel Poirion, "Semblance du Graal dans la *Queste*," in *Mélanges de littérature et de philologie médiévales offerts à J.R. Smeets*, ed. Quirinus Ignatius Maria Mok, Ina Spiele, and P.E.R. Verhuyck (Leyden: n.p., 1982), pp. 227-41, esp. 237, stresses the rarity of the term *graal* as a common noun before Chrétien's last romance. On early depictions of the Grail, see Emmanuèle Baumgartner, "Les Scènes du Graal et leur illustration dans les manuscrits du *Conte du Graal* et des *Continuations*," in *Les Manuscrits de Chrétien de Troyes/The Manuscripts of Chrétien de Troyes*, ed. Keith Busby, Terry Nixon, Alison Stones, and Lori Walters, 2 vols. (Amsterdam and Atlanta: Rodopi, 1993), 1: 489-503: illuminations in Chrétien manuscripts are influenced by later conceptions of the Grail.

56. As is confirmed in the Weeping Maiden's interrogation: "Et veïstes vos le Graal? / —Oïl bien" (3522-23) ("And did you see the grail?" —"Quite clearly").

57. See above, pp. 24-25, 65-66.

58. Thus it is ironically fitting that, when he guesses his name, it comes with a surname that openly betrays his origins: "Percevax li Galois" (3541, B3575) (Perceval the Welshman), which, because he has failed at the Grail Castle, the Weeping Maiden

changes to "Percevax li cheitis" (3548, B3582) (Perceval the wretched).

59. Not only his equation of *eleemosyna* and *caritas*, but also his understanding of the metonymic *locutio tropica* in Leviticus 4:3; see above, pp. 68–70. Cf. also "Cor sapientis intelligitur in sapientia, et auris bona audiet cum omni concupiscentia sapientiam. Sapiens cor et intelligibile abstinebit se a peccatis, et in operibus justitiae successus habebit. Ignem ardentem exstinguit aqua, et *eleemosyna* resistit peccatis: et Deus prospector est ejus qui reddit gratiam: meminit ejus in posterum, et in tempore casus sui inveniet firmamentum" (Sirach 3: 31–34, my emphasis) (The heart of the wise is understood in wisdom, and a good ear will hear wisdom with all desire. A wise heart, and which hath understanding, will abstain from sins, and in the works of justice shall have success. Water quencheth a flaming fire, and *alms* resisteth sins: And God provideth for him that sheweth favour: he remembereth him afterwards, and in the time of his fall he shall find a sure stay). Looking forward (below, pp. 104, 131–32), we shall see that, in the last lines Chrétien was ever to write, he again pairs *eleemosyna* and *caritas* in 9161 (B9211).

60. Norris H. Lacy, "Gauvain and the Crisis of Chivalry in the *Conte del Graal*," in *The Sower and His Seed: Essays on Chrétien de Troyes*, pp. 155–64.

Chapter 3

1. "le vis avoit deppicié, / Et out une plaie mout grief / D'une espee par mi le chief, / Et d'andeus pars par mi les flans / Li coroit a randon li sans" (6512–16, B6552–56).

2. Subsequently also referred to as the Orgueilleus de la Roche.

3. Keith Busby, *Gauvain in Old French Literature* (Amsterdam: Rodopi, 1980), p. 107, n. 42. Like *loins* in English, *reins* (lower back) and *flancs* (flanks) in French may refer to the body's center of strength and generative power.

4. Chrétien describes only the palfrey's head: "D'une part noire et d'autre blanche" (6781, B6823) (half black and half white). It could be a black horse with white markings or a black-and-white piebald; elsewhere it is described as *baucent* (dappled) (7220, B7262). Later Chrétien mentions that it is *crenu* (long-maned) (8927; B8975: *grenu*).

5. The garden within a garden inside a fortification within a walled city surrounded by a river serving as a moat gives the impression of *Inferno*-like concentric enclosures with the inner garden at the center.

6. Like the townspeople who warn Erec about the Joie de la Cort (*Erec et Enide*, 5690–5713) or those at the Chastel de Pesme Aventure who similarly attempt to persuade Yvain not to undertake the castle's adventure (*Yvain*, 5108–63)—supreme adventures in both romances. For Gawain at the Roche a l'Estroite Voie, the "adventure" of meeting the Malevolent Maiden is of a much different order.

7. When Greoreas advises Gawain to turn back and avoid the adventure, he replies that "Cist retorners seroit *vilains*: / Ge ne ving pas por retorner. / L'an le me devroit atorner / A trop leide recreantise, / Qant ge ai or la voie anprise, / Se ge de ci m'an retorneroie" (6576–81, B6616–21, my emphasis; B6616: *grevains* [grievous] for *vilains*) (it would be *unchivalric* to turn around: I didn't come here to turn back. It would be imputed as the worst sort of cowardice if I were to turn back after having chosen this road). Gawain responds in similar terms to the giant knight's warning (6756–59, B6798–6801).

8. Maddox, *Arthurian Romances of Chrétien de Troyes*, pp. 95–108, stresses the similarities among the Orgueilleus de la Lande, the Orgueilleus de la Roche, and the Orgueilleuse de Logres and the murders in which they are involved.

9. Or else Chrétien's narrator loses interest in maintaining the trail of evidence. At Biaurepaire Perceval fights Anguigneron on "un cheval" (2122, B2142) (a horse) and Clamadeus on "un cheval norrois" (2614, B2648) (a Norwegian steed), both apparently from the castle's stables. When he leaves in search of his mother, however, he is "Toz armez si com il i vint" (2941, B2975), presumably therefore astride the Red Knight's charger.

10. "Ez vos celui desconforté / Et angoisseus an son coraige" (784–85, B804–05) ([he] was distressed and tormented in his heart), "cil cui jalosie angoisse" (795, B815) ([a] man tormented by jealousy).

11. The Unruly Squire also shares with Arthur's Fool another of the Hideous Damsel's traits (above, pp. 19–20 and Ch. 1, n. 9) in that he utters a prophetic curse against Gawain after Gawain hits him: "La main et le braz an perdroiz / Don vos m'avez le cop doné, / Que je ne vos ert pardoné" (6996–98, B7038–40) (you'll lose the hand

Notes—Chapter 4

and arm with which you gave me that blow), cf. esp. the Fool's accurate prediction that, because Kay struck him and the Smiling Maiden, he will suffer a broken upper arm within forty days (1240–54, B1280–94). Greoreas comments that the squire should be left alone, "Que ja ne li orroiz rien dire / Ou vos doiez enor avoir" (7004–05, B7046–47) (for you'll never hear him say a word to your honor). In any case, the squire's prediction never comes to pass in Chrétien's romance.

12. "Einz vos donroie set destriers, / Se ges avoie si an destre, / Que son roncin, tex puet il estre" (6962–64, B7004–06) (I'd rather give you seven chargers, if I had them here with me, than this poor horse, such as it is).

13. "Vassax, qu'as tu a faire / Ou ge voise ne don je veingne? / Quel voie que ge onques teingne, / Li tuens cors ait male aventure!" (6972–75, B7014–17) ([Low-life], what's it to you where I'm going or where I'm coming from? Whatever road I'm taking, a curse upon you!).

14. Zrinka Stahuljak, Virginie Greene, Sarah Kay, Sharon Kinoshita, and Peggy McCracken, *Thinking Through Chrétien de Troyes*, Gallica 19 (Cambridge: D.S. Brewer, 2011), e.g., pp. 125–26.

15. Later, however (3816, B3850), he (ironically?) repeats his lady's phrase "valet galois" (771, B791) in describing Perceval, as though he has willfully disbelieved her.

16. See Appendix C, also Maddox, *Arthurian Romances of Chrétien de Troyes*, pp. 36–38, and, for the *Conte del Graal*, pp. 104–08.

17. A reflection of the advice of Perceval's mother, who forbids him the "soreplus," the *factum* of the *gradus amoris* (see above, pp. 36–40).

18. *Oan* (3911, B3845) literally means "sometime this year." Kibler justifiably translates "recently"; however, Chrétien's description of the bedraggled lady whom Perceval meets the second time suggests that summer and winter have passed since their first encounter; see above, MS. pp. 31–32 and Ch. 1, n. 29.

19. When the Malevolent Maiden first catches sight of Gawain as he approaches her, she shouts "Mesure, / Mesure, sire!" (Slow down! slow down, sir!) (6642–43, B6684–85), for she is certain that "Vos me volez / Prandre et porter ci contreval / Sor le col de vostre cheval" (You want to grab me and carry me down this hill across your horse's back) (6656–58, B6698–6700), and she is right: "Vos dites bien voir, dameisele!" (6659, B6701). She will not be carried on his or any other knight's horse, but agrees to "follow" him properly on her own palfrey (6660–77, B6702–19).

20. See below, pp. 104–105.

21. Morawski and esp. Schulze-Busacker 463.

22. The nag and its disreputable gear are described in details (7119–35, B7161–77) that recall the Tent Maiden's starving palfrey (3661–81, B3696–3714).

23. Her seamanship rivals that of the Ferryman. She is able to manage a boat large enough to accommodate herself and her palfrey as well as Gawain and his nag, for she asks him to join her with his beast (7221–38, B7263–80). As the craft is equipped with a single *aviron* (7224, B7266) (oar), which she would use as a tiller, it is clearly a sailboat. Her boat and her skills ironically align her with the Fisher King, the Ferryman, and perhaps the seamen whose boat is miraculously blown off course to provide supplies to Biaurepaire. Later she returns to the landing on horseback "led" by her current lover, the Orgueilleus de la Roche (8262–67, B8304–09); she may well have sailed all the way back to his castle by river and/or by sea.

24. Blanchefleur governs both the Biaurepaire episode (1690–2940, B1710–2974), even when she waits in her castle while Perceval is on the battlefield, etc., and the Blood Drops scene (4160–4427, B4194–4461): 1519 lines. The Malevolent Maiden is similarly present in 1125 lines: 6634–7329, B6676–7371; 7406–16, B7448–58; 8262–8566, B8304–8614; 8583–8600, B8631–48; 8862–8956, B8910–9004.

25. Not "yesterday," for Gawain has spent one night with his host the Ferryman and another in Ygraine's castle.

26. See above, pp. 59–60, and Ch. 1, n. 16.

Chapter 4

1. Aside from the implications of the Pietà image, Greoreas declares that "ainz Dex ne fist ne ne volt feire / Plus franche ne plus deboneire, / Plus cortoise, plus afeitiee. / Or me sanble que desheitiee / Est mout por moi, si n'a pas tort, / Que ele me voit pres de mort" (6605–10, B6645–50) (God never made or conceived of a more noble, better-bred, more courteous, or more gracious damsel. I believe she is downcast now on my account, and rightly so, for she sees me near death). Even so, as suggested earlier, he may well

Notes—Chapter 4

have left her alone and unprotected at the outpost in order to "lead" the Malevolent Maiden to the landing across from the Roche de Champguin.

2. Keith Busby, *Gauvain in Old French Literature*, p. 149, n. 50, observes that subsequent references to Gawain's abilities as a healer are frequent in Middle Dutch literature.

3. See Reinhold Köhler's remarks in *Die Lais der Marie de France*, ed. Karl Warnke, (1885; 3rd ed. Halle: Max Niemeyer, 1925), pp. clxxv-clxxix.

4. Although it may well be made of herbs, it was not made by the lady herself: "[D']un onguement me souvient / Que me donna Margue la sage, / Et si me dist que nule rage / N'est en la teste qu'il n'en ost" (*Yvain*, 2952–55) (I remember a salve that wise Morgan gave me, and she told me that there is no madness that it cannot drive out). Yvain's healing and rehabilitation follow his encounter with a charitable hermit; Greoreas's healing is preceded by Perceval's encounter with another charitable hermit.

5. As suggested by Marie de France's *Les Deus Amanz*, 96–108, 133–40. See Alain Touwaide, "The Legacy of Classical Antiquity in Byzantium and the West," *Health and Healing from the Medieval Garden*, ed. Peter Dendle and Alain Touwaide, Woodbridge, Suffolk: Boydell, 2008, pp. 15–28. Also Fulvio Gherli, ed. and trans., *Regola sanitaria salernitana: Regimen sanitatis salernitanum* (Rome: Edizioni & Gestioni Editoriali, n.d.), esp. pp. 43–65.

6. Pedanius Dioscorides, *De materia medica*, ed. and trans. Tess Anne Osbaldeston (Johannesburg: Ibidis Press, 2000). The text was translated into Latin as early as the sixth century and widely disseminated in Europe.

7. See, for example, Rudolph Abresman, "The Concept of the 'Christus Medicus' in St. Augustine," *Traditio* 10 (1954): 1–28. The theme is expressed as *summus Medicus* (supreme Physician) in the source of a St. Audrey miracle, see Pickens, "Marie de France *Translatrix* II: *La Vie seinte Audree*," ed. Logan E. Whalen (Leiden and Boston: Brill 2011), pp. 267–301, esp. 283.

8. Busby, *Gauvain in Old French Literature*, p. 112, remarks that Gawain speaks to Greoreas's distraught lover "with the confidence of a professional."

9. Ms. S (Paris, BnF fr. 1453), early fourteenth century.

10. Usually noted in dictionaries as "Deus vos lo mire" or "D. le vos mire" (God reward you) (e.g., Greimas, *Grand Dictionnaire ancien français*, and Hindley, Langley, and Levy, *Old French-English Dictionary*, s.v. *merir* and *mirer*). In 6922 (B6964), where *li* is a third-person indirect object that combines with the third-person direct object (*le* or *lo*), the latter regularly disappears in Old French.

11. My translation. Cf. "le chevalier / ... de mire eüst grant mestier" (the knight ... was in great need of a doctor) (6865–66, B6909–10).

12. Despite the facts that the nominative form *mires* is grammatically correct and that Chrétien himself is scrupulous in respecting the two-case system at a time when nominative –*s* was beginning to disappear.

13. See Ana Sofia Laranjinha, "Artur, Gauvain e Keu: representações da realeza em Chrétien de Troyes," *Línguas e Literaturas* 13 (1996): 23–39, esp. 30–31. Also in the Vulgate *Merlin*, trans. Pickens, vol. 2 of *Lancelot-Grail: The Old French Arthurian Vulgate and Post-Vulgate in Translation*, gen. ed. Norris J. Lacy (rev. Cambridge: D.S. Brewer, 2010), p. 140: "When he [Gawain] got up in the morning, he had the strength of the best knight of the world; by the time the hour of prime came, it had grown twofold; at tierce, the same thing. At midday, he went back to the strength he had at first, and at nones and all the nighttime hours, he always still had his first strength."

14. Ironic because the moon is not known for its constancy: for example, in the *Carmina burana*, ed. Ernst Buschor (Frankfurt am Main: Insel Verlag, 1964), p. 44: "O Fortuna / velut luna / statu variabilis, / semper crescis / aut decrescis" (O Fortuna, like the moon you are inconstant by nature, always waxing or waning).

15. See above, pp. 62–63.

16. The classic study remains Howard Rollin Patch, *The Goddess Fortuna in Mediaeval Literature* (Cambridge: Harvard University Press, 1927). For other relevant representations, see, for example, Norris J. Lacy, "The Ambiguous Fortunes of Arthur: The Lancelot-Grail and Beyond," in *The Fortunes of King Arthur*, ed. Norris J. Lacy, Arthurian Studies 64 (Cambridge: D.S. Brewer, 2005), pp. 92–103.

17. "... se tu [Perceval] demandé l'eüsses, / Li riches rois qui mout s'esmaie / Fust la toz gariz de sa plaie, / Et si tenist sa terre an pes, / Dont il ne tandra point ja mes" (4636–40) (if you had asked [the questions], the rich king who suffers so would already be healed of his wound and would be ruling in peace the land he'll never again rule).

Notes—Chapter 4

18. On this subject, see Sara Sturm-Maddox, " 'Tenir sa terre en païs': Social Order in the *Brut* and the *Conte del Graal*," *Studies in Philology* 81 (1984): 82–94.

19. See above, p. 53.

20. In addition to the fact that much information throughout the passage regards the Malevolent Maiden herself, she inhabits it by her visibility in the distance from where Guiromelant and Gawain stand (8505, B8561) (see above, p. 99 and Ch. 3, n. 24).

21. In a subset of manuscripts, Norgres (*BR*) or Nogres (*EMQT*), see variants in ed. Busby, ed., B8639 (=8591); unlike Roach, his predecessor in editing *T* (followed by Maddox in *Arthurian Romances of Chrétien de Troyes*), Busby adopts the common lesson.

22. Clarissant admits later that she has granted her love to Guiromelant from afar, for they have never met and have seen each other only from opposite sides of the river below the Roche de Champguin. She is astonished to hear that she might rather have her brother dead, although she believes that she has never laid eyes on him, than see Guiromelant slightly injured: he has lied on that point (8961–92, B9009–40).

23. The lesson in Busby, ed. is superior. In 8878, in Guiot's copy (*A*) and related manuscripts, gender agreement in the past is not respected: "Que por li a grant poinne tret" (since he has endured so much [grief] for her sake), cf. B8926: "Que por li a grant paine traite."

24. See above, pp. 60, 65–66, and esp. Ch. 2, n. 33.

25. Arthur reshapes and amplifies the proverb "Bel prometrre e nient doner fait fol conforter" (Morawski 230, cf. 1726) (Eloquent promising and giving nothing give comfort to a fool): "Vilenie est d'autrui gaber / Et de promette sanz doner" (997–78, B1017–18) (It is a wicked thing to mock another and to promise without giving), not cited by Schulze-Busacker. In light of Morawski 230, Perceval has indeed "taken comfort" in Kay's "promise" and brought it to fruition.

26. Gawain's brother Agravain is also surnamed "li Orguilleus" (4734, B4768). Gawain adds a second epithet when he speaks to Ygraine of King Lot's sons: "Agravains, / li Orguilleus as dures mains" (8097–98, B8139–40) (Agravain, the Proud Knight with tough hands). At Carlion Agravain prevents Gawain from striking Guiganbresil, who has accused him of murdering the king of Escavalon, and offers to defend his brother (4714–54, B4648–88). In the Lancelot-Grail Cycle, the youthful Agravain is known for his quick temper and, significantly, later becomes an ally of Mordred.

27. It is of interest that Guiromelant is the only one who has recently heard news that Arthur is in Orkney for Pentecost court, which surprises Gauvain (cf. 8848–53, B8896–8901).

28. "Celui qui plus li sanbla estre / Vistes et preuz et servïables / Et plus saiges et plus resnables" (9028–30, B9078–80) (the one who seemed the most eager and worthy and helpful, the wisest and most clever).

29. Issues involving Gawain's name are linked to a reflective sequence beginning with Perceval's encounter with the five knights and finds expression in his mother's advice to ask worthy men their names or surnames. For Perceval the sequence peaks in his self-naming in response to the Weeping Maiden, who is the first ever to ask his name; the sequence resurfaces in the Blood Drops episode, in the second Carlion episode, where the Hideous Damsel knows his name in advance, and finally at the Hermitage. Gawain willingly gives his name to Perceval when they meet in the Blood Drops episode (4450–52, B4484–86), but is reluctant to reveal it outside Arthur's court. He explains to Tiebaut de Tintagel that he must give his name whenever he is asked for it, but he does not reveal it otherwise (5588–91, B5622–25). Except for Tiebaut's enthusiastic response when he learns who Gawain is, he is shamed every time he is recognized or his identity is revealed (Escavalon, Greoreas, Guiromelant). He pointedly asks Ygraine not to ask him his name for a week after he becomes lord of her castle (8308–11, B8350–53), which will coincide with the day of his combat with Guiromelant.

30. Basic studies on the dating of Chrétien's works include Anthime Fourrier, "Encore la chronologie des œuvres de Chrétien de Troyes," *BBSIA* 2 (1950): 69–88, and Jean Misrahi, "More Light on the Chronology of Chrétien de Troyes," *BBSIA* 11 (1959): 89–120. More recently, June Hall McCash, "Reconsidering the Order of Chrétien de Troyes's Romances," in *Li Premiers Vers Essays in Honor of Keith Busby*," ed. Catherine M. Jones and Logan E. Whalen (Amsterdam and New York: Rodopi, 2011), pp. 245–60, argues that *Yvain* was begun after *Erec et Enide* and completed after *Cligés* and before the *Conte del Graal*.

31. The potential importance of Orkney in the *Conte del Graal* is suggested by the fact

that the toponym occurs more times than that of any other city or castle in the romance except one and in the space of just 300 lines to boot (8841, 9051, 9113, 9141; B8889, 9101, 9163, 9191); compare with Biaurepaire (4 times), Carlion (3), Disnadaron (2), and Carlion (2). Guiromelant's castle bears a related name: Orqueneles (8578, B8626).

32. The "ardant" suffer from burning or itching diseases such as mange, as translated, erysipelas, shingles, certain forms of gangrene, etc., which produce painful red weals and eruptions.

33. Kibler aptly translates *estranges*, but the word may also have sinister connotations (below, p. 141).

34. On Arthur's Fool and the power of prophesy in the *Conte del Graal*, see Sara Sturm-Maddox, "King Arthur's Prophetic Fool," *Marche Romane* 29 (1979): 101–08. The Charcoal Burner, Perceval's mother's serfs, and the commoners of Escavalon and Orkney—as well the Wise Vavassor of Escavalon, no doubt, but perhaps not the Unruly Squire—possess the gifts of insight and verediction.

35. William Roach, ed., *The Continuations of the Old French Perceval of Chrétien de Troyes*, vol. 1: *The First Continuation: Redaction of TVD* (Philadelphia: University of Pennsylvania Press, 1949), vv. 1–278.

36. See also Martín de Riquer, "La Composición de 'Li Contes del Graal' y el 'Guiromelant,'" *Boletín de la Réal Academia de Buenas Letras de Barcelona* 27 (1957–1958): 279–320, esp. 304–20, who suggests that the Gawain adventures originally constituted an independent romance written by Chrétien in tandem his *Perceval*.

37. Annie Combes, "The Continuations of the *Conte du Graal*," in *A Companion to Chrétien de Troyes*, ed. Norris J. Lacy and Joan Tasker Grimbert, pp. 191–201, here p. 193. The felicitous term "host romance" is Keith Busby's, in "The Continuations," in *The Arthur of the French*, ed. Glyn S. Burgess and Karen Pratt (Cardiff: University of Wales Press, 2006), pp. 222–47, here p. 224. For a more complete overview of the complex subject of the Continuations in their various redactions, see Roach's Introduction in *The Continuations*, vol. 1; for in-depth analyses of literary aspects of the Continuations, see Bruckner, *Chrétien Continued*, and Thomas Hinton, *The* Conte du Graal *Cycle* (Cambridge: D.S. Brewer, 2012).

38. Duggan, *The Romances of Chrétien de Troyes*, comments on the paradoxical nature of the Roche de Champguin: "[it] is not a land of the living, even though its fields teem with game. It is not a land of the dead either but, rather, an Other-world kingdom" (p. 84).

39. Although, according to G.D. West, *An Index of Proper Names in French Arthurian Verse Romances 1150-1300* (Toronto: University of Toronto Press, 1969), pp. 38, 139, it may perhaps survive as the Chastel as Puceles in the Second Continuation.

Conclusion

1. See Maddox, *Arthurian Romances*, pp. 113–16 and n.78.

2. Is he the same vavassor who discovers Gawain and the king's sister *in flagrante dilecto* (5798–5802, B5832–36, see above, p. 20)? Here an odd wording in the majority of manuscripts leads to the supposition that there may two counselors: "un vavasor" (6054, B6055), who is an advisor of long standing, and "uns sages vavasors" (6115, in *ABFLPQTV*, cf. *S*: ".i. sien v."; B6149: "li sages vavasors," in *CEHMRU*, which bears the definite article). In point of fact, although the difference here is of little consequence, Busby's choice of the latter provides the superior reading.

3. *Brut*, ed. Arnold, 1063–1250; cf. Geoffrey of Monmouth, *Historia*, ed. Wright, ch. 16. See Pickens, "Arthurian Time and Space."

4. Despite the fact that a generally accepted the chronology of Chrétien's romances in terms of Arthurian time is such that the *Conte del Graal* occurs at the end of the cycle rather than near the beginning, see Pickens, "Arthurian Time and Space." Perhaps Chrétien means to suggest that the chronology of the *Conte del Graal* embraces other romances, much as *Lancelot* and *Yvain* are demonstrably simultaneous.

5. Wace does not recount these adventures, but in one manuscript (*R*), Chrétien's five Arthurian romances, with the First Continuation following the *Conte del Graal*, are inserted into the *Brut* after 9798. In *A*, the *Conte del Graal* is preserved with *Brut* and other Arthurian romances by Chrétien; *H*, which begins with *Brut* and ends with the *Conte del Graal*, transmits other texts pertaining to British and English history.

6. See Philippe Ménard, "Problématique de l'aventure dans les romans de la table

ronde," in *Arturus Rex: Acta Conventus Lovaniensis 1987*, 2 vols., ed. Willy Van Hoecke, Gilbert Tournoy, and Werner Verbeke (Louvain: Leuven University Press/Presse, 1991), 2: 89–119, esp. 101. Also Sturm-Maddox, "King Arthur's Prophetic Fool."

7. Cazelles, *The Unholy Grail*, p. 96.

8. The lesson *les* (them) in Pickens, ed., is unique to MS. *A*; the common reading, as in Busby, ed., is superior.

9. See above, pp. 70–73.

10. Cf. Pickens, ed., p. 453n. See Cazelles, *The Unholy Grail*, pp. 94–101, who answers the question by suggesting that Escavalon and Gomeret were inimical to Arthur because of Gawain's alleged murder of the king of Escavalon and, she argues, his rivalry with Lancelot, son of a King Ban. See below, Conclusion. 5, n. 14.

11. As opposed to Avalon, which figures in its name. On Escavalon as a reference to Avalon, see William A. Nitze and Harry F. Williams, *Arthurian Names in the Perceval of Chrétien de Troyes* (Berkeley and Los Angeles: University of California Press, 1955), p. 272.

12. For example, see below, pp. 147–48.

13. See Glyn Sheridan Burgess, *Contribution à l'étude du vocabulaire pré-courtois* (Geneva: Droz, 1970), pp. 104–13.

14. See West, *An Index of Proper Names*, p. 13. Louis-Fernand Flutre, *Table des noms propres ... dans les romans du moyen âge ...* (Poitiers: Centre d'Études Supérieures de Civilisation Médiévale, 1962), p. 25, confuses, as does Cazelles, *The Unholy Grail*, p. 96, Ban de Gomeret with Ban de Benoïe (or Benoic), who is the father of Lancelot in the Lancelot-Grail Cycle. The kingdom of Gomeret is either in North Wales (Gwynneth) or in southern Brittany: Vannes (Morbihan), Breton Wenet or Guenet, see Nitze and. Williams, *Arthurian Names in the Perceval of Chrétien de Troyes*, p. 267. Meanwhile Benoïe (Benoic) is another petty kingdom in western France or Brittany, see Norris J. Lacy, "Ban de Benoic," in *The New Arthurian Encyclopedia*, gen. ed. Norris J. Lacy (1991; rev. New York and London: Garland, 1996), p. 32, and the *Vulgate Merlin*, Sommer, ed., 2: 97. Chrétien's emphasis on the youth of Ban's men in *Erec et Enide* in contrast to the very old men in the train of Quarron of Ariel, beloved of Arthur, the youngest of whom is 140 years old (1981–88), may well anticipate the company of 500 squires in the Roche de Champguin, each group of 100 of whom represents five ages of man.

15. Renaut de Bâgé, *Le Bel Inconnu*, ed. Karen Fresco, trans. Colleen P. Donagher (New York and London: Garland, 1992).

16. *Logres* : *ogres*, see above, p. 134.

17. The image is strangely reminiscent of the branches woven by the Good Friday penitents to mark the way that Perceval follows to the Hermitage (6287–96, B6321–30).

18. "Fili mi Absalom, Absalom fili mi: quis mihi tribuat ut ego moriar pro te, Absalom fili mi, fili mi Absalom" (My son Absalom, Absalom my son: would to God that I might die for thee, Absalom my son, my son Absalom). Perceval's elder brother served the king of Escavalon, and it is he whose eyes were pecked out by birds of prey. It can be no coincidence that his torment signals breaches of filial piety (above, pp. 70–71), as does Guiganbresil's allusion to Absalom.

19. Maddox, *The Arthurian Romances of Chrétien de Troyes*, p. 105, rightly characterizes the whole Greoreas episode as "bizarre."

20. He is certain that Gawain will find the Bleeding Lance because, as he has told the king, no task is too difficult for him to accomplish (6088–90, B6122–24).

21. See also Maddox, *Arthurian Romances of Chrétien de Troyes*, p. 116, n. 78. Duggan appears not to account for this point when he suggests that "it seems distinctly possible that if [the *Conte del Graal*] had been completed, Gawain would have found the lance and would have given it to the king of Escavalon, who would have employed it successfully against Arthur" (*The Romances of Chrétien de Troyes*, pp. 258–29, where he also points out that Perceval's elder brother was a knight in the previous king of Escavalon's court and intriguingly raises the question of whether Gawain killed the king in the same battle in which Perceval's brother was killed).

22. Maddox, *Arthurian Romances of Chrétien de Troyes*, p. 113, n. 70, his emphasis. He follows Jean Frappier, "Le Cortège du graal," in *Lumières du graal*, ed. René Nelli (Paris: Cahiers du Sud, 1951), p. 119, and Guy Vial, *Le Conte du Graal: Sens et unité: La première continuation*, Geneva: Droz, 1987), pp. 80–82.

23. The Grail may be associated with abundance, but, contrary to what happens in the First Continuation, it does not serve those feasting in the great hall in the *Conte del Graal.*

24. Robert de Boron, *Joseph d'Arimathie: A Critical Edition of the Verse and Prose Ver-*

sions, ed. Richard O'Gorman (Toronto: Pontifical Institute of Mediaeval Studies, 1995), where Joseph collects Christ's blood in the Grail (verse version, 562–72, cf. 907–09; prose, 206–11), and *Merlin, roman du XIIIe siècle*, ed. Alexandre Micha, Textes Littéraires Français 281 (Paris: Droz, 1980), ch. 16, etc.; also attributed to Robert by some is *The Didot Perceval*, ed. William Roach (Philadelphia: University of Pennsylvania Press, 1941), p. 208 (Grail with Bleeding Lance), p. 240 (Longinus), etc.; the First Continuation (also pre-1200), vol. 1, ed. Roach, 1194–1509; and the later Vulgate *Merlin* Continuation, ed. Sommer, 2: 159, 334–35. Robert's work is a major foundation of the Lancelot-Grail Cycle, see Pickens, "Histoire et commentaire chez Chrétien de Troyes et Robert de Boron: Robert de Boron et le livre de Philippe de Flandre," in *The Legacy of Chrétien de Troyes*, ed. Norris J. Lacy, Douglas Kelly, and Keith Busby, 2:17–39.

25. See *Raimundi de Agiles historia Francorum qui ceperunt Ierusalem*, Migne, PL 155: 610–14, ch. 14–15.

26. See Nina Rowe, *The Jew, the Cathedral, and the Medieval City* (Cambridge: Cambridge University Press, 2011), pp. 41–78 (history of the motif), 86–138 (Notre-Dame de Reims), 191–247 (Notre-Dame de Strasbourg); and Heinz Schreckenberg, *The Jews in Christian Art: An Illustrated History*, trans. John Bowdon (New York: Continuum, 1996), pp. 31–56 and 66–74 (examples from the ninth through the thirteenth centuries).

27. Cf. the miniature dated ca. 1185 in Schreckenberg, *The Jews in Christian Art*, p. 43.

28. As in William Farina, *Chrétien de Troyes and the Dawn of Arthurian Romance* (Jefferson, NC, and London: McFarland, 2010), pp. 195–202, implications of the Ecclesia-Synagoga motif in the *Conte del Graal* may be advanced without subscribing to a "Judeo-Christian interpretation" of the romance as advocated by my revered mentor, Urban T. Holmes, Jr.; cf. Holmes, "A New Interpretation of Chrétien's *Conte del Graal*," *Studies in Philology* 44 (1947): 453–76, Holmes and M. Amelia Klenke, *Chrétien, Troyes, and the Grail* (Chapel Hill: University of North Carolina Press,1959), pp. 108–61, 195–204, and Mario Roques, "Le Graal de Chrétien et la demoiselle au Graal," *Romania* 76 (1955), 1–27.

29. Arthur may well be subject to the sin of *tristitia*, as are Perceval when he visits the Hermitage and the Malevolent Maiden before her rehabilitation (see above, Ch. 2, n. 33).

30. Wace, *Brut*, 9617–40. In the traditional sources, Gonvais (a name not far from Gauvain in Francien or Walwein in Norman) is king of Orkney in Arthurian times (*Brut*. 10309, etc.). Lot is known first as king of Lothian (Old French Loënis) (*Brut*, 8822, etc.); later he invades Norway and seizes the throne (9799–9862). In Robert de Boron's *Merlin*, the Didot *Perceval*, and the Vulgate *Merlin* Continuation, he is also designated as king of Orkney. In fact, Chrétien's association of Orkney with Gawain may well be the earliest allusion to his father's links to Orkney.

31. Wace, *Brut*, 8813–22. Anna is also known as Morgause, a name later confused with Morgan. See Norris J. Lacy, "Morgause," p. 329, and Suzanne Wilson, "Anna," in *New Arthurian Encyclopedia*, ed. Norris J. Lacy, p. 8. Anna-Morgause, Gawain's mother, is the unnamed Young Queen at the Roche de Champguin and mother of Clarissant.

32. Maddox, *Arthurian Romances of Chrétien de Troyes*, p. 116, assumes that Lot is dead at this point, which runs counter to traditional sources, where both Lot and Gawain fight against the Romans with Arthur in France before he returns to Britain to face Mordred (e.g., Wace, *Brut*, 12366). In the Didot *Perceval* (2567–2608), Lot and Gawain are killed together as they land with Arthur in Britain, but cf. Wace, *Brut*, 13100–01, who, like Geoffrey of Monmouth, *Historia*, ch. 177, mentions only the death of Lot's brother Anguissel, king of Scotland (cf. *Brut*, 10249). Maddox convincingly argues, on the other hand, that in his first romance, *Cligés*, "By conceptualizing *the* crisis in the earlier Arthurian tradition represented by Geoffrey and Wace, touched off by Mordred's betrayal of Arthur and the fall of the Arthurian state that ensued, Chrétien reorients the Arthurian matter, substituting a positive outcome for a tragic dénouement, thus rehabilitating the *matière* for new objectives" throughout his *oeuvre* (*Arthurian Romances of Chrétien de Troyes*, p. 120, his emphasis, cf. pp. 8–23, 119–22); consequently, Chrétien reshapes traditional chronology as well and reconfigures Mordred as insolent intruders who threaten Arthur's kingdom such as Meleagant de Gorre and the Red Knight. At the Roche de Champguin, Ygraine speaks of Lot ambiguously "... or me dites del roi Lot, / De sa fame quanz filz *il ot*" (8093–94, B8135–36, my emphasis) (tell me now about King

Lot: how many sons *did he have* by his wife?), and, after Gawain names them, including himself, she comments: "Car pleüst Deu que tuit ansanble / Fussent or ci avoeques nos!" (8106-07, B8148-49) (Would to God they were all here with us now). Does her wish include or exclude Lot? Comic irony also arises from the fact that the Queen does not know who her interlocutor is; moreover, as she appears to inhabit a land of the dead, she seems to wish that her grandsons (and their father?) were no longer among the living but with her.

33. As in *La Mort le roi Artu*, the conclusion of the *Lancelot-Grail*, ed. Sommer 6: 201-63; cf. Geoffrey of Monmouth, *Historia*, ed. Wright, ch. 177-78; Wace's *Brut*, ed. Arnold, 13010-13293; etc.

34. Maddox, *Arthurian Romances of Chrétien de Troyes*, pp. 116-17. Duggan is more explicit: "The prediction that the Bleeding Lance would lead to the destruction of the kingdom of Logres ... makes it likely that a completed [*Conte del Graal*] would have included a cataclysmic battle" (*Romances of Chrétien de Troyes*, p. 260).

35. On the fall of Utherpendragon's kingdom to Arthur, cf. 409-31 (B427-49) and 8671-8723 (B9719-71).

36. According to the Ferryman, no knight who enters the great hall at the Roche de Champguin may be one "Qui de covoitise soit plains / Ne qui ait an lui nul mal vice / De losange ne d'avarice. / Coarz ne traït[r]es n'i dure / Ne formantie ne parjure" (7514-18, B7556-60) ([who] is filled with covetousness or has within him any stain of pride or avarice. Cowards and traitors cannot endure, nor can perjurers or oath-breakers). On pride, see esp. Sirach 10:14-18: "Initium superbiae hominis apostatare a Deo: quoniam ab eo qui fecit illum recessit cor ejus, quoniam initium omnis peccati est superbia. Qui tenuerit illam adimplebitur maledictis, et subvertet eum in finem. Propterea exhonoravit Dominus conventus malorum, et destruxit eos usque in finem. Sedes ducum superborum destruxit Deus, et sedere fecit mites pro eis. Radices gentium superbarum arefecit Deus, et plantavit humiles ex ipsis gentibus" (The beginning of the pride of man, is to fall off from God. Because his heart is departed from him that made him: for pride is the beginning of all sin: he that holdeth it, shall be filled with maledictions, and it shall ruin him in the end. Therefore hath the Lord disgraced the assemblies of the wicked, and hath utterly destroyed them. God hath overturned the thrones of proud princes, and hath set up the meek in their stead. God hath made the roots of proud nations to wither, and hath planted the humble of these nations).

37. See discussion above in Ch. 5, n. 32.

Appendix A

1. Cf. Chapter 2, p. 67.
2. See also Psalm 50:7/51:5: "ecce enim in iniquitatibus conceptus sum et in peccatis concepit me mater mea" (For behold I was conceived in inquities; and in sin did my mother conceive me).
3. *Enarratio in Psalmum CVIII*, Migne, *PL* 37: 1437, my translation.

Appendix B

1. Cf. Chapter 2, pp. 68-70.
2. The following remarks are informed by Conleth Kearns, *The Expanded Text of Ecclesiasticus* (Berlin and New York: De Gruyter, 2011); James VanderKam and Peter Flint, *The Meaning of the Dead Sea Scrolls* (New York: Harper Collins, 2012), esp. pp. 185-87; Albert Pietersma and Benjamin G. Wright, eds., *A New English Translation of the Septuagint* (NETS), (2007; rev. Oxford: Oxford University Press, 2009), pp. 715-16.
3. A.E. Cowley and Ad. Neubauer, eds., *The Original Hebrew of a Portion of* Ecclesiasticus *(XXXIX.15 to XLIX.11)* ... (Oxford: Clarendon Press, 1897), p. xi.
4. Protestant bibles (Luther, AV and its descendants, etc.) revert to the Hebrew canon and regard Sirach and other books of the Jewish apocrypha as deuterocanonical.
5. For a view of the passage in the pre-Vulgate Latin tradition compared with LXX and the Vulgate, see *Sirach (Ecclesiasticus)*, ed. Walter Thiele, in *Vetus Latina: Die Reste der altlateinischen Bibel*, fasc. 3 (Freiburg: Verlag Herder, 1989), pp. 226-29.
6. "13 κἂν ἀπολείπῃ σύνεσιν, συγγνώμην ἔχε καὶ μὴ ἀτιμάσῃς αὐτὸν ἐν πάσῃ ἰσχύι σου 14[a] **ἐλεημοσύνη γὰρπατρὸς** οὐκ ἐπιλησθήσεται [14b] καὶ **ἀντὶ ἁμαρτιῶν** προσανοικοδομηθήσεταί σοι 15 ἐν ἡμέρᾳ θλίψεώς σου ἀναμνησθήσεταί σου ὡς εὐδία ἐπὶ παγετῷ οὕτως ἀναλυθήσονταί σου αἱ ἁμαρτίαι" (my emphasis) (13 But if he fails in comprehension, excuse him, and do not dishonor him in the fullness of your strength. 14[a] For *charity for a father* will

not be forgotten, [14b] and it will be credited to you *against sins*. 15 In a day of affliction it will be remembered of you; as fair weather upon frost, so will your sins be dissolved.) The Greek text is from *Septuagint*, ed. Alfred Rahlfs, 2 vols. (1935; rpt. in 1 vol. Stuttgart: Deutsche Bibelgesellschaft, 1979); the translation is that of *A New English Translation of the Septuagint* (NETS), which accounts for the Hebrew original when it has survived in the manuscripts from the Cairo *genizah*.

7. LXX vv. 3–4, Vul. vs. 11/LXX vs. 9, Vul. vs. 18/LXX vs. 16 likewise respect the parallel structure. In place of LXX vv. 3–4, Vul. substitutes as vs. 4: "Qui diligit Deum exorabit pro peccatis, et continebit se ab illis, et in oratione dierum exaudietur" (He that loveth God, shall obtain pardon for his sins by prayer, and shall refrain himself from them, and shall be heard in the prayer of days), which seems extraneous to the theme of filial piety. Pairing does not occur in the prologue to the passage, Vul. vs. 2/LXX vs. 1, where the textual voice is that of the father. In Vul. vs. 13/LXX vs. 11, the father is mentioned twice in Vul.; in fact, by mentioning the father instead of the mother in LXX, the Vulgate avoids an anomalous opposition: "Gloria enim hominis ex honore patris sui, et dedecus filii pater sine honore" (For the glory of a man is from the honour of his father, and a father without honour is the disgrace of the son) as opposed to LXX, which attributes a particular kind of fault to the mother: "ἡ γὰρ δόξα ἀνθρώπου ἐκ τιμῆς πατρὸς αὐτοῦ καὶ ὄνειδος τέκνοις μήτηρ ἐν ἀδοξίᾳ" (For a person's repute comes from his father's honor, and a mother in ill repute is a reproach to children).

Appendix C

1. Cf. Chapter 3, pp. 92–93.

Bibliography

Editions and Translations of the Conte del Graal

Chrétien de Troyes. *Le Conte du Graal ou le Roman de Perceval*. Ed. and trans. Charles Méla. Lettres Gothiques. Paris: Livre de Poche, 1990.

———. *Perceval or the Story of the Grail*. Trans Ruth Harwood Cline. Athens: University of Georgia Press, 1985.

———. *Perceval ou le Conte du graal*. Ed. Alfons Hilka. Trans. Jean Dufournet. Paris: Flammarion, 1997.

———. *Le Roman de Perceval ou le Conte du Graal*. Ed. Keith Busby. Tübingen: Max Niemeyer Verlag, 1993.

———. *Le Roman de Perceval ou le Conte del Graal*. Ed. William Roach. Textes Littéraires Français 71. Geneva: Droz and Paris: Minard, 1959.

———. *The Story of the Grail (Li Contes del Graal), or Perceval*. Ed. Rupert T. Pickens, trans. William W. Kibler. New York and London: Garland, 1990.

Der Percevalroman von Christian von Troyes. Ed. Alfons Hilka. Christian von Troyes' Sämtliche Werke, gen. ed. Wendelin Foerster, 5. Halle: Niemeyer, 1932. Rpt. Amsterdam: Rodopi, 1966.

Manuscripts of the Conte del Graal *Cited*

A   Paris, Bibliothèque Nationale de France, f. fr. 794 (Guiot's copy).
B   Bern, Burgerbibliothek, 354.
C   Clermont-Ferrand, Bibliothèque Municipale et Interuniversitaire, 248.
E   Edinburgh, National Library of Scotland, Advocates' 19. 1. 5.
F   Florence, Biblioteca Riccardiana, 2943.
H   London, College of Arms (Heralds' College), Arundel XIV.
L   London, British Library, Additional 36614.
M   Montpellier, Bibliothèque Interuniversitaire, Section Médecine H 249.
P   Mons, Bibliothèque Universitaire et Publique, 331/206.
Q   Paris, Bibliothèque Nationale de France, f. fr. 1429.
R   Paris, Bibliothèque Nationale de France, f. fr. 1450.
S   Paris, Bibliothèque Nationale de France, f. fr. 1453.
T   Paris, Bibliothèque Nationale de France, f. fr. 12576.
U   Paris, Bibliothèque Nationale de France, f. fr. 12577.
V   Paris, Bibliothèque Nationale de France, nouv. acq. fr. 6614.

Editions of Other Works by or Attributed to Chrétien de Troyes

Chrétien de Troyes. *Le Chevalier au lion ou le Roman d'Yvain*. Ed. and trans. David Hult. Lettres Gothiques. Paris: Livre de Poche, 1994.

———. *Le Chevalier de la Charrete*. Ed. Charles Méla. Lettres Gothiques. Paris: Livre de Poche, 1992.

———. *Cligés*. Ed. Charles Méla. Lettres Gothiques. Paris: Livre de Poche, 1994.

———. *Erec et Enide*. Ed. Jean-Marie Fritz. Lettres Gothiques. Paris: Livre de Poche, 1992.

———. *Guillaume d'Angleterre*. Ed. Anne Berthelot. In Chrétien de Troyes, *Œuvres complètes*. Gen. ed. Daniel Poirion. Bibliothèque de la Pléiade. Paris: Gallimard, 1994, pp. 953–1036, 1410–51.

———. *Philomena*. Ed. Anne Berthelot. In Chrétien de Troyes, *Œuvres complètes*, pp. 916–52, 1391–1410.

Other Texts and Translations

Andreas Capellanus on Love. Ed. and trans. P.G. Walsh. 1982. Rpt. London: Duckworth, 1993.

André le Chapelain. *Traité de l'amour courtois*. Trans. Claude Buridant. Paris: Klincksieck, 1974.

The Apocrypha According to the Authorized Version. Oxford: Oxford University Press, n.d.

Aquinas, St. Thomas. *Summa Theologica: Latin Text and English Translation*. Ed. and trans. Thomas R. Heath. Vol. 35 (*Secunda Secundae* 34–36). Cambridge, New York, etc.: 1976. Rpt. Cambridge: Cambridge University Press, 2006.

Augustine of Hippo. *Enarratio in Psalmum CVIII*. Migne, *PL* 37: 1431–1445.

Aurelii Augustini, Sancti, Hipponensis episcopi, Operum supplementum quarta. Ed. D.A.B. Caillau. Paris: Parent-Desbarres, 1839.

Biblia sacra iuxta Vulgatam clementinam. Madrid: Biblioteca de Autores Cristianos, 1994.

Carmina burana. Ed. Ernst Buschor. Frankfurt am Main: Insel Verlag, 1964.

The Confessions of Augustine. Ed. John Gibb and William Montgomery. Cambridge: Cambridge University Press, 1908.

Cowley, A.E., and Ad. Neubauer, eds. *The Original Hebrew of a Portion of Ecclesiasticus Together with the Early Versions and an English Translation Followed by the Quotations from Ben Sira in Rabbinical Literature*. Oxford: Clarendon Press, 1897.

The Didot Perceval. Ed. William Roach. Philadelphia: University of Pennsylvania Press, 1941.

Eneas: Roman du XIIe siècle. Ed. J.-J. Salverda de Grave. 2 vols. Paris: Champion, 1964–1968.

Geoffrey of Monmouth. *History of the Kings of Britain*. Trans. Sebastian Evans, rev. Charles W. Dunn. New York: Dutton, 1958.

Guillaume de Lorris and Jean de Meun, *Le Roman de la Rose*. Ed. Armand Strubel. Lettres Gothiques. Paris: Librairie Générale Française, 1992.

The Historia regum Britannie of Geoffrey of Monmouth. Ed. Neil Wright. Vol. 1. Cambridge: D.S. Brewer, 1984.

The Holy Bible [Authorized King James Version]. Cleveland and New York: World Publishing Company, n.d.

The Holy Bible [Douay-Rheims Version]. Baltimore: John Murphy, 1899.

The Holy Bible [Douay-Rheims Version]. With commentary by George Leo Haydock. 3 vols. 1811–1814. Rpt. in 1 vol. New York: Thomas Kelly, 1873.

Hugh of St. Victor. *De sacramentis christianae fidei*. Migne, *PL* 176: 173–618.

Isidori Hispanensis episcopi Etymologiarum sive Originum Libri XX. Ed. W.M. Lindsay, 2 vols. 1911. Rpt. Oxford: Clarendon Press, 1957.

Johannis Saresberriensis Opera Omnia. Ed. J.A. Giles. Vol. 4 Oxford: J.H. Parker, 1848.

Lais de Marie de France. Ed. Karl Warnke. Trans. Laurence Harf-Lancner. Lettres Gothiques. Paris: Livre de Poche, 1990.

Die Lais der Marie de France. Ed. Karl Warnke. Bibliotheca Normannica 3. 1885; 3rd ed. Halle: Max Niemeyer, 1925.

Matthieu de Vendôme. *Ars versificatoria*. In *Arts poétiques du XIIe et du XIIIe siècles*. Ed. Edmond Faral. Paris: Champion, 1962.

The Medieval French Roman d'Alexandre. Vol. 2: *Version of Alexandre de Paris*. Ed. E.C. Armstrong, D.L. Buffam, Bateman Edwards, and L.F.H. Lowes. Princeton: Princeton University Press, 1938. Rpt. New York: Kraus, 1965.

Merlin, roman du XIIIe siècle. Ed. Alexandre Micha. Textes Littéraires Français 281. Paris: Droz, 1980.

A New English Translation of the Septuagint [NETS]. Ed. Albert Pietersma and

Benjamin G. Wright. 2007. Rev. Oxford: Oxford University Press, 2009.
Pedanius Dioscorides. *De materia medica.* Ed. and trans. Tess Anne Osbaldeston. Johannesburg: Ibidis Press, 2000.
Ovid. *Metamorphoses.* Ed. and Trans. Frank Justus Miller. Loeb Classical Library. 2 vols. 1921–1922. Rpt. London: W. Heinemann and Cambridge, MA: Harvard University Press, 1960.
Rabanus Maurus, *Commentarium in Ecclesiasticum.* Migne, PL 109: 763–1126.
Raimundi de Agiles historia Francorum qui ceperunt Ierusalem. Migne, PL 155: 610–12.
Regola sanitaria salernitana: Regimen sanitatis salernitanum. Ed. and trans. Fulvio Gherli. Rome: Edizioni & Gestioni Editoriali, n.d.
Renaut de Bâgé. *Le Bel Inconnu (Li Biaus Desconneüs; The Fair Unknown).* Ed. Karen Fresco, trans. Colleen P. Donagher. New York and London: Garland, 1992.
Robert de Boron. *Joseph d'Arimathie: A Critical Edition of the Verse and Prose Versions.* Ed. Richard O'Gorman. Toronto: Pontifical Institute of Mediaeval Studies, 1995.
Le Roman de Brut de Wace. Ed. Ivor Arnold. 2 vols. Paris: Société des Anciens Textes Français, 1938–40.
Septuagint. Ed. Alfred Rahlfs. 2 vols. 1935. Rpt. in 1 vol. Stuttgart: Deutsche Bibelgesellschaft, 1979.
Sirach (Ecclesiasticus). Ed. Walter Thiel. In *Vetus Latina: Die Reste der altlateinischen Bibel.* 9 fascicules. Freiburg: Verlag Herder, 1987–2005.
The Song of Roland: An Analytical Edition. Ed. and trans. Gerard J. Brault. 2 vols. University Park and London: Pennsylvania State University Press, 1978.
The Story of Merlin. Trans. Rupert T. Pickens. In *Lancelot-Grail: The Old French Arthurian Vulgate and Post-Vulgate Versions in Translation.* Gen. ed. Norris J. Lacy. Vol. 1. New York and London: Garland, 1993, pp. 167–424. Rev. Cambridge: Boydell and Brewer, 2010, vol. 2.
Vergil's Aeneid, Books I-VI. Ed. Clyde Pharr. Boston: D.C. Heath, 1930.
Villon, François. *Poésies complètes.* Ed. Claude Thiry. Lettres Gothiques. Paris: Livre de Poche, 1991.
The Vulgate Version of the Arthurian Romances. Ed. Oskar Sommer. 8 vols. Washington: The Carnegie Institute, 1908–1916. Rpt. New York: AMS Press, 1969.
Wace's Roman de Brut: A History of the British. Rev. and trans. Judith Weiss. Exeter: University of Exeter Press, 1999, rev. 2002.

Critical Studies and Reference Works

Abresman, Rudolph. "The Concept of the 'Christus Medicus' in St. Augustine." *Traditio* 10 (1954): 1–28.
Andersen-Wyman, Kathleen. *Andreas Capellanus on Love? Desire, Seduction, and Subversion in a Twelfth-Century Latin Text.* New York: Palgrave Macmillan, 2007.
Armstrong, Grace. "The Scene of the Blood Drops on the Snow: A Crucial Narrative Moment in the *Conte del Graal.*" *Kentucky Romance Quarterly*, 19 (1972): 127–47.
Armstrong, Karen. *The Bible: A Biography.* New York: Grove/Atlantic, 2007.
Astell, Ann. *The Song of Songs in the Middle Ages.* Ithaca and London: Cornell University Press, 1990.
Baldwin, John W. "Chrétien in History." In *A Companion to Chrétien de Troyes*, ed. Norris J. Lacy and Joan Tasker Grimbert, pp. 3–13.
Baumgartner, Emmanuèle. "Les Scènes du Graal et leur illustration dans les manuscrits du *Conte du Graal* et des Continuations." In *Les Manuscrits de/The Manuscripts of Chrétien de Troyes*, ed. Keith Busby, *et al.*, 1: 489–503.
Bogdanow, Fanni. "The Mystical Theology of Bernard de Clairvaux and the Meaning of Chrétien de Troyes' *Conte du Graal.*" In *Chrétien de Troyes and the Troubadours: Essays in Memory of the Late Leslie Topsfield.* Ed. Peter S. Noble and Linda Paterson. Cambridge: St. Catherine's College, 1984, pp. 249–82.
Brandsma, Frank. "Mirror Characters." In

Bibliography

Courtly Arts and the Art of Courtliness: Selected Papers from the Eleventh Triennial Congress of the International Courtly Literature Society, University of Wisconsin-Madison, 29 July–4 August 2004. Ed. Keith Busby and Christopher Kleinhenz. Cambridge: D.S. Brewer, 2006, pp. 275–82

Bruckner, Matilda Tomaryn. *Chrétien Continued: A Study of the* Conte du Graal *and Its Verse Continuations*. Oxford: Oxford University Press, 2009.

———. *Narrative Invention in Twelfth-Century French Romance: The Convention of Hospitality (1160–1200)*. Lexington, KY: French Forum, 1980.

———. "Weaving a Tapestry from Biblical Exegesis to Romance Textuality: Caught in the Web of Chrétien's *Conte du Graal*." Forthcoming.

Buettner, Bonnie. "The Good Friday Scene in Chrétien de Troyes' *Perceval*." *Traditio* 36 (1980): 415–26.

Burgess, Glyn Sheridan. *Contribution à l'étude du vocabulaire pré-courtois*. Geneva: Droz, 1970.

Busby, Keith. *Chrétien de Troyes, Perceval (Le Conte du Graal)*. London: Grant and Cutler, 1993.

———. "The Continuations." In *The Arthur of the French*. Ed. Glyn S. Burgess and Karen Pratt. Cardiff: University of Wales Press, 2006, pp. 222–47.

———. *Gauvain in Old French Literature*. Amsterdam: Rodopi, 1980

———, Terry Nixon, Alison Stones, and Lori Walters, eds. *Les Manuscrits de/The Manuscripts of Chrétien de Troyes*. 2 vols. Amsterdam and Atlanta: Rodopi, 1993.

Campbell, Joseph. *The Masks of God: Creative Mythology*. New York: Viking, 1970.

Cazelles, Brigitte. *The Unholy Grail: A Social Reading of Chrétien de Troyes's "Conte del Graal."* Stanford: Stanford University Press, 1996.

Colby[-Hall], Alice M. *The Portrait in Twelfth-Century French Literature: An Example of the Stylistic Originality of Chrétien de Troyes*. Histoire des Idées et Critique Littéraire 6. Geneva: Droz, 1965.

Combarieu du Grès, Micheline de. "Les Enjeux de la langue dans *Le Conte du Graal*." In *Le Conte du Graal*, ed. Danielle Quéruel, pp. 43–61.

Combes, Annie. "The Continuations of the *Conte du Graal*." In *A Companion to Chrétien de Troyes*. Ed. Norris J. Lacy and Joan Tasker Grimbert, pp. 191–201.

Cook, Eleanor. *Enigmas and Riddles in Literature*. Cambridge: Cambridge University Press. 2009.

Curtius, Ernst Robert. *European Literature and the Latin Middle Ages*. Trans. Willard Trask. 1953. Rev. Princeton: Princeton University Press, 1990.

Dällenbach, Lucien. *Le Récit spéculaire: Essai sur la mise en abyme*. Paris: Seuil, 1977.

D'Arcy, Marie Anne. "*Li Anemis meismes*: Satan and Synagogue in *La Queste del Saint Graal*." *Medium Ævum* 66 (1997): 207–35.

DeVries, Kelly, and Robert D. Smith. *Medieval Weapons: An Illustrated History of Their Impact*. Santa Barbara, CA: ABC-CLIO, 2007.

Douglas, R.W., and Susan Frank. *A History of Glassmaking*. Henley-on-Thames: Foulis, 1972.

Duggan, Joseph J. *The Romances of Chrétien de Troyes*. New Haven and London: Yale University Press, 2001.

Edelman, Nathan. "A Scriptural Key to Villon's *Testament*." *Modern Language Notes* 72 (1957): 345–51. Rpt. in Edelman, *The Eye of the Beholder: Essays in French Literature*. Ed. Jules Brody. Baltimore and London: Johns Hopkins University Press, 1974, pp. 31–37.

Farina, William. *Chrétien de Troyes and the Dawn of Arthurian Romance*. Jefferson, NC: McFarland, 2010.

Flutre, Louis Fernand. *Table des noms propres avec toutes leurs variantes figurant dans les romans du moyen âge écrits en français ou en provençal et actuellement publiés ou analysés*. Poitiers: Centre d'Études Supérieures de Civilisation Médiévale, 1962.

Foulet, Alfred. "Chrétien's Indebtedness to the *Alexandre décasyllabique*." In *The Romances of Chrétien de Troyes: A Symposium*, ed. Douglas Kelly, pp. 305–09.

———, Gen. Ed. *The Medieval French*

Roman d'Alexandre. Vol. 2: *Version of Alexandre de Paris*. Ed. E.C. Armstrong, D.L. Buffam, Bateman Edwards, and L.F.H. Lowes. Princeton: Princeton University Press, 1938. Rpt. New York: Kraus, 1965.

Fourrier, Anthime. "Encore la chronologie des œuvres de Chrétien de Troyes." *BBSIA* 2 (1950): 69-88.

Fowler, David C. *Prowess and Chivalry in the Perceval of Chrétien de Troyes*. Seattle: University of Washington Press, 1959.

Frappier, Jean. "Le Cortège du graal." In *Lumières du graal*. Ed. René Nelli. Paris: Cahiers du Sud, 1951, pp. 175-221.

Freeman, Michelle A. *The Poetics of Translatio Studii and Conjointure: Chrétien de Troyes's Cligés*. Lexington, KY: French Forum, 1979.

Friedman, Lionel J. "Gradus amoris." *Romance Philology* 19 (1965): 167-77.

Goering, Joseph. *The Virgin and the Grail*. New Haven/London: Yale University Press, 2005.

Goldin, Frederick. *The Mirror of Narcissus in the Courtly Lyric*. Ithaca, NY: Cornell University Press, 1967.

Groos, Arthur, and Norris J. Lacy, eds. *Perceval/Parzifal: A Casebook*. Arthurian Characters and Themes 6. New York and London: Routledge, 2002.

Gravdal, Kathryn. *Ravishing Maidens: Writing Rape in Medieval French Literature and Law*. Philadelphia: University of Pennsylvania Press, 1991.

Greimas, Algirdas-Julien. *Grand Dictionnaire ancien français*. 1979. Rpt. Paris: Larousse, 2007.

Grimbert, Joan Tasker. *"Yvain" dans le miroir: Une poétique de la réflexion dans le Chevalier au lion de Chrétien de Troyes*. Purdue Monographs in Romance Languages 25. Amsterdam and Philadelphia: John Benjamins, 1988.

Guerin, M. Victoria. *The Fall of Kings and Princes: Structure and Destruction in Arthurian Tragedy*. Stanford: Stanford University Press, 1995.

Haidu, Peter. *Aesthetic Distance in Chrétien de Troyes: Irony and Comedy in Cligès and Perceval*. Geneva: Droz, 1968.

———. "The Hermit's Pottage: Deconstruction and History in *Yvain*." In *The Sower and His Seed: Essays on Chrétien de Troyes*, ed. Rupert T. Pickens, pp. 127-45. Rpt. *Romanic Review* 74 (1983): 1-15.

Harty, Kevin, ed. *Cinema Arthuriana: Twenty Essays*. Rev. Jefferson, NC: McFarland, 2002.

Hindley, Alan Hindley, Frederick W. Langley, and Brian J. Levy, eds. *Old French-English Dictionary*. Cambridge: Cambridge University Press, 2000.

Hinton, Thomas. *The Conte du Graal Cycle: Chrétien de Troyes' Perceval, the Continuations, and French Arthurian Romance*. Cambridge: D.S. Brewer, 2012.

Hoggan, David G. "Le Péché de Perceval: pour l'authenticité de l'épisode de l'ermite dans le *Conte du Graal* de Chrétien de Troyes." *Romania* 93 (1972): 50-76.

Holmes, Urban T., Jr. "A New Interpretation of Chrétien's *Conte del Graal*." *Studies in Philology* 44 (1947): 453-76.

———, and M. Amelia Klenke. *Chrétien, Troyes, and the Grail*. Chapel Hill: University of North Carolina Press, 1959.

Hunt, Tony. "The Prologue to *Li Contes del Graal*." *Romania* 92 (1971): 359-79.

Irvine, Ian. "Acedia, *Tristitia* and Sloth: Early Christian Forerunners to Chronic Ennui." *Humanitas* 12.1 (1999): 89-103.

James-Raoul, Danièle. *Chrétien de Troyes, la greffe d'un style*. Paris: Champion, 2007.

———. *La Parole empêché dans la littérature arthurienne*. Paris: Champion, 1997.

Kearns, Conleth. *The Expanded Text of Ecclesiasticus: Its Teaching on the Future Life as a Clue to Its Origin* .... Ed. Pancratius C. Beentjes. Berlin and New York: De Bruyter, 2011.

Kelly, Douglas. "The Logic of the Imagination in Chrétien de Troyes." In *The Sower and His Seed: Essays on Chrétien de Troyes*, ed. Rupert T. Pickens, pp. 9-30.

———, ed. *The Romances of Chrétien de Troyes: A Symposium*. Lexington, KY: French Forum, 1985.

Köhler, Reinhold. "Vergleichende Anmerkungen." In *Die Lais der Marie de France*, ed. Karl Warnke, pp. xcix-clxxxiv.

Lachet, Claude. "La Confession de Perceval chez l'ermite: étude littéraire des vers 6136 à 6217 [=6314–99, B6348–6475]." In *Le Conte du Graal: Chrétien de Troyes*, ed. Danielle Quéruel, pp. 62–72.

Lacy, Norris J. "The Ambiguous Fortunes of Arthur: The Lancelot-Grail and Beyond." In *The Fortunes of King Arthur*. Ed. Norris J. Lacy. Arthurian Studies 64. Cambridge: D.S. Brewer, 2005, pp. 92–103.

———. "Ban de Benoic." In *The New Arthurian Encyclopedia*, gen. ed. Norris J. Lacy, p. 32.

———. "Gauvain and the Crisis of Chivalry." In *The Sower and His Seed: Essays on Chrétien de Troyes*, ed. Rupert T. Pickens, pp. 155–64.

———. "Morgause." In *The New Arthurian Encyclopedia*, gen. ed. Norris J. Lacy, p. 329.

———. Gen. ed. *The New Arthurian Encyclopedia*. 1991; rev. New York and London: Garland, 1996.

———, Douglas Kelly, and Keith Busby, eds. *The Legacy of Chrétien de Troyes*. 2 vols. Amsterdam: Rodopi, 1987–1988

———, and Joan Grimbert, eds. *A Companion of Chrétien de Troyes*." Cambridge: Boydell and Brewer, 2005.

Laranjinha, Ana Sofia. "Artur, Gauvain e Keu: representações da realeza em Chrétien de Troyes." *Línguas e Literaturas* 13 (1996): 23–39.

Le Nan, Frédérique. "La *Male Pucele* aux bornes de Galvoie." In *"Le Conte du Graal: Chrétien de Troyes,"* ed. Danielle Quéruel, pp. 74–88.

Lubac, Henri de. *Exégèse médiévale: Les quatre sens de l'Écriture*. Vol. 1.2. Paris: Auber, 1959.

Maddox, Donald. *The Arthurian Romances of Chrétien de Troyes: Once and Future Fictions*. Cambridge: Cambridge University Press, 1991.

———. *Fictions of Identity in Medieval France*. Cambridge: Cambridge University Press, 2000.

McCash, June Hall. "Chrétien's Patrons." In *A Companion to Chrétien de Troyes*, ed. Norris J. Lacy and Joan Grimbert, pp. 15–25.

———. "Reconsidering the Order of Chrétien de Troyes's Romances." In *"Li Premerains Vers": Essays in Honor of Keith Busby*. Ed. Catherine M. Jones and Logan E. Whalen. Amsterdam and New York: Rodopi, 2011, pp. 245–60.

Melchior-Bonnet, Sabine. *The Mirror: A History*. Trans. Katherine H. Jewett. New York: Routledge, 2001.

———. "Présentation: Réflexions sur le miroir." In *Miroirs et jeux de miroirs*, ed. Fabienne Pomel, pp. 17–26.

Ménard, Philippe. "Problématique de l'aventure dans les romans de la table ronde." In *Arturus Rex: Acta Conventus Lovaniensis 1987*. 2 vols. Ed. Willy Van Hoecke, Gilbert Tournoy, and Werner Verbeke. Louvain: Leuven University Press, 1991, 2:89–119.

Miner, Robert. *Thomas Aquinas on the Passions*. Cambridge, New York, etc.: Cambridge University Press, 2009.

Misrahi, Jean. "More Light on the Chronology of Chrétien de Troyes." *BBSIA* 11 (1959): 89–120.

Monson, Don A. *Andreas Capellanus, Scholasticism, and the Courtly Tradition*. Washington: Catholic University of America Press, 2005.

Morawski, Joseph, ed. *Proverbes français antérieurs au XVe siècle*. Classiques Français du Moyen Age 47. Paris: Champion, 1925.

Müller, Ulrich. "Blank, Syderberg, and the German Arthurian Tradition." In *Cinema Arthuriana: Twenty Essays*, ed. Kevin J. Harty, pp. 177–84.

Nightingale, Jeanne A. "Erec in the Mirror: The Feminization of the Self and the Re-invention of the Chivalric Hero in Chrétien's First Romance." In *Arthurian Romance and Gender/Masculin-Féminin dans le roman arthurien médiéval/Geschlechtlicherrollen im mittelalterlichen Artusroman*. Ed. Wolfgang Wolfzettel. Amsterdam and Atlanta: Rodopi, 1995, pp. 130–46.

Nitze, William A., and Harry F. Williams. *Arthurian Names in the Perceval of Chrétien de Troyes: Analysis and Commentary*. Berkeley and Los Angeles: University of California Press, 1955.

Nouvet, Claire. "An Allegorical Mirror: The Pool of Narcissus in Guillaume de Lorris' *Romance of the Rose*." *Romanic Review*, 91 (2002): 353–74.

O'Gorman, Richard. "Grail." In *The New Arthurian Encyclopedia*, ed. Norris J. Lacy, p. 212–13.

Ollier, Marie-Louise. *Lexique et concordance de Chrétien de Troyes d'après la copie de Guiot*. Montreal: Institut d'Études Médiévales, Université de Montréal/Paris: Vrin, 1986.

Owen, D.D.R. *The Evolution of the Grail Legend*. St. Andrews University Publications 58. Edinburgh and London: Oliver and Boyd, 1968.

Patch, Howard Rollin. *The Goddess Fortuna in Mediaeval Literature*. Cambridge, MA: Harvard University Press, 1927.

Pickens, Rupert T. "Arthurian Time and Space: Chrétien's *Conte del Graal* and Wace's *Brut*." *Medium Ævum* 75 (2006): 219–46.

———. "Arthur's Channel Crossing: Courtesy and the Demonic in Geoffrey of Monmouth and Wace's *Brut*." *Arthuriana* 7 (1997): 3–19.

———. "*Le Conte del Graal (Perceval)*." In *The Romances of Chrétien de Troyes: A Symposium*, ed. Douglas Kelly, pp. 232–86, 335–39.

———. "*Le Conte du Graal*: Chrétien's Unfinished Last Romance." In *A Companion of Chrétien de Troyes*," ed. Norris J. Lacy and Joan Grimbert, pp. 169–87.

———. "Courtesy and *Vasselage* in Chrétien de Troyes's *Conte del Graal*." In *Echoes of the Epic: Studies in Honor of Gerard J. Brault*. Ed. David P. Schenck. Birmingham, AL: Summa Publications, 1998, pp. 189–221.

———. "Grail." In *Medieval France: An Encyclopedia*. Ed. William W. Kibler and Grover A. Zinn. New York and London: Garland, 1995, pp. 409–10.

———. "Histoire et commentaire chez Chrétien de Troyes et Robert de Boron: Robert de Boron et le livre de Philippe de Flandre." In *The Legacy of Chrétien de Troyes*, ed. Norris J. Lacy, Douglas Kelly, and Keith Busby, 2: 17–39.

———. "Marie de France Translatrix II: *La Vie seinte Audree*." In *A Companion to Marie de France*. Ed. Logan E. Whalen. Leiden and Boston: Brill, 2011, pp. 267–301.

———. "*Perceval* and the Book of Sirach." Paper read at the 48th International Congress on Medieval Studies, Western Michigan University, Kalamazoo, May 11, 2013.

———. "Rencontres culturelles: monde francophone et matière de Bretagne." In *A French Forum: Mélanges de littérature française offerts à Raymond C. et Virginia A. La Charité*. Ed. Gérard Defaux and Jerry C. Nash. Paris: Klincksieck, 2000, pp. 21–30.

———, ed. *The Sower and His Seed: Essays on Chrétien de Troyes*. Lexington, KY: French Forum, 1983.

———. *The Welsh Knight: Paradoxicality in Chrétien's Conte del Graal*. French Forum Monographs, 6. Lexington, KY: French Forum, 1977.

Pierrevieille, Corinne. "Figures féminines dans *Le Conte du Graal*." In *Le Conte du Graal*, ed. Danielle Quéruel, pp. 89–101.

Poirion, Daniel. "L'Ombre mythique de Perceval dans le *Conte du Graal*." *Cahiers de Civilisation Médiévale* 16 (1973): 191–98.

———. "Semblance du Graal dans la Queste." In *Mélanges de littérature et de philologie médiévales offerts à J.R. Smeets*. Ed. Quirinus Ignatius Maria Mok, Ina Spiele, and P.E.R. Verhuyck. Leiden: n.p., 1982, pp. 227–41.

Pomel, Fabienne, ed. *Miroirs et jeux de miroirs dans la littérature médiévale*. Rennes: Presses Universitaires de Rennes, 2003.

Prestwich, Michael. *Armies and Warfare in the Middle Ages: The English Experience*. New Haven and London: Yale University Press: 1999.

Prior, Joseph G. *The Historical Critical Method in Catholic Exegesis*. Rome: Editrice Pontifica Università Gregoriana, 2001.

Roques, Mario. "Le Graal de Chrétien et la demoiselle au Graal." *Romania* 76 (1955): 1–27.

Quéruel, Danielle, ed. *Le Conte du Graal: Chrétien de Troyes*. Paris: Ellipses, 1998.

Rackham, Oliver. *Ancient Woodland: Its History, Vegetation and Uses in England*. London: Edward Arnold, 1980.

———. *Woodlands*. London: Harper Collins, 2006.

Bibliography

Rey-Flaud, Henri. *Le Chevalier, l'Autre et la Mort: Les aventures de Gauvain dans Le Conte du Graal*. Paris: Payot & Rivages, 1998.

———. "Le Sang sur la neige: analyse d'une image-écran de Chrétien de Troyes." *Littérature* 37 (1980): 15–24.

Rider, Jeff. "The Perpetual Enigma of Chrétien's Grail Episode." *Arthuriana* 8.1 (1998), 6–21.

———. " 'Wild Oats': The Parable of the Sower in the Prologue of Chrétien de Troyes' *Conte del Graal*." In *Philologies Old and New: Essays in Honor of Peter Florian Dembowski*. Ed. Joan Tasker Grimbert and Carol J. Chase. Edward C. Armstrong Monographs on Medieval Literature 12. Princeton, NJ: Edward C. Armstrong Monographs, 2001, pp. 251–66.

———, Richard Hull, and Christopher Smith, with Michael Carnes, Sasha Foppiano, and Annie Hesslein. "The Arthurian Legend in French Cinema: Robert Bresson's *Lancelot du Lac* and Eric Rohmer's *Perceval le Gallois*." In *Cinema Arthuriana: Twenty Essays*, ed. Kevin J. Hardy, pp. 148–62.

Riquer, Martín de. "La Composición de 'Li Contes del Graal' y el 'Guiromelant.'" *Boletín de la Réal Academia de Buenas Letras de Barcelona* 27 (1957–1958): 279–320.

Roques, Mario. "Le Graal de Chrétien et la demoiselle au Graal." *Romania* 76 (1955): 1–27. Rpt. Publications Romanes et Françaises 50. Geneva: Droz, 1955.

Rose, Paul Lawrence. *Wagner: Race and Revolution*. New Haven and London: Yale University Press, 1992.

Rowe, Nina. *The Jew, the Cathedral and the Medieval City: Synagoga and Ecclesia in the Thirteenth Century*. Cambridge: Cambridge University Press, 2011.

Rutledge, Amelia A. "Perceval's Sin: Critical Perspectives." *Œuvres et Critiques* 5.2 (1981): 53–60.

Saly, Antoinette. "Beaurepaire et Escavalon." In *Mélanges d'études romanes du Moyen-Âge et de la Renaissance offerts à Jean Rychner*. *Travaux de Linguistique et de Littérature*, 16 (1978): 469–81.

———. "La Récurrence des motifs en symétrie inverse dans la structure du *Perceval* de Chrétien de Troyes." *Travaux de Linguistique et de Littérature*, 21 (1983): 21–41.

Sargent-Baur, Barbara N. "Alexander and the *Conte du Graal*." In *Arthurian Literature* 14. Ed. James P. Carley and Felicity Riddy. Cambridge: Brewer, 1996, pp. 1–18.

———. "L'Autre chez Chrétien de Troyes." *Cahiers de Civilisation Médiévale*, 10 (1967): 199–205.

———. *La Destre et la senestre: Étude sur le* Conte del Graal *de Chrétien de Troyes*. Amsterdam and Atlanta: Rodopi, 2000.

———. "Medieval *ris, risus*: A Laughing Matter?" *Medium Ævum* 43 (1974):116–32.

Sherwin, Michael S. "Aquinas, Augustine, and the Medieval Scholastic Crisis Concerning Charity." In *Aquinas the Augustinian*. Ed. Michael Dauphinais, Barry David, and Matthew Levering. Washington: Catholic University of America Press, 2007, pp. 182–204.

Schreckenberg, Heinz. *The Jews in Christian Art: An Illustrated History*. Trans. John Bowdon. New York: Continuum, 1996.

Schulze-Busacker, Elisabeth. *Proverbes et expressions proverbiales dans la literature narrative du moyen âge français*. Paris: Champion, 1985.

Schwartz, Debora B. " 'A la guise de Gales l'atorna': Maternal Influence in Chrétien's *Conte del Graal*." *Essays in Medieval Studies* 12 (1996): 94–118.

———. "*Par bel mentir*: Chrétien's Hermits and Clerkly Responsibility." In *Translatio Studii: Essays by His Students in Honor of Karl D. Uitti for His Sixty-Fifth Birthday*. Ed. Renate Blumenfeld-Kosinski, Kevin Brownlee, Mary B. Speer, and Lori J. Walters. Birmingham, AL: Summa, 2000, pp. 287–309.

Simpson, James R. *Troubling Arthurian Histories: Court, Culture, Performance and Scandal in Chrétien de Troyes's* Erec et Enide. Medieval and Early Modern Studies 5. Oxford: Peter Lang, 2007.

Slojka, Ewa. "Escape from Paradox: Perceval's Upbringing in the *Conte du Graal*." *Arthuriana* 18.4 (2008): 66–86.

Sturm-Maddox, Sara. "King Arthur's Prophetic Fool: Prospection in the *Conte del Graal*." *Marche Romane* 29 (1979): 101–08.

———. " 'Tenir sa terre en pais': Social Order in the *Brut* and the *Conte del Graal*." *Studies in Philology* 81 (1984): 82–94.

La Tapisserie de Bayeux/The Bayeux Tapestry/Wandtepppich von Bayeux.Reproduction intégrale au 1/7ᵉ .... Bayeux: Édition Ville de Bayeux, n.d.

Touwaide, Alain. "The Legacy of Classical Antiquity in Byzantium and the West." In *Health and Healing from the Medieval Garden*. Ed. Peter Dendle and Alain Touwaide. Woodbridge, Suffolk: Boydell, 2008, pp. 15–28.

Uitti, Karl D., with Michelle A. Freeman. *Chrétien de Troyes Revisited*. New York: Twayne, 1995.

———. "Christian de Pisan and Chrétien de Troyes: Poetic Fidelity and the City of Ladies." In *The Legacy of Chrétien de Troyes*, ed. Norris J. Lacy, Douglas Kelly, and Keith Busby, 2: 229–53.

Valette, Jean-René. *La Pensée du Graal: Fiction littéraire et théologique (XIIᵉ-XIIIᵉ siècle)*. Paris: Champion, 2008.

VanderKam, James, and Peter Flint. *The Meaning of the Dead Sea Scrolls: Their Significance for Understanding the Bible, Judaism, Jesus, and Christianity*. New York: Harper Collins, 2002.

Vauthier, Michèle. "Le Paradoxe des fenêtres colorées dans *Le Conte du Graal*: une interprétation possible à la lecture des couleurs chez Chrétien de Troyes." In *Les Couleurs au moyen âge*. Senefiance 24. Aix-en-Provence: Publications du CUER-MA, 1988, pp. 423–48.

Vial, Guy. *Le Conte du Graal: Sens et unité: La première continuation*. Geneva: Droz, 1987.

Viereck, Peter. "Metapolitics Revisited." *Humanitas* 16 (2003): 48–75.

Vitz, Evelyn Birge Vitz. *Orality and Performance in Early French Romance*. Cambridge: D.S. Brewer, 1999.

Walters, Lori. "The Image of Blanchefleur in Montpellier, BI, Sect. Méd. H 249." In *Les Manuscrits de/The Manuscripts of Chrétien de Troyes*, ed. Keith Busby, et al., 1: 437–52.

Weever, John. *Antient [sic] Funeral Monuments of Great-Britain, Ireland, and Islands Ajdacent...* London: W. Tooke, 1767.

West, G.D. *An Index of Proper Names in French Arthurian Verse Romances 1150–1300*. Toronto: University of Toronto Press, 1969.

Whalen, Logan E., and Rupert T. Pickens. "Gardens and Anti-Gardens in Marie de France's *Lais*." *Romance Philology* 66 (2012): 185–210.

Wielockx, Robert. "La Discussion scolastique sur l'amour d'Anselme de Laon à Pierre Lombard d'après les imprimés et les inédits." Diss. Université Catholique de Louvain, 1981.

———. "La Sentence '*De caritate*' et la discussion scolastique sur l'amour." *Ephemerides Theologicae Lovanienses* 58 (1982): 50–86, 334–56; 59 (1983): 26–45.

Wilson, David M. *The Bayeux Tapestry*. New York: Thames & Hudson, 1985.

Wilson, Suzanne. "Anna." In *The New Arthurian Encyclopedia*, ed. Norris J. Lacy, p. 8.

Zink, Michel. "The Prologue to the *Historia de Preliis*: A Pagan Model of Spiritual Struggle." In *The Medieval French Alexander*. Ed. Donald Maddox and Sara Sturm Maddox. Albany: State University of New York Press, 2002, pp. 21–27.

———. "Renouart et Perceval: le tinel et le javelot." In *Literatur, Geschichte und Verstehen: Festschrift für Ulrich Mölk zum 60. Geburtstag*. Ed. Hinrich Hugge and Udo Schöning with Friedrich Wolfzettel. Heidelberg: Winter, 1997, pp. 277–86.

Zrinka, Stahuljak, Virginie Greene, Sarah Kay, Sharon Kinoshita, and Peggy McCracken. *Thinking Through Chrétien de Troyes*. Gallica 19. Cambridge: D.S. Brewer, 2011.

Index

Numbers in **_bold italics_** indicate pages with photographs.

Abraham 79, 80, 175*n*54
Absalom 139, 140, 141, 142, 181*n*18
absolution 61, 62, cf. 68, 89, 105, 121*n*23
acedia (ennui) 60, 173*n*33
Adam 67, 172–73*n*28
Adoration of the Cross *see* Easter Triduum
adventure 1, 3, 5, 6, 8, 20, 22, 23, 24, 26, 27, 29, 34, 47, 48, 50, 54, 63, 66, 73, 82, 86, 87, 101, 104, 115, 123, 131, 133, 135, 138, 141, 176*n*6
Æneid 168*n*50
Agravain li Orguilleus (brother of Gawain) 179*n*26
Alexander the Great 12, 13, 147, 163*n*9; *see also* Romances *of Alexander*
Alexandre (*Cligés*) 168*n*49
Alexandria (Egypt) 156
allegiance 139, 142
alloquium see *gradus amoris*
almosne, aumosne (act of mercy; penance) 83, 84, 104, 128, 131, 172*n*15, 174*n*40; *see also eleemosyna*
alms 13, 68, 128, 163*n*11, 176*n*59
amor purus (erotic enjoyment short of coitus) 45–46
amorous couple 36–47, 87; *see also* reflective sequence
Amorous Maiden (*Charrete*) 92, 93, 96, 103, 158
anchorites 170*n*13
Andreas Capellanus 45, 167*n*38
angarde (defensive mound) 54, 85, 86, 87, 88, 89, 100, 101, 104, 105, 178*n*1
Anguigneron 4, 8, 19, 20, 26, 27, 35, 40, 41, 42, 43, 79, 84, 129, 168*n*47, 172*n*24, 176*n*9
Anguissel (king of Scotland, brother of King Lot) 182–83*n*32
Anna 148, 182*n*31; *see also* Morgause, Young Queen
Antioch 145
antiphrasis 42, 43, 46
Antiquity 12, 14, 147

Apollonian powers (attributed to Gawain) 108, 109, 149; *see also* sun; sunlight
Apotheosis 108
Aquinas, St. Thomas 171*n*18, 171*n*20, 173*n*33
armor, arms 3, 9, 17, 18, 19, 21, 22, 23, 24, 26, 27, 32, 33, 34, 46, 47, 48, 49, 54, 57, 58, 59, 61, 62, 82, 87, 88, 97, 100, 119, 127, 135, 137, 138, 142, 152, 166*n*31, 166*n*22; *see also* weapons
Arthur 1, 3–9, 17, 19–28, 31, 32, 33, 36, 51, 53, 57, 58, 59, 66, 71, 79, 87, 82, 84, 88, 92, 95, 103, 114, 115, 116, 118–24, 126–31, 135, 136, 138, 139, 141, 142, 143, 147–51, 152, 166*n*22, 168*n*47, 168*n*49, 172*n*22, 173*n*33, 177*n*22, 179*n*25, 179*n*27, 180*n*5, 181*n*14, 182*n*29, 182–83*n*32, 183*n*35; *see also* court; reflective sequence
aumosne see *almosne*
Authorized King James Version (AV) *see* Bible
Avalon 181*n*11

Ban de Benoïe (Benoïc) (father of Lancelot) 181*n*
Ban of Gormeret 21, 137, 138–39, 181*n*10, 181*n*14
basia see *gradus amoris*
Baumgartner, Emmanuèle 175*n*55
Bayeux Tapestry 36, 164*n*5, 167*n*35
Bed of Marvels 6, 35, 49, 50, 101, 117
Bel Inconnu 139
Ben Ezra Synagogue (Cairo) 156
Ben Sira 155; *see also* Bible: Sirach
Bernard of Clairvaux *see* St. Bernard of Clairvaux
Biaurepaire 3, 4, 23, 25, 30, 35, 38, 40, 43, 47, 51, 52, 53, 73, 76, 79, 80, 81, 86, 124, 126, 134, 148, 151, 166*n*19, 168*n*47, 170*n*9, 170*n*15, 172*n*24, 174*n*44, 176*n*9, 177*nn*23–24, 179–80*n*31
Bible 14: Authorized King James Version (AV) 2, 155, 156, 157; Colossians ch. 3 171*n*20; I Corinthians 13; ch. 13 2, 13, 14,

195

Index

58, 61, 120, 151; II Corinthians ch. 9 11, 12; Deuteronomy ch. 5 153; ch. 6 171*n*18; Douay-Rheims (translation of Vulgate) 2, 69; Ecclesiastes 155; ch. 3 76, 174*n*46; Ecclesiasticus 155; Ephesians ch. 4 151; Exodus ch. 20 68, 153; John ch. 19 145; I John ch. 4 13; Leviticus ch. 4 69, 176*n*59; ch. 19 171*n*18; Luke ch. 8 162*n*2; Luther (translation) 183*n*4; Mark ch. 4 162*n*2; Matthew ch. 5 68; ch. 6 13, 163*n*11; ch. 13 162*n*2; ch. 22 171*n*18, 171*n*20; New English Translation of the Septuagint (NETS) 156; New Testament 12, 155; Old Testament 69, 156; Parable of Lazarus and the Rich Man (Luke 16) 175*n*54; Parable of the Prodigal Son (Luke 15) 84; Parable of the Sower (Mark 4, Matthew 13, Luke 8) 12, 18; Passion Gospel (John ch. 18, Luke ch. 22–23, Matthew ch. 26–27, Mark ch. 14–15) 144, 172*n*25; pre-Vulgate Latin tradition 183*n*5; Protestant 183*n*4; Proverbs 155; ch. 10 75, 175*n*50; ch. 16 120; ch. 19 68, 76; ch. 30 70; Psalm 50 174*n*36; 108/109 12, 67, 162–63*n*4; II Samuel/II Kings 13–18 140; Romans ch. 15 163*n*5; ruler of the synagogue's daughter (Luke ch. 8, Mark ch. 5, Matthew ch. 9) 107; Septuagint (LXX) 69, 156; Sirach 10, 70, 75, 76, 83, 155–57, 174*n*39; ch. 3 67, 68, 69, 77, 84, 156–57, 174*n*39, 176*n*59, 183*n*4; ch. 20 75, 175*nn*49–50; ch. 27 174*n*46; ch. 38 108; Vulgate 2, 67, 70, 75, 155, 156–57, 174*n*42

black *see* color

blanche (white) 166*n*25; *see also* color

Blanchefleur 3, 19, 20, 23, 25, 29, 30, 31, 32, 38, 41, 42, 43, 44, 45, 46, 47, 48, 51, 55, 56, 58, 79, 80, 82, 99, 115, 124, 166*n*19, 166*n*24, 167*n*38, 170*n*5, 170*n*15, 170–71*n*16, 174*n*44, 177*n*24

Bleeding Lance 4, 5, 33, 35, 48, 50, 53, 62, 73, 74, 82, 129, 130, 131, 133, 136, 139, 141, 143, 144, 145, 148, 150, 152, 181*nn*20–21, 181–82*n*24, 183*n*34; *see also* Holy Speer; reflective sequence

blood 5, 17, 20, 29, 32, 33, 34, 85, 145, 146, 181–82*n*24; *see also* reflective sequence

Blood Drops in the Snow 4, 8, 28–36, 47, 174*n*46, 177*n*24, 179*n*29; *see also* mirror; reflective sequence

blue *see* color

book (mentioned in Chrétien's text) 106, 107, 147

Book of Sirach *see* Bible

Bo(r)ne de Galvoie (Galloway frontier) 53

Brault, Gerard J. 167*n*35

bread 9, 51, 81, 126, 136, 170*n*13; *see also* reflective sequence

bridge 52, 53, 65, **71**, 74, 77, 79, 86–89, 125; *see also* reflective sequence

Britain 135, 138, 147, 148, 165*n*15, 180*n*5, 182–83*n*32

Brittany 181*n*14

Bruckner, Matilda 40, 162*n*1, 166*n*19, 172–73*n*28

Brun de Branlant (First Continuation) 130, 131

Brut see Wace

Brutus (of Troy) 134–35

Busby, Keith 85, 131, 178*n*2, 178*n*8, 180*n*37, 180*n*2

Calogrenant (*Yvain*) 123
Campbell, Joseph 172–73*n*28
candelabra 49, 143, 144
caritas see charity
Carlion 4, 5, 8, 9, 20, 23, 24, 28, 51, 59, 66, 88, 129, 130, 131, 138, 139, 142, 179*n*26, 179*n*29, 179–80*n*31
Carlisle (Carduel) 4, 8, 19, 22, 23, 25, 34, 36, 42, 51, 82, 87, 88, 122, 126, 129, 149
Carmina burana 178*n*14
carving platter 49, 143
Castle of Maidens 139
Cazelles, Brigitte 136, 181*n*10
chalice 145, 146
Champagne 1
Champguin 147, 150, 151; *see also* Roche de Champguin
chanson de geste 87
chaplain 89, 105
Charcoal Burner 22, 126, 127, 180*n*34
charger *see* equestrian propriety
Charitable Hermit (*Yvain*) 169*n*1, 170*n*13, 177*n*4, 178*n*4
charitas see charity
charité see charity
charity 12, 13, 14, 18, 37, 55, 56, 57, 58, 60, 61, 66, 68, 70, 71, 80, 83, 84, 97, 103, 104, 110, 120, 121, 128, 131, 147, 149, 151, 152, 155, 157, 163*n*10, 163*n*12, 166*n*32, 171*n*18, 174*n*38, 176*n*59, 178*n*4, 183*n*1; uncharitable 20, 25, 28, 42, 119, 141; *see also* lex caritatis
Charrete see Chrétien de Troyes: *Chevaliers de la Charrete* (*Lancelot, Charrete*)
Chastel de Pesme Aventure (Castle of Direst Adventure) (*Yvain*) 176*n*6
Chevaliers au lion see Chrétien de Troyes: *Chevaliers au lion* (*Yvain*)
chivalry 3, 21, 23, 24, 25, 29, 37, 56, 58, 83, 89, 93, 112, 123, 129, 131, 135, 141, 152, 176*n*7; *see also* adventure; knighthood

Index

Chrétien de Troyes 1, 2, 3, 7, 8, 9, 10, 12, 13, 14, 18, 20, 23, 24, 28, 29, 30, 31, 33, 36, 40, 41, 82, 91, 123, 129, 130, 131, 133, 138, 141, 143, 146, 147, 148, 150, 151, 157, 161*n*2, 163*n*9, 165*n*7, 166*n*29, 168*n*49, 168–69*n*50, 169–170*n*3, 170*n*13, 173*n*32, 175*n*55, 176*n*3, 178*n*12, 180*n*4, 182–83*n*32: *Chevaliers au lion* (*Yvain*) 1, 36, 106, 108, 122, 123, 170*n*13, 173*n*32, 176*n*6, 180*n*4; *Chevaliers de la Charrete* (*Lancelot, Charrete*) 1, 23, 44, 92, 93, 96, 126, 148, 150, 164*n*4, 180*n*4; *Cligés* 1, 124, 163*n*8, 168*n*45, 168*n*49, 182–83*n*32; *Erec et Enide* 1, 93, 119–20, 124, 163*n*8, 168*n*49, 169–70*n*3, 176*n*6, 181*n*14; *Guillaume d'Angleterre* (attributed) 1; lost texts 161*n*2; *Philomena* (attributed) 1; *see also* Prologue (*Conte del Graal*)

Chrétien's narrator 30, 31, 32, 38, 41, 42, 43, 44, 45, 52, 54, 59, 74, 75, 76, 78, 80, 81, 88, 92, 95, 96, 106, 108, 117, 120, 122, 124, 126, 127, 138, 139, 140, 141, 144, 166*n*21, 174*n*44, 176*n*9

Chrétien's romances 19, 20, 23, 40, 82, 91, 131, 141, 150, 172–73*n*28, 176–77*n*11, 180*n*4

Christ 12, 13, 58, 60, 61, 69, 85, 107, 109, 145, 146, 149, 154, 171*n*20, 172*n*24, 172–73*n*28, 178*n*7, 181–82*n*24

Christendom 169–70*n*3

Christian 12, 55, 60, 61, 155, 156, 163*n*9, 170*n*14

Christianity 145, 163*n*9, 170*n*14

Christus medicus (Christ the Physician) 109, 149

church 3, 8, 12, 25, 48, 51, 55, 62, 79, 126, 141, 145, 146, 169*n*56, 170*nn*14–15; *see also* Ecclesia

ciborium 146

Clamadeus of the Islands (des Isles) 3, 8, 19, 23, 27, 35, 40, 43, 44, 46, 79, 84, 126, 129, 150, 165*n*15, 168*n*47, 170–71*n*16, 176*n*9; *see also* Island(s)

Clarissant (Gawain's sister) 30, 31, 47, 53, 118, 130, 131, 140, 165*n*11, 179*n*22, 182*n*31

Cligés see Chrétien de Troyes: *Cligés*

clothing 24, 34, 46, 58, 82, 88, 95, 128, 151, 166*n*22

coitus see gradus amoris

colloquium see gradus amoris

color 2, 15, 24, 29, 30, 31, 32, 59, 58, 164*n*20: black 49, 164*n*1; blue 17, 49, 164*n*1; dappled 176*n*4; gold, golden 3, 14, 17, 24, 47, 48, 49, 50; green 17, 49, 164*n*1; indigo 49; piebald (black and white) 176*n*4; rosiness, rosy 29, 30; silver 14, 15, 17, 29, 47, 50, 81, 143, 164*n*1; vermilion 29, 49, 164*n*1; white 29, 30, 31, 32, 33, 34, 117, 139; *see also* Red Knight

Colossians *see* Bible

combat 5, 7, 19, 35, 36, 42, 53, 66, 110, 118, 121, 124, 134, 137, 139, 140, 141

Combes, Annie 130

communion 25, 84, 89, 105

confession 5, 8, 19, 20, 21, 25, 55, 62, 84, 89, 104, 105, 108, 115, 116, 118, 121, 144, 108, 121, 172*n*23

congressio see gradus amoris

contactus see gradus amoris

"conte de Gauvain" (story about Gawain within the *Conte del Graal*) 20, 94, 97, 117, 123, 147, 152, 165*n*10; *see also* reflective sequence

"conte de la demoiselle" 94, 95; *see also* reflective sequence

"conte de Perceval" (story about Perceval within the *Conte del Graal*) 19, 20, 28, 59, 65, 94, 95, 129, 147; *see also* reflective sequence

"conte del Graal" (story about the Grail within the *Conte del Graal*) 8, 32–33, 19, 62, 94, 147

Continuators 28, 40, 41, 129, 130, 131, 133, 141, 144, 145, 146, 175*n*53, 181*n*23, 181–82*n*24

Corinthians, I and II *see* Bible

Count Phillip *see* Philippe of Alsace

court 1, 4, 5, 8, 17, 18, 19, 20, 21, 24, 25, 26, 28, 33, 59, 66, 82, 84, 88, 95, 121, 122, 123, 124, 127, 128, 129, 130, 137, 138, 168*n*47, 179*n*27, 179*n*29; *see also* reflective sequence

courtesy 24, 36, 39, 51, 52, 91, 120, 138, 177*n*1; discourteous 20, 15, 28, 42, 90

courtier 126, 127, 129

courtliness 3, 18, 20, 29, 32, 39, 41, 44, 48, 55, 58, 60, 114, 116, 118, 151, 166*n*22, 164*n*4, 166*n*22, 170*n*5, 171*n*18

cowardice 28, 52, 114, 176*n*7, 183*n*36

credo 66

crossbow 34, 35, 36

Crucifixion (of Christ) 58, 61, 146

curse 67, 87, 110, 113, 174*n*38, 176*n*11, 177*n*13; *see also* adventure

custom 6, 50, 99, 100–2, 103, 116, 118, 121, 122, 144, 148, 149, 150–51; *see also* reflective sequence

Custom of Logres 9, 37, 38, 92–94, 96–97, 99, 103, 104, 116, 119, 120, 140, 158–59, 165*n*11; *see also* reflective sequence

cutting platter 50, 81, 143, 144

Dällenbach, Lucien 2

Dame de Noroisson (*Yvain*) 106

197

Index

Danek, Martha 9
dappled *see* color
David (King of Israel) 140, 142
Day of Judgment 69
decapitation 4, 6, 54, 85, 87, 88, 93, 96, 100, 102, 103, 118
defial, defiance 59, 102, 170–71*n*16
depression 59–60, 173*n*33
description 28–32, 89–90; *see also* reflective sequence
desert 57, 170*n*11
despair 20, 60–62, 64, 65, 66, 119, 173*n*33
destrier see equestrian propriety
Deuteronomy *see* Bible
DeVries, Kelly 167*n*35
Didot Perceval see Robert de Boron
discourse 18, 37, 58, 65, 95, 117, 144, 145
discourteous *see* courtesy
disgrace 98, 192, 104, 110, 183*n*36, 184*n*7
dishonor 12, 97, 110, 159
disloyalty 92
Disnadaron 4, 51, 124, 129, 168*n*47, 179–80*n*31
disorder 58, 92
Douay-Rheims translation *see* Bible
downfall *see* fall
dragonwart 107
drawbridge *see* bridge
druërie (love) 41, 43
duel 121
Duggan, Joseph 150, 168*n*50, 180*n*38, 181*n*21, 183*n*34

Easter Triduum (Adoration of the Cross, Maundy Thursday liturgy, Mass of the Presanctified, Paschal Vigil, Easter Mass) 25, 58, 61, 62, 84, 104, 124, 141, 169*n*56, 172*n*23, 172–73*n*28
ebony 49, 50, 169*n*50
Ecclesia (Church) 145, **146**, 147, 182*n*28
Ecclesiastes *see* Bible
Ecclesiasticus *see* Bible: Sirach
Edelman, Nathan 12
Egypt 156
Eleanor of Aquitaine 1
eleemosyna (alms) 68, 69, 71, 77, 95, 128, 156, 176*n*59; *see also almosne*
Eliduc see Marie de France
England 170*n*12, 180*n*5
Ephesians *see* Bible
equestrian propriety 26, 27, 87–92, 92, 97, cf. 92–99, 123; charger (*destrier*) **26**, **72**, 82, 86, 87, 88, 89, 91, 92, 97, 98, 99, 100, 110, 176*n*9, 177*n*12 (*see also* Gringalet); hunting horse (hunter) (*chaceor*) 17, 26, **27**, **71**, 77, 82, 86, 87, 92, 123; mare 98; mule 90, **112**; nag (*roncin*) 6, 89, 90, **91**, 92, 97, 98, 177*n*12, 177*nn*22–23; palfrey 31, 86, 87, 88, 89, **90**, 90–91, 93, 97, 98, 100, 176*n*4, 177*n*19, 177*nn*22–23; *see also* horse; reflective sequence
Erec 176*n*6
Erec et Enide see Chrétien de Troyes: *Erec et Enide*
Escavalon 4, 8, 20, 21, 27, 33, 35, 47, 51, 52, 53, 54, 85, 86, 103, 129, 131, 133, 138, 139, 140, 141, 142, 143, 147, 150, 179*n*26, 180*n*34, 181*n*11, 181*n*18
Etheldred the Unready 174*n*38
Eucharist 9, 145; *see also* reflective sequence
Europe 156
Excalibur 36
Exodus *see* Bible
Exultet 172–73*m*28

factum see gradus amoris
faith (*fides*) 14, 19, 58, 59, 60, 62, 66, 79, 102, 109, 117, 124, 130, 170–71*n*16
fall 3, 19, 21, 33, 41, 52, 56, 59, 63, 65, 66, 77, 78, 79, 82, 83, 115, 129, 137, 138, 150, 155, 162*n*2, 176*n*58, 182–83*n*32, 183*n*35; *see also* reflective sequence
Farina, William 182*n*28
fealty 138, 148
felix culpa (happy fault) 172–73*n*28
Fenice (*Cligés*) 168*n*45
Ferryman 6, 49, 50, 99, 100, 101, 103, 116, 117, 121, 151, 177*n*23, 177*n*25, 185*n*36
filial piety 63, 68, 70, 73, 77, 80, 83, 137, 141, 157, 181*n*18, 184*n*7; *see also* reflective sequence
fin' amors (refined love) 25, 38, 48, 119, 121
First Continuation *see* Continuator
First Crusade 145
Firth of Forth 148
Fisher King 4, 23, 28, 32, 34, 49, 50, 62, 63, 73, 81, 85, 114, 133, 138, 144, 147, 150, 165*n*17, 172–73*n*28, 177*n*23, 178*n*17
Fool 23, 25, 36, 55, 120, 127, 135, 141, 176–77*n*11; *see also* reflective sequence
foot soldier 36, 167*n*35
forest 3, 4, 8, 18, 22, 48, 51, 52, 57, 60–61, 64, 73, 77, 82, 86, 134, 170*n*12; *see also* Waste Forest
forgiveness 5, 84, 121, 118, 169*n*2, 174*n*38; *see also* mercy
fortified space 51–54; *see also* reflective sequence
Fortuna, Fortune, fortune 32, 42, 43, 63, 64, 98, **111**, 112–14, 115, 173*n*33, 178*n*14, 172–73*n*28
France 1, 147, 170*n*12, 181*n*14, 182–83*n*32

Index

Francien (Old French dialect of Ile-de-France) 182*n*30
French (language) 18

Galloway 17, 20, 45, 50, 52, 53, 54, 55, 84, 85, 88, 92, 100, 102, 102, 103, 104, 116, 117, 130, 131, 150, 159, 170*n*9, 175*n*53
Galloway Section 5–7, 15, 30, 53, 54, 104, 113, 115, 121, 129, 131, 139, 141, 148, 163*n*12, 169*n*55
garden 86, 87, 89, 99, 100, 176*n*5
Gaste Forest *see* Waste Forest
Gauvain (Francien form of Gawain) 182*n*30; *see also* "contes de Gauvain"
genealogy 3, 21, 22, 23, 67, 70, 153; *see also* reflective sequence
Geoffrey of Monmouth 22, 150, 152, 165*n*15, 180*n*5, 182–83*n*32, 183*n*33
God 12, 13, 17, 25, 48, 51, 58, 59, 60, 62, 65, 66, 67, 68, 69, 75, 77, 79, 82, 83, 102, 103, 104, 108, 141, 154, 156, 157, 170–71*n*16, 171*n*18, 171*n*20, 172*n*24, 173*n*33, 174*n*38, 176*n*59, 177*n*1, 182–83*n*32, 183*n*36
gold *see* color
Gomeret *see* Ban of Gomeret
Gonvais (traditional king of Orkney) 182*n*30
Good Friday 4, 9, 25, 60, 61, 69, 73, 115, 141, 144, 147, 170*n*13, 172*n*25, 181*n*17
Gornemant de Gohort 3, 19, 23, 24, 34, 39, 55, 56, 58, 59, 60, 62, 70, 72–76, 78, 81, 82, 83, 84, 93, 115, 117, 165*n*7, 170*n*5, 174*n*45, 175*n*50
Gorre (*Charrete*) 150
Gotland 22
grace 83–84, 103, 121, 173*n*33, 177*n*1; *see also* disgrace
gradus amoris (stages of love) 37, 38, 45, 94, 177*n*17: *accessus* (approach) 39, 167*n*38; *alloquium* (conversation) 37, 39, 43; *basia* (kisses) 37, 38; *blandimentum* (caressing) 167*n*38; *coitus* 37, 38; *colloquium* (conversation) 37, 167*n*38; *concupiscientia* (desire) 167*n*38; *congressio* (meeting) 37, 38, 167*n*38; *contactus* 37, 38; *factum* (deed, i.e., coitus) 37, 38, 45, 177*n*17; *intuitus* (looking) 37, 167*n*38; *visus* (sight) 37, 39; *see also* reflective sequence; *soreplus*
grail 1, 2, 49, 81, 143, 175*n*56
Grail 1, 9, 19, 33, 47, 49, 50, 51, 61, 63, 64, 65, 73, 74, 81, 109, 130, 133, 134, 136, 141, 143, 144, 145, 146, 148, 150, 165–66*n*17, 175*n*55, 181*n*23, 181–82*n*24
Grail adventure 63, 82, 133
Grail Castle 4, 5, 8, 17, 19, 20, 23, 25, 28, 48, 49, 50, 51, 52, 53, 55, 57, 59, 63, 64, 73, 76, 80, 82, 84, 86, 113, 118, 131, 133, 139, 143, 144, 151, 168–69*n*50, 169*n*53, 170*n*7, 170*n*15, 174–75*n*47, 175*n*58
Grail King 22, 73, 80, 84, 109, 138, 144, 147, 148, 165*n*17
Grail kingdom 22, 23, 131, 137, 138, 143, 144, 148, 150, 152
Grail Procession 4, 32–33, 50, 76, 79, 81, 143–44, 145, 146, 175*n*55
Grail question 81
Gravdal, Kathryn 175*n*51
green *see* color
Greoreas 5, 10, 20, 47, 50, 66, 85, 86, 87, 89, 90, 91, 92, 96, 97, 100, 101–6, 109, 110, 112, 113, 115, 119, 120, 121, 129, 141, 149, 159, 165*n*11, 176*n*7, 177–78*n*1, 178*n*8, 179*n*29, 181*n*19; nephew 35, 98, 99, 100, 100–1, 102, 165*n*11
grief 19, 21, 60, 63, 64, 65, 70
Grimbert, Joan 2
Gringalet (Le) 6, 53, 86, 89, 91, 97, 98, 99, 110, 113, 118
guardian of the borderland, of Galloway *see* Orgueilleus de la Roche
guardian's castle *see* Roche a l'Estroite Voie
Guenet *see* Vannes
guest 40, 81, 133, 134, 138
Guiganbresil 20, 21, 102, 131, 133, 139, 140, 141, 142, 150, 179*n*26, 181*n*18
Guigemar see Marie de France
Guildeluec (wife of Marie de France's Eliduc) 106
guilt 4, 58, 61, 64, 66, 96, 110, 140, 151
Guiromelant (Le) of Orqueneles 6, 7, 21, 36, 47, 53, 66, 85, 103, 116, 117, 118, 120, 121, 123, 130, 131, 139, 140, 159, 165*n*11, 179*n*20, 179*n*22, 179*n*27, 179*n*29, 179–80*n*31
Gwyneth (North Wales) 181*n*10

Hadrian's Wall 148
Haidu, Peter 169*n*51
hand (left vs. right) 13, 80, 120, 147, 152, 163*n*10
Harrowing of Hell 58, 61
hauberk 164*n*1
Haydock, George Leo 69
healer 97, 107, 108, 109, 110, 136, 178*n*2
healing 103, 105, 107, 108, 144, 149, 178*n*4; *see also* Bible: ruler of the synagogue's daughter
"heavy petting" 44, 45
Hebrew 155, 156, 166, 183*n*4, 183–84*n*6; *see also* Jews

Index

Hell 99, 108, 168n50, 175n54; see also Harrowing of Hell
helmet 34, 164n1
Henry the Liberal (count of Champagne) 1
herb 6, 9, 89, 105, 106, 107, 170n13, 178n4
Hermit 8, 9, 20, 51, 57, 59, 60, 61, 62, 63, 64, 65, 66, 73, 80, 81, 82, 83, 84, 115, 133, 143, 144, 165n17, 169n1, 170n6, 172n22, 172n26, 173n33, 175n52, 178n4; see also Charitable Hermit
Hermitage 4, 5, 8, 19, 20, 22, 25, 51, 52, 54–58, 62, 63, 66, 71, 72, 73, 76, 82, 84, 96, 104, 105, 109, 110, 115, 121, 145, 151, 170n7, 172–73n28, 173n33, 179n29, 181n17, 182n29; see also reflective sequence
Hideous Damsel 5, 8, 19, 20, 22, 23, 31, 32, 33, 36, 59, 63, 76, 82, 84, 89, 112, 113, 114, 131, 136, 144, 148, 174–75n47, 176n11, 179n29; see also reflective sequence
history 22, 23, 117, 130, 134, 136, 138, 147, 148, 180n5, 132n26
Holmes, Urban T., Jr. 182n28
Holy Names of God 172n26
Holy Spear 145, 146
Holy Trinity 104
honor 28, 35, 37, 58, 68, 80, 83, 88, 93, 108, 109, 114, 115, 140, 142, 143, 151, 157, 168n49, 176–77n19, 183–84n6, 184n7
hope (spes) 14, 41, 43, 55, 58, 60, 80, 119, 120–21, 167n38
horn 168n50
horse 6, 8, 10, 17, 24, 26, 32, 34, 34, 35, 52, 53, 74, 77, 78, 86, 87, 89, 90, 92, 97, 99, 100, 101, 105, 115, 123, 137, 169n9, 170n13, 176n4, 176n9, 177n12, 177n19, 177n23; see also equestrian propriety
hospitality 5, 28, 54, 134, 139, 143, 169n58
host 6, 49, 64, 81, 82, 99, 117, 118, 139, 131, 142, 144, 148, 169n56, 177n25, 180n37
Host (hostia: sacrificial victim, consecrated bread) 51, 64, 68, 69, 70, 73, 81, 109, 145, 165n17
hour 59, 113, 178n13
hubris 149
Hugh of St. Victor 171n18
hunter, hunting horse see equestrian propriety
hypocrisy 13, 120, 163n10

Iceland 22
iconography 145
Igerne see Ygraine
Incarnation 61
incest 64, 66, 140
indigo see color
indolence 173n33; see also Oiseuse
insanity 5, 73, 115, 132, 141, 169n1

interrogation 4, 17–18, 19, 20, 24, 25, 33, 35, 37, 58, 60, 62, 63, 64, 65, 73, 74, 81–82, 90, 99, 112–13, 116, 117–18, 133, 143, 172nn26–27, 172–73n28, 175n56, 178n17, 179n29; see also question; reflective sequence
intertextuality 9, 12–14, 59
intuitus see *gradus amoris*
Ireland 22
irony 35, 42, 50, 57, 81, 83, 87, 97, 109, 118, 122, 124, 127, 139, 152, 158, 175–76n58, 177n15, 177n23, 178n14, 182–83n32
Isidore of Seville 14
Island(s) 19, 22, 23, 40, 138, 148, 150, 165n15
Israel 140
ivory 49, 168n50

James-Raoul, Danièle 162n1, 174n46
javelin 17, 21, 24, 32–36, 50, 82, 151, 167n35
Jerusalem 12, 155
Jesus 171n18; see also Christ
Jewers, Caroline 10
Jews 58, 61, 155, 156, 183n4; see also Hebrew
Johab 140
John (Gospel of) see Bible
John, I see Bible
Joie de la Cort (*Erec et Enide*) 176n6
Joseph d'Arimathie see Robert de Boron
joy (*joie*) 43, 44, 45, 47, 64, 70, 77, 79, 98, 121, 122, 126–30, 134, 135, 137, 168nn48–49, 171n18
Judaism 145
Judas 153, 154
Judeo-Christian interpretation 182n 28

Kay 20, 23, 24, 25, 26, 27, 34, 36, 42, 119, 126, 127, 135, 166n32, 176–77n11, 179n25
Kibler, William W. 84, 172–73n28, 177n18, 180n33
King Arthur's land see Logres
King Ban (de Benoïe, father of Lancelot) 181n10; see also Ban de Benoïe (Benoïc)
King Ban (of Gomeret) see Ban of Gomeret
King Lot 7, 38, 53, 103, 118, 138, 140, 147, 148, 149, 179n26, 182n30, 182–83n31–32
king of Escavalon (elder) 5, 21, 137, 138, 179n26, 180n10, 181n18, 181n21
king of Escavalon (younger) 5, 33, 47, 103, 136, 139, 140, 141, 181n21
King Rion of Denmark 165n15
King Ryon see Ryon, king of the Islands
kingdom 5, 22, 23, 24, 33, 52, 63, 92, 92, 114, 124, 126, 127, 128, 131, 134, 135, 136, 137, 138, 139, 142, 143, 144, 147, 148, 149, 150, 151, 152, 158, 165n15, 168nn49–50, 174n38, 180n38, 181n14, 182–83n32, 183nn34–35; see also realm

200

Index

Kings, II *see* Bible
knight 1–128 *passim*, 136, 137, 139, 140, 147, 149, 150, 151, 152, 158, 159, 164*n*3, 164*n*6, 165*n*15, 166*n*29, 167*nn*35–36, 169*n*57, 170*n*10, 170–71*n*16, 172*n*27, 173*n*33, 174*n*44, 176*n*7, 177*n*19, 178*n*11, 178*n*13, 179*n*29, 181*n*21, 183*n*36; *see also* spurs
knighthood 18, 21, 25, 48, 56, 57, 61, 75, 79, 83, 92, 93, 97, 100, 109, 131, 138, 147, 150, 151, 152; *see also* chivalry
Köhler, Reinhold 178*n*3

Lacy, Norris J. 2, 103
Lady Lore (Laurel) 129, 130, 141
lance 4, 29, 32, 33, 34, 35, 36, 51, 64, 65, 82, 85, 86, 88, 98, 103, 134, 143, 142, 144, 145, 146, 164*n*1, 167*nn*35–36, 169*n*54, 181*n*21
Lancelot 23, 44, 92, 93, 150, 181*n*10
Lancelot see Chrétien de Troyes: *Chevaliers de la Charrete*
Lancelot-Grail Cycle 150, 178*n*13, 179*n*26, 181*n*14, 181–82*n*24, 182*n*30, 183*n*33: *Merlin* 165*n*15, 178*n*13, 181*n*14, 181–82*n*24, 182*n*30; *Mort le roi Artu* 150, 183*n*36; *Queste del Saint Graal* 41
Last Supper 145
Latin 106, 147, 178*n*6
Laughing Maiden *see* Smiling Maiden
Law of Christ 61, 171*n*20; *see also* lex caritatis; charity
Le Nan, Frédérique 166*n*27
lèse-majesté 24
lex caritatis (Law of Charity), *lex Christi* (Law of Christ) 61, 69, 171*n*20
lex militiae (law of knighthood) 61
light 2, 9, 17, 30, 47–48, 48–49, 50, 81, 84, 109, 136, 143, 164*n*1, 173*n*33; *see also* sun, sunlight
Lit de la Merveille see Bed of Marvels
Locrinus (son of Brutus of Troy) 135
Loënis *see* Lothian
Logres 4, 5, 23, 33, 52, 63, 92, 96, 114, 124, 131, 134, 135, 138, 139, 142, 147, 148, 149, 150, 152, 158, 159, 165*n*15, 181*n*16, 182–83*n*32, 183*n*35, 184*n*34
Longinus 85, 145, 146, 181–82*n*24
Lot *see* King Lot
Lothian 147, 148, 182*n*30
Louis VII, king of France 11
loyalty 12
Luke *see* Bible
Lunette (*Yvain*) 109

Mabonagrain's lady (*Erec et Enide*) 119
Maddox, Donald 2, 21, 84, 150, 176*n*8, 179*n*21, 181*n*19, 182–83*n*32
Malevolent Maiden 6, 7, 21, 30, 47, 51, 53, 58, 66, 84, 86, 87, 89, 93, 96, 97, 98–99, 100, 101, 103, 105, 109, 112, 115, 116, 117, 118, 119, 121, 140, 159, 165*n*11, 166*n*27, 173*n*33, 176*n*6, 177*n*19, 177*n*24, 177–78*n*1, 179*n*20, 182*n*29; *see also* Orgueilleuse de Loges; reflective sequence
Manessier *see* Continuator
manuscript 53, 63, 64, 108, 156, 161*n*1, 166*n*21, 167*n*41, 170*n*4, 172*n*22, 172*n*26, 173*n*29, 174*n*34, 175*n*55, cf. 178*n*9, 179*n*21, 179*n*23, 180*n*2, 180*n*5, 181*n*8, 183–84*n*6
mare 98; *see also* equestrian propriety
Marie de Champagne (wife of Henry the Liberal) 1
Marie de France 34, 106, 178*n*5: *Deus Amanz* 178*n*5; *Eliduc* 106; *Guigemar* 167*n*34
Mark *see* Bible
Mass(es) 58, 59, 62, 79, 83, 169*n*56, 172*n*23; *see also* Easter Triduum
matricide 83
Matter (substance) 1, 2, 69, 70, 76, 83, 87, 92, 102, 131, 133, 139, 144, 150, 155, 165*n*11, 182–83*n*32
Matthew *see* Bible
Matthieu de Vendôme 39, 167*n*38
McCash, June Hall 179*n*30
meal 8, 9, 39, 44, 51, 81, 144; *see also* reflective sequence
Medieval West 145
Meleagant de Gorre (*Charrete*) 182–83*n*32
Meliant de Liz 47, 52
men-at-arms 124–26
mercy 8, 55, 59, 60, 68, 73, 84, 93, 95, 96, 121, 151, 153, 170*n*14; *see also* forgiveness
Merlin see Robert de Boron
merveille (wonder) 48, 73–74, 88, 121, 135, 168*n*48
Middle Ages 2, 15, 85
mirror 2, 4, 9, 11, 13–14, 15, 17, 23, 27, 28–36, 37, 46, 47–51, 55, 57, 63, 70, 72, 73, 83, 87, 89, 92, 96, 100, 103, 104, 114, 124, 126, 128, 129, 130, 135, 147, 149, 151, 152, 164*n*20, 166*nn*26–27, 170*n*13; *see also* reflective sequence
misadventure 53, 63
mise en abyme 18
misfortune 42, 43, 63, 64, 86, 114, 172–73*n*28
modernity (medieval concept) 12, 147
monster 165*n*9
Mont St. Michel 165*n*15
Montesclere 131
moon 49, 109, 178*n*14
Mordred 141, 150, 152, 179*n*26, 182–83*n*32
Morgan 178*n*4

201

Index

Morgause 182*n*31; *see also* Anna
Mort le roi Artu see Lancelot-Grail
mule *see* equestrian propriety
Murray, Sarah-Jane 10

nag *see* equestrian propriety
name 1, 3, 4, 13, 24, 25, 33, 35, 40, 51, 53, 60, 62, 63, 64, 85, 86, 93, 101, 103, 117, 118, 122, 128, 131, 135, 139, 147, 148, 156, 159, 163*n*8, 165*n*7, 165*n*15, 166*n*26, 169*n*53m 169–70*n*3, 172*nn*26–27, 175*n*58, 179*n*29, 179–80*n*31, 181*n*11, 182*n*30–31, 182–83*n*32; *see also* reflective sequence; surname
Narcissus 166*n*27
Nature 30
New Law 60, 146, 154, 171*n*20
New Testament *see* Bible
New Troy 135
nones *see* hour
Norman (Old French dialect of Normandy) 182*n*30
Norman Conquest 167*n*35
North Wales *see* Gwyneth
Norway 182*n*30
Norwegian steed 176*n*9
Notre-Dame de Paris 172*n*25

oath 26, 84, 142–43, 183*n*36
Oiseuse (*Romance of the Rose*) (Indolence) 30, 166*nn*27–28
Old French 33, 64, 75, 76, 168*n*48, 170–71*n*16, 175*n*55, 178*n*19, 182*n*30
Old Law 146, 154, 171*n*20
Old Queen *see* Ygraine
Old Testament *see* Bible
order 32, 43, 57, 58, 75, 92, 147, 150, 151, 161*n*3, 173*n*33, 176*n*6
Orgueilleus de la Lande (Proud Knight of the Heath) 4, 8, 19, 20, 27, 28, 31, 35, 47, 51, 55, 66, 84, 85, 88, 92, 93, 94, 95, 102, 120, 121, 129, 130, 159, 166*n*21, 166*n*22, 167*n*38, 176*n*8
Orgueilleus de la Roche a l'Estroite Voie (Proud Knight of the Stone at the Narrow Pass) 35, 53–54, 55, 85, 87, 98, 99, 100, 101, 102, 103, 112, 115, 116, 117, 118, 119, 120, 131, 150, 151, 165*n*11, 176*n*2, 176*n*8, 177*n*23
Orgueilleuse de Logres (Proud Maiden of Logres) 6, 86, 117, 120, 176*n*8, 179*n*21; *see also* Malevolent Maiden
Original Sin 67, 153–54, 172–73*n*28
Orkney (Orquenie) 7, 22, 23, 33, 51, 59, 114, 122, 122, 124, 126, 127, 129, 131, 138, 141, 147, 148, 149, 151, 165*n*10, 170*n*9, 173*n*33, 179*n*31, 182*n*30
Orqueneles 21, 53, 115, 117, 129, 130, 179–80*n*31; *see also* Guiromelant (Le) of Orquenelles
Otherworld 130, 150, 168*n*50, 180*n*38
Ovid 1, 161*n*2, 169*n*54
Oxford *Roland* 167*n*35

pagan 12, 87, 163*n*9
palfrey *see* equestrian propriety
Parable of Lazarus and the Rich Man *see* Bible
Parable of the Sower *see* Bible
paradox 78, 118, 172–73*n*28, 180*n*38; *see also felix culpa*
paraphrase 2, 75, 96, 167*n*38
parole (word, words, speech, power of speech) 56, 65–66, 74, 82–83, 84, 107–8, 119, 166*n*32, 170*n*6, 174*n*34, 174*n*45
Parsifal (neo-Nazi *nom de guerre*) 171–172*n*21
Paschal Vigil 172–73*n*28; *see also* Easter Triduum
passion 118, 173*n*33
Passion (of Christ) 58, 145; *see also* Bible: Passion Gospel
Passion play 172*n*25
pasties *see* bread
Paul *see* St. Paul
pax arthuriana (Arthurian time of peace) 23, 135, 138
peace 4, 22, 23, 26, 75, 76, 135, 144, 178*n*17; *see also* pax arthuriana
peccatum matris (mother's sin) 67, 68, 69, 70, 73, 76, 77, 82, 83, 114, 151, 153–54, 155–57
"pechié … de ta mere" (your mother's sin) 63–65, 66, 70, 73
Pedanius Dioscorides 107, 178*n*6
peg-leg (*eschacier*) 50, 169*n*51
penance 83, 84, 172*n*23, 174*n*40
penitent 55, 57, 58, 60, 61, 62, 147, 181*n*17
Pentecost 7, 122, 123, 124, 129, 179*n*27; *see also* Whitsuntide
Perceval: brothers 21, 70–71, 77, 82, 138, 173*n*33, 181*n*21; father 21, 34, 50, 64, 77, 136–37, 138, 173*n*33; mother 3, 17, 18, 19, 21–22, 23, 25, 34, 36, 37, 38, 40, 41, 47, 48, 52, 55, 56, 57, 58, 59, 61, 63, 64, 65, 66, 70, **71**, 73, 76, 77, 78, 78–79, 80, 82, 83, 84, 113, 114, 115, 148, 165*n*15, 165–66*n*17, 166*n*18, 166*n*19, 170*n*6, 171*n*22, 172*n*24, 172*n*26, 172–73*n*28, 176*n*9, 177*n*17, 180*n*34; mother's manor 3, 18, 19, 21, 22, 38, 47, 51, 52, 53, 56, 57, **71**, 78, 80, 86, 114, 170*n*10; *see also* reflective sequence; Welshman
Perceval *see* Chrétien de Troyes: *Conte del Graal (Perceval)*

202

Index

Perilous Bed *see* Bed of Marvels
Perilous Ford 6, 53, 115, 117
perjurer 183n36
Philippe of Alsace, count of Flanders 1, 12, 13, 28, 119, 147
physician 106, 107, 108, 178n7
piebald *see* color
Pietà 85, 88, 177n1
pigritia (sloth) 173n33
plank *see* bridge
point of view 44, 119, 124, 127, 128, 133
Poirion, Daniel 175n55
prayer 65, 66, 67, 82, 83, 162–63n4, 170n6, 172nn24–25, 173n33, 184n7
Prestwich, Michael 167n35
pride 4, 6, 12, 35, 42, 55, 85, 86, 97, 119, 120, 166n32, 179n26, 183n36
prime *see* hour
procession 105, 136; *see also* Grail Procession
Prologue (*Conte del Graal*) 3, 11–15, 17, 18, 20, 55, 58, 66, 80, 97, 104, 119, 120, 128, 128, 147, 151–52, 162n1, 162n3, 163n7, 163n9, 169n1
proverb (Old French) 11–12, 75, 76, 97, 179n25
Proverbs *see* Bible
Psalms *see* Bible
Pucele aus Manches Petites (Maiden with the Small Sleeves, Tiebaut of Tintagel's younger daughter) 20, 52, 129
pyx 146

Quarron of Ariel (*Erec et Enide*) 181n14
Queen (Arthur's wife) 24, 44, 45, 95, 122, 129, 130
quest 4, 8, 20, 29, 33, 35, 53, 57, 59, 76, 80, 84, 129, 130, 131, 133, 136, 142, 172n22; *see also* reflective sequence
Queste del Saint Graal see Lancelot-Grail
question 4, 18, 19, 24, 61, 62, 63, 65, 81, 81, 82, 116, 117, 118, 129, 144, 172–73n28, 178n17; *see also* interrogation; reflective sequence

Rabanus Maurus 68–69, 73, 84, 174–75n47, 175n49
ramprosnes (sarcastic jibes) 28
realm 23, 61, 84, 114, 131, 147, 149, 150, 165n15; *see also* kingdom
reconciliation 88, 95, 121, 151, cf. 19, 115, 121
Red Knight (from the Forest of Quinqueroy) 3, 19, 24, 25, 26, 34, 55, 82, 87, 119, 126, 135, 149, 182–83n32
Red Knight (Perceval) 44, 147
redemption 20, 21, 59, 70, 73, 84, 96, 103, 104, 105, 110, 115, 144, 147, 172–73n28, 173n28
reflection 8, 11, 12, 13, 15, 17, 18, 20, 21, 24, 28, 29, 32, 34, 36, 45, 47, 48, 50, 53, 55, 57, 58, 60, 66, 70, 73, 75, 78, 84, 85, 92, 99, 103, 105, 109, 112, 118, 120, 121, 124, 126, 129, 131, 132, 136, 137, 139, 141, 147, 148, 149, 150, 151, 165n10, 169n3, 168n47, 172n26, 174–75n47, 177n17
reflective sequence/specular sequence 2, 3, 7–9, 17, 18–19, 19–21, 21–28, 30, 32–34, 36–54, 56, 57–58, 60–63, 64, 65, 66, 72, 76–84, 86–89, 92–99, 117–18, 180n34: *see also* amorous couple; armor, arms; Bleeding Lance; blood; Blood Drops in the Snow; bread; bridge; "conte de la demoiselle"; "contes de Gauvain"; "contes del Graal"; "contes de Perceval"; court; custom; Custom of Logres; description; equestrian propriety; Eucharist; fall; filial piety; Fool; fortified space; genealogy; *gradus amoris*; Hermitage; Hideous Damsel; interrogation; Malevolent Maiden; meal; mirror; name; Perceval, mother; quest; question; Smiling Maiden; *soreplus*; specular encounter; Tent Maiden; Two Queens; venison; Waste Forest; Weeping Maiden; wine; Wise Vavassor; Ygraine; Young Queen
reflexivity 2, 124
regicide 136, 139
Resurrection of Christ 58
rhetoric 80, 163n14, 168n44
rich king *see* Fisher King
Rider, Jeff 162n3, 164n6
Riquer, Martín de 180n36
Roach, William 130, 179n21, 180n37
Robert de Boron 145; *Didot Perceval* (attributed) 150, 182n30, 182–83n32; *Joseph d'Arimathie* 181–82n24; *Merlin* 181–82n24, 182n30
Roche a l'Estroite Voie 86, 100, 176n6
Roche de Champguin 6, 7, 15, 17, 22, 23, 35, 36, 49, 50, 51, 53, 60, 84, 98, 99, 100, 114, 115, 116, 118, 122, 126, 129, 130, 147, 148, 149, 151, 168n50, 173n33, 177n25, 177–78n1, 179n22, 181n14, 182n31, 182–83n32, 183n36
Rohmer, Eric, *Perceval le Gallois* (1978) 172n25
Roman d'Eneas 168–69n50
Romance of the Rose 30
Romances of Alexander 12, 163n9
Romans 182–83n32
Rome 147
rosiness, rosy *see* color
Round Table 22

203

Index

Ryon, king of the Islands 22, 23, 25, 126, 149, 165*n*15

Sagremor 36
St. Audry 178*n*7
St. Augustine of Hippo 14, 67, 153, 165*n*9, 171*n*20, 174*n*38
St. Bernard of Clairvaux 14
St. Paul 2, 11, 12, 13, 17, 151, 163*n*13, 171*n*20
Salernitan pharmaceutics 107
Salomon Rashi 156
Saly, Antoinette 2, 35, 85, 170*n*7
Samuel II *see* Bible
sang froid 123; *see also* "thinking on the spot"
Saracen *see* topos
sarcasm 42, 119
Sargent-Baur, Barbara N. 172*n*22
Satan 120
Saxon 23, 165*n*15
School of Laon 171*n*18
Scotland 135, 148
Second Continuator *see* Continuator
seminal word *see* topos
serf 18, 127, 172*n*27, 180*n*34
service 1, 6, 7, 21, 24, 25, 37, 39, 51, 54, 57, 58, 62, 70, 74, 79, 81, 86, 110, 116, 118, 133, 137, 144, 146, 148, 151, 153, 157, 169*n*53, 171*n*18, 175*n*55, 176*n*5, 181*n*23
Sherwin, Michael S. 171*n*18
shield 36, 88, 117, 134, 164*n*1
silence 39, 50, 55, 63, 74, 76, 81, 105, 113, 126, 129, 144, 174*nn*44–46, 174–75*n*47
sin 5, 41, 55, 60–72, 75, 82, 83, 84, 89, 103, 105, 110, 115, 119, 120, 147, 153–54, 156–57, 172–73*n*28, 173*n*33, 174*n*36, 174*n*38, 174*n*40, 176*n*59, 182*n*29, 183*n*36, 183*AppAn*2, 183–84*n*6, 184*n*7; *see also* Original Sin
Sirach *see* Bible
Smiling Maiden 25, 26, 27, 28, 36, 55, 129, 135, 176–77*n*11; *see also* reflective sequence
Smith, Robert D. 167*n*35
"smother love" 66
Solomon 75, 83; *see also* Bible: Proverbs
Song of Wisdom 155
Soredamors (*Cligés*) 168*n*49
soreplus (the rest, i.e., coitus) 37, 38, 40, 41, 44, 159, 166*n*19, 177*n*17; *see also* reflective sequence
spear 167*n*35; *see also* Holy Spear
specular encounter 2, 18, 19, 21–28, 34, 36, 138; *see also* reflective sequence
specular sequence *see* reflective sequence
specularity 2, 9, 13, 17, 18, 30
speculum see mirror

speech 7, 24, 28, 39, 42, 43, 68, 75, 76, 82, 83, 108, 119, 120, 139, 140, 151, 164*n*4, 166*n*32, 168*n*45, 174*n*44, 174*n*45, 174–75*n*47, 175*n*48
spurs (giving, receiving) 24, 58, 82; *see also* knight
"stage left," "stage right" 146; *see also* hand
Sturm-Maddox, Sara 179*n*18
succession 23, 114, 131, 137, 138, 140, 147, 148, 149, 150
"suicide by knight" 119, 173*n*33
Summus Medicus (Supreme Physician) 178*n*7
sun, sunlight 17, 29, 32, 47, 48, 49, 108–109, 164*n*1; *see also* Apollonian powers;, light
Sunday 25, 124
surname 24, 62–63, 113, 172*n*26, 175–76*n*58, 179*n*26, 179*n*29; *see also* name
sword 28, 35, 36, 80, 85, 165*n*15, 166*n*21
Syderberg, Jürgen: *Parsifal* (1982) 171–72*n*21
Synagoga (Synagogue) 145, 146, 147, 182*n*28

Talmud 155, 156
Tent Maiden 3, 4, 7, 8, 9, 19, 25, 28, 31, 38, 55, 58, 66, 78, 80, 82, 87, 93, 96, 98, 115, 159, 166*n*27, 166*n*29, 167*nn*38–39, 168*n*47, 170*n*15, 177*n*22; *see also* reflective sequence
"thinking on the spot" 91, 113; *see also sang froid*
Thursday 122
Tiebaut of Tintagel 27, 47, 89, 119, 120, 179*n*29; *see also* Pucele aus Manches Petites
time 2, 14, 63, 74, 75–76, 81, 124, 130, 135, 138, 140, 148, 155, 158, 163*n*12, 166*n*1, 174–75*n*47, 176*n*59, 180*n*4, 182*n*30
tint *see* color
Tintagel 4, 20, 27, 35, 51, 52, 53, 54, 129, 165*n*10
topos 18, 163*n*9
Torah 155
tradition 67, 106, 120, 124, 150, 155, 156, 163*n*10, 170*n*4, 171*n*18, 182*n*29, 182–83*n*32, 183*n*5
traitor 141, 183*n*36
translation 18, 19, 83, 147
treachery 47, 98, 104, 110, 141
treason 139, 140, 142
Triduum *see* Easter Triduum
Tristan 1
tristitia (extreme sadness) 60, 65, 119, 128, 149, 151, 173*n*33, 182*n*29
tropica locutio (figure of speech) 176*n*59;

204

Index

tropica locutione (in a figure of speech) 68
Troy 147
Troyes, Jewish school in 156
True Cross 172n24
"Truth or Consequences" 117–18
Two Queens (Ygraine and her daughter) 23, 47, 51, 84, 114; *see also* reflective sequence; Ygraine, Young Queen

Unruly Squire 89–90, 97, 196n11
Utherpendragon 21, 22, 34, 50, 114, 118, 135, 147, 148, 165n15
Utherpendragon's queen *see* Ygraine

vainglory 13, 120, 163n10
Vannes (Morbihan) (Breton Guenet or Wenet) 181n14
Varro 165n9
vavassor 20, 52, 56, 83, 134, 180n2; *see also* Wise Vavassor
venison 81, 144, 170n13; *see also* reflective sequence
verbosity 175n50
vermilion *see* color
viewpoint *see* point of view
Villon, François: *Testament* 12, 174n38, 171n38
visus see *gradus amoris*
Vulgate *see* Bible
Vulgate *Merlin* *see* Lancelot-Grail Cycle

Wace 135, 150: *Brut* 22, 23, 134, 135, 138, 141, 147, 152, 165n15, 179n18, 180n3, 180n5, 182nn30–32, 183n33
Wales 135, 168n49; *see also* Gwyneth
Walters, Lori 40
Walwein (Norman form of Gawain) 182n30
Waste Forest (Gaste Forest) 3, 8, 9, 17, 19, 22, 33, 47, 49, 51, 52, 53, 56, 57, 58, 62, 64, **71**, 72, 78, 79–80, 81, 82, 86, 87, 170nn7–9, 170n12, 175n53; *see also* reflective sequence
wasteland 57, 61, 170n9
water 117, 145, 169n56, 170n13
weapons 17, 34, 36, 134, 142, 167n35; *see also* armor, arms

Weeping Maiden 4, 8, 19, 22, 28, 33, 62, 63, 64, 65, 76, 82, 85, 93, 113, 144, 148, 175n56, 175n58, 179n29; *see also* reflective sequence
Welsh (language, culture, people) 18, 24, 34, 88, 173n33
Welshman 34, 87, 94, 63, 147, 165n8, 175n58
Wends (land of the Wends along the eastern Baltic coast) 22
Wenet *see* Vannes
white doe 34
Whitsuntide 20; *see also* Pentecost
Wielockx, Robert 191n18
window (stained-glass) 15, 29, 35–36, 49, 164n20
wine 9, 25, 43, 49, 51, 92, 126; *see also* reflective sequence
Wisdom of Yeshua (or Jesus) Ben Sira 155
Wisdom tradition 67
Wise Vavassor 134, 136, 141, 142, 143, 152, 180n34; *see also* reflective sequence; vavassor
Wolfram von Eschenbach: *Parzifal* 172–73n28, 175n55
word 3, 18, 24, 25, 26, 33, 35, 36, 38, 42, 43, 46, 48, 63, 66, 71, 74, 75, 82, 83, 92, 93, 94, 97, 104, 107, 119, 136, 140, 141, 142, 163n12, 166n32, 168n45, 174n46, 175n50, 177n11, 180n33
wound 4, 6, 21, 22, 23, 25, 29, 33, 34, 36, 50, 54, 63, 85, 87, 89, 100, 101, 103, 104, 105, 106, 107, 108, 145, 146, 148, 178n17
Wright, Monica E. 166n29

Ygraine (mother of Arthur) 6, 22, 53, 60, 99, 100, 101, 103, 117, 118, 123, 147, 148, 149, 169n55, 179n26, 179n29, 182–83n32; *see also* Two Queens
Ygraine's castle *see* Roche de Champguin
Yonet 8, 19, 20, 23, 26, 82, 129, 135
Young Queen (daughter of Ygraine, mother of Gawain and Clarissant) 53, 118, 147, 182n31; *see also* Anna; Morgause; Two Queens
Yvain see Chrétien de Troyes: *Chevaliers au lion* (*Yvain*)
Yvain 170n13, 176n6, 178n4

www.ingramcontent.com/pod-product-compliance
Ingram Content Group UK Ltd.
Pitfield, Milton Keynes, MK11 3LW, UK
UKHW042004140426
5217IPUK00015B/975